AFRICAN AMERICANS AND POPULAR CULTURE

AFRICAN AMERICANS AND POPULAR CULTURE

VOLUME III
MUSIC AND POPULAR ART

Edited by Todd Boyd

PRAEGER

Westport, Connecticut
London

Library of Congress Cataloging-in-Publication Data

African Americans and popular culture / edited by Todd Boyd.
    p. cm.
  Includes bibliographical references and index.
  ISBN 978-0-275-98922-4 (set : alk. paper) — ISBN 978-0-275-98923-1 (v. 1 : alk. paper) —
ISBN 978-0-275-98924-8 (v. 2 : alk. paper) — ISBN 978-0-275-98925-5 (v. 3 : alk. paper)
  1. African Americans in popular culture—History. 2. Popular culture—United States—
History. 3. United States—Civilization—African American influences. 4. African
Americans—Intellectual life. I. Boyd, Todd.
  E185.625A384 2008
  973'.0496073—dc22   2008024474

British Library Cataloguing in Publication Data is available.

Library of Congress Catalog Card Number: 2008024474

ISBN: 978-0-275-98922-4 (set)
      978-0-275-98923-1 (vol. 1)
      978-0-275-98924-8 (vol. 2)
      978-0-275-98925-5 (vol. 3)

First published in 2008

Praeger Publishers, 88 Post Road West, Westport, CT 06881
An imprint of Greenwood Publishing Group, Inc.
www.praeger.com

Printed in the United States of America

The paper used in this book complies with the
Permanent Paper Standard issued by the National
Information Standards Organization (Z39.48-1984).

10 9 8 7 6 5 4 3 2 1

Contents

Introduction

AFRICAN AMERICAN POPULAR CULTURE

The argument can be made that it is in the broad area of popular culture that African Americans have had their greatest and most profound effects on American society. This is most certainly the case from the beginning of the twentieth century on. My intention is not to discount the role of the social and the political in contextualizing the African American experience, but to point out the overwhelming influence that popular culture has had in shaping the image of African Americans internally and in the larger society.

The relationship between African Americans and various forms of popular culture—such as music, sports, film, and television—is both complicated and congratulatory. Relative to this relationship is the way in which, over time, certain issues have evolved while other issues—such as the need for African Americans to control the means of cultural production, and the continued prevalence of certain stereotypes—in spite of the particular form of culture in question. Interestingly enough, these various forms of popular culture have often been written about and discussed exclusively of one another. I have long been a proponent of discussing these forms of culture as part and parcel of a larger body of work defined collectively as African American popular culture rather than limiting the influence of one form exclusively to its own domain. It makes sense that what is happening at a given time in film, for instance, may be influenced by what is taking place in the world of music. On the other hand, each medium requires that specific attention be paid to it in order to determine what is going on internally within that specific field of inquiry.

It is important to point out that in discussing popular culture, I am concerned with the culture consumed by "the people," as it were. Some may find the exclusion of literature from these volumes to be an omission, but it is the point of view of this project that much has been written about literature but little penned about African American representation in less well-regarded genres such as comic books that nonetheless deserve our attention. In some ways, my distinctions are motivated by class concerns that have often tended to exclude the "popular" in popular culture when celebrating those works that have animated discussions about African American identity over the years. This is not to dismiss the impact of a Langston Hughes or Toni Morrison as much as it is to recognize the fact that those watching a boxing match or a Blaxploitation film could indeed be excluded from discussions that might overlook such endeavors because of their overtly popular nature. It is this populist appeal that underscores the aim and scope of articles selected for this series of volumes.

For many years, African Americans were simply objects within popular culture whose representation tended to be quite stereotypical and especially problematic. At a certain point though, African Americans attempted to harness the means of production and create their own representations instead of being represented by others. This is the point at which things began to get interesting. For example, it is the utterly hideous and overtly racist representation of African Americans in a monumental film like D. W. Griffith's *Birth of a Nation* (1915) that creates the space for the beginning of an independent Black film movement, a movement that began with people such as Emmett J. Scott, Oscar Micheaux, and George and Nobel P. Johnson and continued up to such a prolific and contemporary mainstream figure as Spike Lee.

The tragedy and the triumph of African American imagery in popular culture is a situation where the two seemingly opposite poles are often interwoven. A good example of this can be found in the reasoning surrounding baseball player Jackie Robinson's integration of Major League Baseball in 1947—the point here being that there would have been no need for Robinson to break the "color line" in baseball had there not been a policy of racial segregation instituted in the first place. As this example indicates, African Americans in popular culture have often found themselves operating somewhere between the reality of racism and the possibilities of redemption through cultural engagement.

To this end, the core of African American cultural expression has often been located in music, which is itself an extension of the oral tradition that has long defined the Black presence in American society. A discussion of American music is a discussion that must recognize the centrality of African American music in this context. To exclude African American music from this discussion ultimately means that no discussion can take place.

The various forms of Black music—from gospel and the blues to jazz, soul, and, more recently, hip hop—have helped define the culture over time and have also provided a running soundtrack to American life. Black music, in the forms of blues and rhythm and blues, was the original source for what would eventually become "rock 'n' roll," a popular but derivative genre of music that went on to reach mainstream mass appeal—often at the expense of its Black roots. The everlasting influence of music has been represented over time in phrases like "the Jazz Age," the role of bebop in defining the "Beat Generation," the place of both gospel music and Motown in the Civil Rights movement, and the transformation of American culture brought by hip hop in contemporary society, among many other examples. The joys and pain, the triumphs and tribulations—all have been expressed both in and by the music. A list of social, political, and economic issues have been uniquely represented by the various sounds that emerge from the oral tradition. The music has served to inspire, inform, soothe, and enrage all those who might choose to listen, as well as all those preferring to ignore what was going on but unable to get away from the prevalence of the particular music in question. The role of Black radio at various points in history has helped to spread this music while also serving as an important nexus between the culture and the community in the process. Black music is a life force as well as a source of history, and the influence of this music has been felt throughout the culture.

If music represents the heart and soul of Black popular culture, sports represents the body itself. The success and struggles of African Americans in sports helps provide a physical example of the long, arduous journey that Black people have traveled over time in America. From once being excluded from certain sporting activities to now being the standard by which others measure their success, Black athletes have served a vital role in pushing the social and political boundaries that have often limited Black advancement in society.

The success of such a great boxer as Joe Louis and such a great sprinter as Jesse Owens helped solidify America's image and position in the world during the lead-up to World War II. Yet neither of these figures was afforded the treatment of a first-class citizen after their athletic success was no longer needed for the country's uplift. The aforementioned Jackie Robinson was successful at integrating baseball well before the public schools were desegregated and before the Civil Rights movement had gained national attention. Some might even call this "Act One" of what would become the Civil Rights movement, helping to bring attention to the push for social justice on a national stage in an otherwise unjust society.

There is perhaps no better example of the shift in attitude about Black athletes in America than the saga of Muhammad Ali. The gentleman originally known as Cassius Clay was one of the most hated Americans in the turbulent 1960s because of his membership in the controversial Nation of Islam, and especially because of his refusal to be drafted into the Vietnam War. Ali was stripped of his title, his passport was taken, and his ability to make a living was seriously denied based on such actions. Over time, however, Ali prevailed in the courts and in the ring as well. Eventually his triumphant story caused a new generation to begin reconsidering his legacy in the 1990s—so much so that he is often considered one of America's greatest heroes and most influential icons in the present. Yet, for many

African Americans, Ali was always a hero who stood up for what he believed, who spoke his mind, and who used his status as a prominent athlete to push for social change.

Since the heyday of Ali in the 1960s and 1970s, Black athletes have transcended new heights, becoming successful corporate sponsors and cultural icons of the highest order. This transition is best exemplified by Michael Jordan, whose incredible skill set and success as a basketball player was his passport to an unprecedented reign as a global sports and cultural icon in the 1980s and 1990s. In his time, Jordan was embraced across the racial spectrum, but there were also many African Americans who felt that Jordan should have used his position to further political issues as Ali had done before him. But Jordan was of a different era and generation from Ali. His across-the-board appeal and monumental success set new standards for Black athletes and the role of athletics in the larger society. Figures like Jordan help make sports an integral area of popular culture, their images moving freely through so many different areas within the culture itself.

In contemporary society, some African Americans entrepreneurs now occupy places in the sports world other than just participating as athletes—for example, figures like Robert Johnson, founder of the BET network and the owner of the NBA's Charlotte Bobcats. Johnson's success demonstrates the link between entertainment and sports, thus fully foregrounding the importance of popular culture as a vehicle, as well as the upward mobility of African Americans now having a hand in the ownership of teams, as opposed to simply being players. The presence of a prominent figure from the hip-hop world, such as mogul Jay-Z, who owns portions of the New Jersey Nets, is but another example of the link between various spheres of popular culture and the existence of those who now have enough resources to be capital investors as well. Many African Americans have also moved into the executive suites of various teams and assume the roles of managers and coaches as well. Though there is still a lot of room to grow in terms of full Black participation in all levels of the sporting world, progress has been made since the racially problematic days of Owens, Louis, and Robinson.

In the worlds of film and television, African Americans have fared somewhat less well than their counterparts in music and sports, although the presence of African Americans in these venues has been something of note throughout the history of both. The visibility and influence of media has meant a constant struggle over issues of representation as it pertains to African Americans. In addition to the above-mentioned Micheaux and his fledgling efforts as an independent filmmaker, other African Americans such as Spencer Williams and, later, Melvin Van Peebles used the screen as a way of representing their own version of Black life in America. Van Peebles and his provocative work *Sweet Sweetsweetback's Baadasssss Song*

(1971) took the notion of independent cinema to uncharted territory with a stunning political critique that spoke to the sentiment of many people invested in the ideology of Black nationalism. The film represented a moment when culture and politics tended to work hand in hand. Hollywood took its cue from Van Peebles's critical and financial success and began what came to be known as the Blaxploitation movement, which defined Black presence in the 1970s. For the first time, cinema assumed a unique position among other aspects of Black culture in which visual representation came to be debated for its central role in defining African Americans relative to the larger society.

In 1986 filmmaker Spike Lee released his debut feature *She's Gotta Have It* and in so doing revived the Black independent film movement. Lee, with his shrewd marketing skills, tapped into the emerging sentiment of hip-hop culture and went on to redefine what it meant to be a Black filmmaker, managing to get his films made by the mainstream Hollywood studio system and maintain his own unique style at the same time. After Lee's success, several other young Black filmmakers—Robert Townsend, Reginald and Warrington Hudlin, John Singleton, and Allen and Albert Hughes, among others—began making their own way into Hollywood, turning the late 1980s and early 1990s into an extremely fertile period for African American images on film.

In addition to African American filmmakers attempting to control the means of production, the overall image of African Americans in Hollywood has long been an issue. Demeaning stereotypes often accompanied actors such as Stephin Fetchit and Hattie McDaniels in the 1930s; an actor such as Sidney Poitier enjoyed groundbreaking success in the 1960s, in more recent times, Denzel Washington's critically acclaimed performances have garnered Oscars, and the financial clout of Will Smith has made a mark on box-office proceeds. The historical evolution of the African American image in Hollywood is a journey filled with peaks and valleys, often defined by promises of inclusion set against a tradition of exclusion.

To the extent that African Americans in film have been defined by a conflicted history, something similar can be said about the role that African Americans have played on television. African Americans on film and in television have functioned differently from those in sports or music. Issues of representation, especially pertaining to stereotypes, for instance, continue to animate discussions about both film and television; yet the desire for dramas about African Americans on television has been the consistent cry as well. Many regard television's focus on Black situation comedies limiting and especially problematic. Though African Americans have long used stand-up comedy as an effective forum for the dissection of racial politics, the limitations inherent to confining Black television representation primarily to the genre of the situation comedy remains in question. Here the

focus is on genre. Comedies have often tended to feature Black performers in roles that are taken less than seriously, thus the desire to see a
broader palette for African American images remains a demand put forth
by the offended party.

For African Americans on television, Bill Cosby tends to function in a
manner similar to Sidney Poitier on film. Bill Cosby made a name for himself as the first African American in a starring role on television with *I Spy*
in the 1960s, his animated cartoon *Fat Albert* in the 1970s, and his mega-hit
The Cosby Show, which dominated 1980s network television, revived the sit-
com, and became in the process one of the most important television programs ever. Since that time though, much discussion has taken place about
what was not being represented on television—rather than what was.

The 1970s also featured several prominent African American sitcoms,
including *Sanford and Son, Good Times*, and *The Jeffersons. The Flip Wilson
Show*, an hour-long variety show, revolved around the many personas of
comic Flip Wilson. The ground breaking miniseries *Roots* was another landmark television event during this decade. Based on the best-selling book by
Alex Haley, *Roots* unfolded over seven nights in 1977 and traced the history
of Haley's family from its African roots to its enslavement in America and
the resulting aftermath. This popular narrative exposed many Americans
to the horrors of slavery for the first time and also sparked an interest in
genealogy as people from all races became interested in tracing their own
roots. In the 1960s, television played a vital role in broadcasting the pivotal
moments of the Civil Rights movement, and the 1970s inaugurated a fertile period for Black representation on television. Since that time, some
might say that little has changed in these representations, even though the
landscape of television has broadened substantially since then.

The proliferation of cable ushered in the era of Black Entertainment
Television (BET), a network originally owned by Robert Johnson. This all-
Black cable channel, long controversial for its heavy emphasis on hip-hop
music videos, infomercials, and religious programming, was the result of
Johnson's strategy of maximizing profit, though many of his critics felt that
the network should be a venue for education, filling in the blanks left by
the exclusion of African American representation on other networks. More
recently, the cable network TV1 debuted in 2004, part of the media empire
of Cathy Hughes, a prominent and successful African American woman
who also owns the radio conglomerate Radio One.

One of the most significant figures in the history of television has been
Oprah Winfrey. As an African American woman, Winfrey developed a massive following from the mid-1980s forward based on her extremely popular
television program; from this, she has branched out into other areas of the
culture—film, magazines, theater—creating a pervasive brand name that
has few peers throughout the larger history of American popular culture.

Winfrey's popularity has been so broad-based that she decided to use her weighty mass appeal to endorse and campaign for Illinois senator Barack Obama in his historic quest for the presidency in 2008.

To the extent that popular culture is produced and consumed, its ability to reach the hearts and minds of common people is illuminating. To trace the history of African Americans through the twentieth century is to observe the drama, comedy, politics, and soul of Black cultural expression. When focusing on several different modes of representation, from early silent film to theater and from the Delta blues to hip-hop and beyond the breadth and depth of the Black experience is evident in all its attendant celebration and controversy. The contents of these volumes cut across medium, genre, and style to be both focused and eclectic. It is in the accumulation of these individual parts as a whole that we may begin to recognize the many common themes that animate this uniquely American set of circumstances, located deep within the African American existence.

Dr. Todd Boyd
May, 2008
Los Angeles, CA

1

Black Radio Stations and the Community

Carmen L. Manning-Miller

AFRICAN AMERICAN MUSIC: UNIVERSAL APPEAL

Black radio in the United States is born from the African American experience. African Americans are the primary target audience members for these stations. Since the early days of radio, African Americans have set important trends in America's popular culture, because, clearly, the black listening audience has not been the only audience for black radio stations. Black radio is recognized as influencing the career of Elvis Presley, introducing white listeners to rhythm and blues, and fueling the rock 'n' roll culture. Issues of race and community still make the role of black radio in popular culture distinctive and crucial.

Soul, rhythm and blues, gospel/inspirational, jazz, rap, and hip-hop are always fair game as descriptors of black radio formats. For some African Americans, in spite of computer technology, black radio is their only link to some forms of black culture.

American popular culture has been enhanced by the genius of African American musical traditions because African Americans, in a peculiar context, have been involved in the development of popular music. Selective expropriation of African American culture has existed since slavery. American popular culture is periodically infused with the latest in African American music, dance, and comedy, although these cultural transactions are sometimes misguided and condescending. Historically, African American song, dance, and humor were vulnerable to commercial exploitation. White entrepreneurs and entertainers routinely appropriated black cultural innovations and tailored them to appeal to a white audience. In return, African Americans were forced to compromise their artistry in order to gain entrance into a white-controlled and racially segregated entertainment industry. By the 1920s, radio broadcasting played a decisive role in determining the form and context of African Americans cultural and economic development and political participation in the United States.[1]

With the invention and subsequent mass production of the phonograph in the 1920s, blues, jazz, and gospel were made more accessible, to black people in particular. The formation of the race record industry enabled blues and jazz to surface as national phenomena. The recordings were called "race records" because they were produced by and for African Americans. The records were played on the radio and youth—not only black but increasingly white—liked the sounds. Within these parameters, the race record business served as an important catalyst in helping blues and jazz become a part of the mainstream of popular American culture.[2]

The period before the end of World War II was the era of big bands, fancy ballrooms, and live music for radio. By and large, live music on radio meant live music performed by white musicians. (As a rule, black musicians were barred from radio performances.) Exceptions, however, included the likes of Duke Ellington at the Cotton Club, Chuck Hubb, Count Basie, and others. These broadcasts weren't aimed at African American audiences. Broadcasters and advertisers were simply meeting white Americans' demand for big band music.

As the swing era declined, rhythm and blues became popular in African American communities. With the added boost of increased affluence after World War II, African Americans were able to spend more money on recorded music. In 1952, Dolphin's, a Hollywood record shop and black retail outlet, reported that its business suddenly consisted of almost as many white customers as blacks. The growth was attributed to deejays playing rhythm and blues records. As the market for African American popular music expanded, so did the number of stations playing it.[3]

Wilson notes that in the early 1940s less than 25 percent of stations in the United States were independent, unaffiliated with the ABC, NBC, CBS, or Mutual Radio Networks. To attract an audience, independent stations specialized in types of programming not offered by the networks. Until the 1940s, independent radio stations and networks included African Americans only in selected radio programs because of advertisers' fears of alienating white audiences by associating their products with too much programming for black people. Popular shows were *Amos 'n' Andy* and *The All-Negro Hour*. Celebrities such as Paul Robeson, Nat King Cole, and Ella Fitzgerald were featured performers. However, at the end of World War II the purchasing power of African Americans had caught the eyes of some struggling white entrepreneurs.[4]

BLACK RADIO: COMMERCIAL APPEAL AND POLITICAL PARTICIPATION

One of the first radio stations in the United States to develop programming by blacks for blacks with white ownership was WDIA of Memphis, Tennessee. In the early 1950s, the station's ratings skyrocketed. WDIA was rated first in the Memphis radio market and had one of the highest ratings of any independent station in the nation. A. C. Williams, a pioneer WDIA disc jockey, said, "Before we were six months old, stations from all over were sending representatives who stayed two or three days observing us." WDIA was one of many stations eventually switching formats from white to black programming.[5]

After the launching of WDIA, other black radio stations broke ground and provided similar community services: WOKJ in Jackson, Mississippi, KOKY in Little Rock, Arkansas, and WENN in Bessemer, Alabama. In the 1950s, Michigan dentist Haley Bell became the first African American to build black radio stations (WHCB-AM and WCHD-FM) from the ground up. Big stations such as WERD in Atlanta, WDAS in Philadelphia, WEDR in Miami, and WLOU in Louisville, Kentucky, had black radio formats by the mid-1960s.[6]

WDIA listeners recalled the core of the community programming broadcast. Shirley Cosby remembers participating in *Quizzen on the Air*, a quiz show developed by the *Memphis Commercial Appeal* and WDIA to feature students from the area's black schools.[7] Another listener, Dorothy Saulsberry, a Memphis educator said, "The station's worthwhile activities in the black community were almost beyond numbering. Cultural activities, philanthropy, youth work, help to the poor, whatever the black community in Memphis and the area needed, WDIA was there to help."[8] The station set up a goodwill fund to buy school buses to transport crippled black children and to make college scholarships available. It established boys' clubs, provided 125 little league teams, and collected funds for low-cost supplemental housing.

The voice of African American disc jockeys was central to black radio's community involvement and economic growth. Barlow contends that with soul music enshrined as the programming choice for black radio stations, the role of the disc jockey became influential. They were a potent force not only on the airways but in the music industry and in their hometowns. In the 1960s, disc jockeys at black radio stations pioneered radio's most creative formats, introduced their audiences to new, socially conscious soul music, championed civil rights causes, and retained the power to make or break the hits in their respective markets.[9]

Deejays at black radio stations nurtured the grapevine on which civil rights information circulated in the black community: "They marched on picket lines, spoke at protest rallies, helped raise money for the civil rights case, and served as officers in local civil rights organizations. These activities kept them closely attuned to the grassroots struggle, which was reflected in what they said and played on the air."[10]

In 1964, KOKY–Little Rock station manager Eddie Phelan explicitly told disc jockeys not to comment on social issues at the station. Still, the station found itself in the forefront of a campaign for justice in the *Curtis Brown Ingram* case. Brown was a black prisoner clubbed to death by a white trustee at the Pulaski County Penal Farm. Deejay Bob Broadwater managed to find two witnesses who testified that the trustee had acted on the orders from one of the guards without provocation from Ingram.[11]

In 1968, WDIA's Chris Turner openly flaunted his membership in a Memphis black power organization called the Black Knights. Turner, hugely popular in the local community, held a minute of radio silence to protest Mayor Henry Loeb's handling of sanitation workers. The strike eventually drew Martin Luther King Jr. to the city and his death was the subject of extensive coverage and comment by Turner and other WDIA announcers. The station seemed to have been important in sustaining community support of the strike.[12]

Jack Gibson, a noted Atlanta disc jockey, was among those who insisted that "if it were not for black radio . . . more cities in the United States would have been burnt to the ground after the death of Martin Luther King." The deluge of commendations and awards received by black radio stations— among them D.C. outlets WOL and WUST and Memphis station WDIA— from law enforcement agencies and civic leaders in recognition of their contribution in restoring order suggests that these stations had played a significant role in preventing a terrible situation from worsening.[13]

Black politicians also heralded black radio in reaching black voters during this era of civil rights history. In Texas, Barbara Jordan noted the value of radio in the 1966 campaign that saw her become the first African American, and first woman, elected to the state's senate. Contrasting her success in that election with two successful earlier bids for election to the Texas House of Representatives, she set much store by her decision to ignore television and concentrate on black-oriented radio: "When we got it broken down into districts, we did not put any funds into television, and only into radio for the two Negro stations that we had."[14]

New York City's WLIB-AM Radio once dubbed itself "the Nation's Top Black Super Station—Your Total Black News and Information Station." The station was cited as a center of communication, a place for dialogue, and a source of news and information. Walker found that the station played a key role in the 1989 election campaign of the city's first African

American mayor, David Dinkins, and that most black elected officials in the New York community viewed WLIB as part of their community outreach strategy.[15]

Martin Luther King surmised in 1967 that black people "were totally dependent on radio as their means of relating to society at large. They do not read newspapers. . . . Television speaks not to their needs but to upper-middle-class America." King said the community had come to appreciate the role that the radio announcer played in the lives of African Americans. In praise of deejays, he contended that "for better or for worse, you are opinion leaders in the community. And it is important that you remain aware of the power which is potential in your vocation."[16]

By the mid-1960s there were only a handful of black-owned radio stations, yet black radio stations were willing to cooperate with the activities of the civil rights movement. Ward provided several reasons for this utility. By 1964 attitudes had changed within the industry toward covering the Southern freedom struggle. Ward noted that the civil rights campaign was perceived as a viable movement allowing deejays, reporters, radio owners, and managers to test the limits of what was acceptable in terms of civil rights advocacy and movement news coverage. Also radio stations were compelled to cover civil rights as it became the major domestic news story of the times because stations were saddled with Fairness Doctrine policies mandating the community coverage.[17] Even white owners who had no reputation of supporting civil rights causes realized that "[black radio] has to be involved in the struggle for integration. You cannot operate a station and not be involved."[18]

One of the most outstanding examples of how radio was positioned to promote community interests was the long campaign against discriminatory practices in the state of Mississippi. The outcomes served to have a profound national implication for efforts to increase African American involvement in radio and other media. In 1964, the United Church of Christ (UCC) led the opposition to the renewal of broadcasting licenses at WJDX and WLBT in Jackson, Mississippi. Complaints were also made against other Jackson facilities—radio stations WSLI and WRBC, and WJTV, a CBS television affiliate owned by *Jackson Clarion Ledger and Daily News*—as well as against the WCBI radio and television franchise in Columbus, Mississippi. Headquartered in New York, the UCC was a two-million strong union of congregational Christian Churches and the Evangelical and Reformed Churches. In March 1964, the UCC monitored a week of radio and television broadcasts in Mississippi. Disturbed by the complete absence of African American voices or viewpoints on these media outlets serving an area with a 45 percent African American population, the UCC had petitioned the FCC on behalf of various groups who wanted to testify in the next round of station license renewal applications.

The UCC petition raised critical questions about the extent to which local people could exercise a measure of control over the radio and television facilities that purported to serve them. This initiative and a slew of other civil rights and media litigation efforts were dedicated to increasing the number of black owners of radio and television stations, to improving the quantity and quality of service broadcasting devoted to black audiences, and to ensuring proper African American representation at the FCC.[19]

BLACK OWNERSHIP

Some scholars claim that two assumptions underwrote the clamor for more black radio ownership. The first was that black owners would hire more black staff at their stations, especially in executive positions. The second was that black ownership and executives would be conspicuously engaged in community activism and politics—and that they would find a balance between news, politics, community affairs, and public service broadcasting and the soul music that dominated black radio stations.[20]

By 1964, only 5 of the 5,500 commercial radio stations operating in the United Sates were owned by African Americans. By 1968, when advertising revenue of the 528 commercial stations featuring regular programming for black audiences brought in $35 million dollars per annum, there were still just eight black-owned stations. By 1970, there were sixteen, ten of which were in the South. Between 1969 and 1989, loans from government-sponsored programs helped fund the purchase of 90 percent of all new black-owned outlets. The number of black-owned facilities had increased nearly twelvefold. In 1978 the FCC introduced for the first time measures designed specifically to increase the level of minority media ownership in America. But these efforts yielded ambiguous results. The new ownership statistics represented less than 2 percent of the total number of radio stations operating in the United States by 1980. Then, too, definitions of what constituted minority-owned stations were in constant flux and were revised in 1982 so that owners selling to companies with as little as 20 percent minority participation could appeal for special tax breaks. African Americans seldom managed to buy the bigger, more lucrative and prestigious metropolitan stations. (Cathy Hughes, owner of the most black radio stations, is a notable exception.[21])

Black radio ownership seemed to have reached a plateau by 2000. The 274 black-owned stations operating in 1995 had dwindled to 200. Within a decade the deregulation of the airwaves and the lapse of federal assistance to black ownership initiatives in the form of distress sale provisions, tax incentives, and restrictions on the number of stations a single owner could have in any market, eroded significant economic gains for African American radio station owners. The legislation also eliminated the requirements that stations include public service programming in their formats.

Scholars fault the 1996 Telecommunications Act for the decline in black radio ownership. Hutchinson posited that rising operating costs, racial discrimination by advertisers, media consolidation, and changes in listener demographics made black stations ripe for the pickings of corporate entities. Hutchinson found that the corporate syndicates appreciated the lucrative nature of the stations and bought them on the cheap.[22]

African American station owners were unable to access capital quickly to make new acquisitions, especially because the 1996 legislation inflated the price of broadcast ownership beyond the reach of most African American owners. Optimistically, owners of the largest black-owned radio companies, such as Cathy Hughes, CEO of Radio One, are buying struggling stations and investing in African American news and information for radio and television.[23]

DEFINING FORMATS

Another industry shift affected the prosperity of black radio, the career potential of some African American artists, and the flexibility of black radio programming. The stronghold that deejays possessed in radio programming in the industry waned when the "Top Forty" format became an industry standard. This programming format affected black radio in that what was played was in the control of the station's management and no longer in control of the deejays. This process decreased deejays' opportunities to expose local artists. The play list, dictated by *Billboard* rankings, dismissed the notoriety of many black artists.

Radio industry leaders justified the shift by blaming deejays who were involved in payola operations for robbing stations. In the aftermath of the scandals, when Top Forty radio emerged, many black radio stations followed suit in an effort to compete in a new market that attracted advertisers to demographics that included black and white listeners of crossover music. The new format shaved the profits and diluted the cultural identity of the once-profitable soul-station formats in the nation's biggest media markets.

Top Forty radio eventually led industry leaders in the direction of the urban contemporary concept. Urban contemporary was designed as a multiracial format. In its original conception, black artists in the soul, funk, and jazz categories were integrated on air with tunes by white artists who performed in similar genres. Barlow argues that urban contemporary simply institutionalized a process of "reverse crossover" that had begun earlier. Although the format provided greater access for white musicians and white personalities on what had been black radio stations, black performers or black radio personalities did not gain any reciprocal access to rock radio.[24] As the style became a successful crossover ploy for attracting white advertising dollars without alienating black listeners, the format was labeled urban contemporary by the radio industry.

Barrow described a similar cycle of innovation, success, competition, and crossover at Washington D.C.'s WHUR-FM. The station's biggest advance in the era of crossover was a format called "The Quiet Storm," a blend of ballads and jazz instrumentals. Stations all over the nation copied the idea. But the crossover trend raised concerns among afrocentric purists who argued that "at some stations the format only paid lip service to the cultural and social diversity of the African American population."[25]

At the beginning of the twenty-first century the concentration of economic power in the radio industry, competing digital technologies, cookie-cutter music, and radio schedules with negligible news and current affairs broadcasting are the order of the day for most commercial black radio stations. In this milieu, the communal aspects of black radio may be preserved by black public radio, black radio networking, and the evolving technologies of high definition and satellite radio.

PUBLIC RADIO, THE AMERICAN URBAN RADIO NETWORK, AND NEW TECHNOLOGY

Black public radio can be categorized in two groups: educational and community. The educational stations are mostly owned and operated by historically black colleges and universities. The community-owned radio stations are most often owned and operated by nonprofit foundations controlled by local boards of directors. These stations usually program jazz, blues, gospel, Caribbean, Brazilian, and African music, the formats abandoned by most commercial stations in pursuit of high ratings and profits. Historically, black college and university public radio stations have most often been attached to academic budgets and academic programs.

Before the mandate of the Corporation for Public Broadcasting and National Public Radio in 1967, which spawned the growth of public radio funding by the federal government, the only black college station on the air was WCSU-FM at Central State University in Ohio. The upsurge began when WSHA-FM at Shaw University in Raleigh, North Carolina, went on the air. During the 1970s, at least twenty other stations emerged.[26]

Another category is the student-intensive cable radio outlet. Cable stations do not need an FCC license to operate, and they have a history on black campuses dating back to World War II. The first cable station was started at Hampton University in 1940. Lincoln University in Pennsylvania also operated a cable station during this period.

In the 1980s, the growth spurt of black-controlled public radio at historically black colleges and universities slacked off because of federal govern-

Tom Joyner speaks at the 2004 Dialogue with America's Families, in which six presidential hopefuls answered questions posed by local residents.

AP Photo/Bruce L. Flashnick

ment cutbacks. Some stations developed alternative operational models to compensate for the lack of funding. Brooklyn, New York's Medgar Evers Community College worked out a time-sharing arrangement on WNYE-FM with its license holder, CUNY Board of Trustees. CUNY continued to broadcast educational programs on WNYE in the day, but evening hours were turned over to a coalition of faculty, students, and community media activists. The news and public affairs programming focused on issues, needs, and concerns affecting central Brooklyn residents.[27]

Twelve outlets were initially charged with serving the interest of African American communities. Over time these stations have broadened their community bases and services. The most successful community radio station serving an African American community is identified as WPFW-FM, a 50,000-watt outlet launched by the Pacifica Foundation in Washington, D.C. Eventually, WPFW became the largest and most listened-to historically African American community radio station in the country. However, the station fell victim to market factors. After a long stint as a jazz station, WPFW decided to switch to a "world" beat format. Quickly the station's ratings and funding base plummeted, and the station renewed its original format.[28]

By the early 1980s, KPOO, "Poor People's Radio in San Francisco," had broadened its base to include San Francisco's Hispanic, Asian, Filipino, and Native American populations. Music, news, public affairs, and cultural programs are presented in the languages of each of the station's targeted ethnic groups. Nevertheless, the station is still marketed as an African American–owned and –operated noncommercial radio station.[29]

Examples also exist in noncommercial radio history of how the most depressed communities, who might benefit from community radio the most, have been penalized by the structural constraints of the model. In 1977, a black nonprofit community organization in rural Warren County, North Carolina, put WVSP on the air. The station began with a paid staff of six and a jazz, blues, local news, and public affairs format. By 1982, the station had expanded its staff and volunteer bases. When funding cuts devastated its operational budget, the station moved to the adjacent Nash County market in search of a more lucrative funding base. The strategy failed and the station went off the air.[30]

In 1991, the historical merger of its two competing black radio network predecessors, National Black Network (NBN) and Sheridan Broadcasting Network (SBN), created American Urban Radio (AURN). AURN became the third-largest and only black radio network in the United States. AURN touts having the largest network reaching urban America, with more than 200 weekly shows and an estimated 25 million listeners. The network broadcasts news, entertainment, sports, and information programming to more than 475 radio stations nationwide. It is the only African American broadcaster with a bureau in the White House, and it has offices and bureaus in New York, Pittsburgh, Atlanta, Chicago, Detroit, Los Angeles, and Washington, D.C.[31] Another aspect of networking in black radio also endures: the *Tom Joyner Morning Show*. It is the most prominent black radio show in decades to be syndicated nationally by a mainstream media corporation. Joyner's show has been successful for several reasons: it has amassed a large influential audience among African American baby boomers, has rejuvenated the careers of "old-school" R&B artists, and has paved the way for other black radio ventures by proving that they can be profitable and competitive in urban markets.[32]

Critics legitimately bemoan the demise of black radio vis-à-vis ownership and programming, but alternatives exist on the digital horizon. Already, the migration of African Diaspora music has survived the transition to digital technology. The concept of "narrowcasting" has renewed the attraction of advertisers to more specifically targeted audiences. Satellite radio so far has offered a variety of afrocentric formats grouped by decade and by genre. African American personalities such as Oprah Winfrey and Jamie Foxx have also launched talk, music, and comedy programming that will attract an African American listening base to satellite radio. Because digital and satellite media technologies are exempt from FCC requirements, the presence of public affairs that meet the specific needs of the African American community is minimal, although present. Similar to the plight of resource-poor noncommercial public radio audiences, the very audiences who benefit from these technologies can ill afford to pay for expensive hardware and monthly subscription fees.

High definition has bolstered the free radio market. HD radio uses a signal that piggybacks on standard frequencies and can be played on digital radio receivers. HD radio allows broadcasters to slice their broadcast streams into several channels, each devoted to a different kind of news or music programming. Listeners' access to this technology also remains a big concern.

Howard University's WHUR-FM launched its HD station, WHUR-WORLD, in 2006. It has allowed the station to revisit the all-black music concept the station employed before market pressures—wrought by innovations in programming for urban audiences—altered its format. In addition, the station can be accessed by Internet. WHUR-WORLD has returned to its original "360-Degree Total Blackness" concept. The station's management claims that because the station is not owned by corporate interests, the programming can cover a broad range of interests throughout the African Diaspora.[33]

AURN has used podcasting as one way to interface its programming digitally. Listeners can download shows to their computers or iPods.[34] Podcasting is one of the Internet's equalizing technologies, allowing anyone with a PC to become a broadcaster. By lowering the cost of broadcasting to nearly nothing, it enables more voices and messages to be heard.

Black radio is a medium of creation, evolution, and dissemination, and it is a home for many African American listeners. It has been in some ways the only forum for a wide spectrum of issues and concerns of black culture and African American people. Black radio is the most ubiquitous means of mass communication for African Americans. It helped define African American music and consciousness because of its appeal, giving it its economic prowess and its place as both a servant and leader of the African American community. On black radio, African Americans speak a different English language, empower politicians and the citizenry, challenge racial supremacy, fuss with and gossip about each other, worship, and reveal their talents to a nation of listeners who embrace the best of what is broadcast. Black radio is a platform for a culture that will continue to claim an important presence in all realms of radio broadcasting, whether over the airwaves or across cyberspace.

NOTES

1. William Barlow, "Black Music on Radio During the Jazz Age," *African American Review* (Summer 1995): 326.

2. William Barlow, "Cashing In," in *Split Images: African Americans in the Mass Media*, eds. Jannette Dates and William Barlow (Washington, D.C.: Howard University Press, 1990), 25.

3. Reebee Garofalo, "Crossing Over: 1939–1989," in *Split Images*, eds. Dates and Barlow, 60.

4. George T. Wilson, "When Memphis Made Radio History," *American Visions* (Aug./Sept. 1993), 22.

5. Wilson, "When Memphis Made Radio History," 24.

6. William Barlow, *Voice Over: The Making of Black Radio*, (Philadelphia: Temple University Press, 1999), 204. See also Brian Ward, *Radio and the Struggle for Civil Rights in the South* (Gainesville, FL: The University of Florida Press, 2004), 183.

7. Wilson, "When Memphis Made Radio History," 24.

8. Ibid.

9. Barlow, *Voice Over: The Making of Black Radio*, 204.

10. Ibid.

11. Ward, *The Struggle for Civil Rights*, 318.

12. Ibid.

13. Ibid., 344.

14. Julian Bond, "Black Candidates' Southern Campaign Experiences," VEP Commissioned Study (1968), quote 37.

15. Annette Walker, "Black-Owned Radio Stations Struggle to Survive," *Black World Today* (online edition), July 27, 2005, http://www.tbwt.org.

16. Martin Luther King, "Transforming a Neighborhood with Brotherhood," *Jack the Rapper* 13 (1989): 1.

17. Ward, *The Struggle for Civil Rights*, 180

18. Egmont Sonderling, *Official Record of Proceedings Before the Federal Communications Commission*, testimony to the FCC, July 11, 1966, 51 file 16533, Vol. 2, box 164, FCC-DOC.

19. Sidney Head, Christopher Sterling, and Lemuel B. Schofield, *Broadcasting in America: A Survey of Electronic Media*, 2nd ed. (Boston: Houghton Mifflin, 1996), 298.

20. Ward, *The Struggle for Civil Rights*, 283.

21. Larry Irving, "The Big Chill: Has Minority Ownership Been Put on Ice?" Assistant Secretary for Communications and Information, National Telecommunications and Information Administration, Department of Commerce (Washington, D.C.: National Association of Black Owned Broadcasters' Annual Meeting, September 11, 1997).

22. Earl Hutchinson, "Endangered Black Radio," http://www.blackjournalism .com/dealth.

23. See http: //www. ntia.doc.gov/opadhome/minown98/blac.htm.

24. Barlow, "Commercial and Noncommercial Radio" in *Split Images*, eds. Dates and Barlow, 222.

25. Ibid.

26. See http: //www.radiostations.com.

27. Barlow, "Commercial and Noncommercial Radio" in *Split Images*, eds. Dates and Barlow, 222.

28. Ibid., 241.

29. Ibid., 235.

30. Ibid., 233. See also www.kpoo.com.

31. See http: //www.aurnol.com.

32. Jounice L. Nealy, "He's Your Wakeup Call," *St. Petersburg Times*, July 6, 1998, 1D, 4D.

33. See http: //www.whurworld.com.

34. See http: //www.aurnol.com.

2

African American Sacred Music: From Folk Spirituals to Urban Gospel

Milmon F. Harrison

The musical legacy of African Americans is arguably their greatest and most enduring contribution to American expressive culture. This essay explores one aspect of that rich musical heritage: African American sacred music. The story of the origins and subsequent development of African American sacred music follows the experience of African Americans from their earliest arrivals in North America as enslaved Africans to the present. It might be thought of as a kind of repository of a people's commentary on the world and their varying positions within it. African Americans translated their particular struggle, and their enduring hope for something better, into the universal language of music.

In order to more fully understand our topic, we must place it within historical contexts that both precede and follow its emergence as a distinct art form in the United States. The goal here is not to provide an exhaustive history of the vast topic of African American sacred music but rather to consider several important moments in its development and its continued influence on American culture beyond the strictly religious community of African Americans. This essay argues that the meanings, uses, and influence of this music extend far beyond the boundaries of the spiritual or religious rites—and that, historically, the relationship between the black Church and the performance of African American sacred music has frequently been marked by a tension that continues today. In other words, although an obvious, close relationship between African Americans' sacred music, faith, and faith-based institutions does indeed exist, African American sacred music is not only church music but occupies a number of important spaces within the broad spectrum of African American culture in particular, as well as American popular culture in general. These linkages will be made clear through illustrative examples in the remainder of this exploratory essay.

WHAT IS AFRICAN AMERICAN SACRED MUSIC?

African American sacred music—whether as spirituals or gospel—refers to the music-making traditions of black people in a North American, primarily Christian, context from the seventeenth century to the present day. These forms of music gave utterance to the spiritual and theological worldview— the Black Sacred Cosmos[1]—of Americans of African descent. African American sacred music also refers to a body of songs (or hymnody) that has come to be accepted and established as traditional within the African American religious community and by scholars of African American music. Such songs include "Didn't My Lord Deliver Daniel?" "Swing Low, Sweet Chariot," and "Steal Away." This body of work also includes standard hymns of Protestant Christianity in general that over time have been reinterpreted according to African American sensibilities. The well-known hymn "Amazing Grace" is one example of this practice.

Like other forms of African American music, African American sacred music also carries within it a particular style of singing and musical performance. This style has its origins in traditional West African performance practices adapted by African Americans, and many of the characteristic elements can usually be found in other forms of African American music. Among these elements are the prevalence of polyrhythms and syncopation (referring to the complexity of the rhythmic structure of the music as well as the vocal performance) and a style of singing that is sometimes highly dramatic and expressive of individual faith and conviction (as in gospel performance).

Melismatic singing, the practice of vocal embellishment in which a singer moves through a range of notes on one syllable within a song's lyric, is another characteristic of African American sacred music performance. The "call and response" modality, in which a lead singer sings or "calls" out a particular line or phrase that is then "answered" by the other singers (or the congregation), is yet another characteristic element adapted by African Americans and can be found in virtually all their music. This emphasis on collectively creating the music through "call and response" is also supported by the simple lyrical structure of the songs and the repetition of certain words and phrases throughout the song.[2]

Like those of jazz and blues that developed alongside it, audiences of black gospel music performance expect a high degree of improvisation, often thought of as making a song a performer's own. Rather than merely rendering a song the same way twice, musicians' and singers' ability to instantaneously improvise, or riff, is highly valued. In terms of overall thematic structure—again like the blues—gospel music's primary concern is to express aspects of the believer's experience in this world, rather than to focus primarily on the deliverance to the next world. It articulates a transcendent faith that is "real-ized" in the struggles of everyday life. Finally, given that a distinctive characteristic of twentieth-century gospel music lies in its marriage of blues music to sacred lyrical content, it has followed musical trends found elsewhere in secular musical culture, and continues to do so even today.

In terms of accompaniment, singing a cappella (without instrumental accompaniment) and using the body as instrument in music making (as in hand-clapping, foot-stomping, and dancing) have been an important part of making African American sacred music that originated in the slave community. Where there were instruments to be found or made, and where there were musicians among the community who might play a banjo or violin, for example, such music might have been included as well in the singing of sacred folk songs during slavery and afterward in the small, Southern churches in which these songs continued to be sung.

Black gospel musicians have included a broad range of instruments into their performances beyond, for example, the pipe organ used in more traditional forms of European sacred works. In contrast, gospel musicians use drums, electric guitars, horns, and any other type of available instruments as accompaniments to the voice. Gospel music carries a long tradition of fusing secular musical idioms—such as blues, jazz, R&B, and, in more recent years, hip-hop—with religious imagery and lyrical content.

RESISTANCE IN AFRICAN AMERICAN SACRED FOLK MUSIC

The music of enslaved Africans contained multiple meanings. These songs expressed hope for deliverance from their experience of enslavement on earth, faith in salvation, and hope that their spirit would be received into heaven upon death, their singular perspective on those who dominated them. These songs played a part in their acts of resistance of their subordinated position as well as made space for them to challenge the negative representations of black people and their culture that enjoyed great currency in the popular imagination of the day.

Enslaved Africans in the United States drew upon their cultural heritage and adapted aspects of it in New World contexts. Because theirs was a life with the central characteristic of long hours of unpaid labor, the work songs and the field hollers were two of the earliest forms of their generalized African cultural background to be adapted. Toiling together in the fields as agricultural workers gave them an opportunity to use the work songs and hollers as a way of not only passing the time but, in certain types of jobs, rhythmically coordinating their efforts when working together on a common task. This rhythmic pattern, or cadence, helped all involved to maintain a steady, common pace in the work. "Call and response" was also an important feature of the work song and field hollers.

The spirituality of Africans and their American-born descendents also occupied an important position in their worldview. As is common with many indigenous peoples, enslaved Africans came from cultural backgrounds where little distinction was made between the sacred and the secular, or profane, realms of existence. According to this view, everything was subject to the spirit world. Out of their secret gatherings under the "brush arbors" (or "hush harbors," as they often referred to these places in which vegetation grew in such as way as to muffle the sound of their worship activities) the plantation churches developed.[3] In their churches and other clandestine religious gatherings African Americans could openly worship together. Thus the spirituals, including the mournful sorrow songs, the jubilee songs of joy and celebration, and also the songs that spoke of deliverance, reflected the consciousness of an enslaved but hopeful people.[4]

But the spirituals also served subversive purposes in the midst of systematic racial subordination of blacks. Not only did these songs reaffirm the spirituality and faith of the community—and in so doing, affirmed their humanity and intrinsic worth in the midst of a social and political system that completely denied their humanity—but they were also drawn upon in the service of collective resistance to the social order. In certain contexts, the singing of particular spirituals was understood to contain coded messages that the slaves used to communicate secretly with each other under the ignorant eyes and ears of their masters and overseers. For example, the well-known spiritual "Steal Away" was often used to convey the message that there would either be a secret meeting taking place soon, or that there would be an escape attempt. In this way the duality—the double meanings—contained within African American music represents another characteristic feature for consideration in our attempts to fully understand African American expressive culture more generally. This duality has been an important part of African American survival: appearing to be resigned to their second-class citizenship while at the same time finding creative ways to express inner or secret ways to oppose and resist structured oppression.[5]

The spirituals, or sacred folk songs, of enslaved Africans and their descendants were also subversive in that they were appropriated politically by the abolitionists and advocates for black civil rights in the nineteenth century (as well as in the mid-twentieth century Civil Rights movement). As part of the abolitionist campaign, written testimony of former, or fugitive, slaves became a literary genre known as (Fugitive) Slave Narratives. These works bore witness to the horrors of life in bondage. Public appearances and speeches by former (often fugitive) slaves such as Sojourner Truth and Frederick Douglass also served the abolitionist movement. The folk spirituals of the Southern slave community were also called into service as an example of the creativity, the expressiveness, and most of all the humanity of enslaved Africans and their free, but still not equal, counterparts. Thus, in addition to their written and spoken testimony, the music of African Africans—particularly their sacred music—served multiple purposes far beyond their particular religious beliefs and practices.

Many historically black colleges and universities (HBCUs), most of which are located in the South, were established during Reconstruction, the period immediately following the Civil War lasting from 1865 to 1877. Among the most notable of these institutions of higher education for newly freed black Americans was Fisk University, founded 1866 in Nashville, Tennessee. A few years later, in 1871, as a means of helping save the struggling university from financial collapse, the university's music director George White assembled a small group of students, some of whom were former slaves, into a group that came to be known as the Fisk Jubilee Singers. Originally the repertoire of the singers was a combination of European choral works and other types of music appropriate for the concert hall. But soon, in response to the overwhelming response of audiences to their renditions of the songs of their slave past, the focus of their concerts came to be primarily spirituals and the jubilee songs of celebration and joy from which their name arose.

The group of singers toured not only the nation but also abroad for more than a decade, some of its original members continuing to sing with newcomers. The original Jubilee Singers of Fisk University are commonly considered the group responsible for once again adapting the culture of enslaved Africans and developing it into an arranged concert format more suitable to white and European musical tastes and aesthetic sensibilities. At this time in American popular culture, the dominant portrayals of black life came through the demeaning caricatures performed by white minstrel show performers in blackface makeup. In that context the Jubilee Singers of Fisk University brought the music of African Americans to an international audience with a dignity and a sense of racial pride uncommon in the representation and popular imagination of African Americans, especially those who had been enslaved. At the same time that they helped challenge prevalent stereotypes of their race, this group of talented young people was able to save their university, helping to make it possible for multitudes of other African Americans to receive a university education in the midst of a still racially restrictive South. Thus the duality of African American expressive culture can once again be appreciated. As did the abolitionists before them, the Jubilee singers called into service the sacred music of African Americans to indirectly subvert the existing order. Their concerts, which increasingly featured folk spirituals sung in complex harmonies, opened a space for new, more dignified representations of African Americans, their culture, and their capabilities. The

Jubilee singers' use of four-part harmonies in the arrangements of their music became the model of the gospel quartets that would dominate the genre from the 1940s to the 1960s, a period commonly referred to as gospel music's Golden Age.[6]

Continuing in the tradition established by the original Fisk Jubilee Singers, a number of similar groups sprang up in African American colleges and universities within a short time. Today, many college and university campuses across the United States have gospel choirs as permanent performing groups that help audiences to learn about, appreciate, and preserve the creativity and faith expressed in the body of songs created in African Americans' slave past for future generations to enjoy.

THE GREAT MIGRATION AND THE RISE OF GOSPEL MUSIC

The reality of blacks' lack of power or protection in the "Jim Crow" South, along with the region's economic instability, provided strong pushes for African Americans looking for a new place to call home. Northern industrial cities such as Chicago, Detroit, and New York became the destination of over 1.5 million African Americans during what is referred to as the Great Migration between the years of 1910 and 1920. African Americans left the South in droves, their imaginations fired by religious images of a promised land of freedom and opportunity.

But for many of these formerly rural and agricultural migrants to urban industrial centers, the North was anything but a promised land. They found that a de facto form of segregation also existed there and that blacks were still subjected to unfair treatment and lack of protection by authorities, just as they had been in the South. To make matters worse, some of those African Americans who already were in the North were less than hospitable to their country cousins from the South. One of the settings in which this sense of alienation for migrants *within* the black community was most strongly felt was in the mainline black churches.

It was not uncommon for black churches in Northern cities to be made up of congregants from a higher social class than that of the migrants. The norms of acceptable emotional display in the worship services within these churches revolved around reserve: being much less spontaneous, less ecstatic, and less demonstrative than was the norm in many of the black churches in the rural South. The songs sung by the large Northern church choirs were frequently classical European choral works rather than the sacred folk songs and high-energy services the Southern migrants were accustomed to. As a result, many of these migrants became disaffected and left these established black churches in favor of an ever-increasing number of new social and religious movements. These movements and new religions were led by colorful, charismatic figures such as Marcus Garvey and

Father Divine. Some of these religious leaders set up their own Southern-style churches in rented storefront spaces. A large number of these store-front churches were some form of Holiness denomination or the recently established Pentecostal church, and others were Baptist—but with a South-ern, revivalistic worship style that closely resembled that found in the Holi-ness–Pentecostal churches that many migrants found more suitable than the worship style they saw at the sterile mainline churches. It is at this juncture that we pinpoint the origins of black gospel music as a distinct musical form.

More than any other form of religion with a substantial African American following, those within the Holiness–Pentecostal tradition became most central to the development of this new music. The Holiness–Pentecostal movement broadened to other parts of the country in the decades during which the Great Migration took place. Emphasizing the free exercise of the charismatic gifts of the spirit, including spontaneous, ecstatic worship, faith healing, prophesy, and glossolalia (also known as speaking in tongues), the type of worship generally found in Pentecostal worship services also had one additional characteristic: the belief in and practice of receiving the Holy Ghost and shouting. Shouting is a highly stylized form of ecstatic dance with origins in the ring shout that enslaved Africans also adapted in their worship services along with their songs and beliefs.

The highly syncopated, fast-tempo shout songs were of great importance in Pentecostal churches. These were accompanied by a much wider array of musical instruments than were commonly allowed in non-Pentecostal churches. Along with piano, organ, guitar, horns, and drums, the music was also collectively produced by the congregation by stomping feet, clapping hands, rhythmic tambourine playing, triangles, sticks, and whatever else congregation members had at hand. The openness of Holiness–Pente-costals to music that may have sounded less like European choral works in favor of lively, rhythmic music made it a perfect breeding ground for the development of gospel music in the future. The black church, in its accept-ance of gospel music in some quarters and in its rejection in others, helped it to develop into the phenomenon it later would become.

The Father of Gospel: Thomas Andrew Dorsey and Other Pioneers

As we have seen, African American sacred music was a well-established part of American culture long before the dawn of the twentieth century. But the term *gospel music* was actually coined by Thomas A. Dorsey (1899–1993), himself a migrant to Chicago from the South.[7] Dorsey was born in Villa Rica, Georgia, to parents who were strongly rooted in the church. His father was a pastor and his mother an organist. After suffer-ing financial difficulty, the family moved to the city of Atlanta, where

Thomas A. Dorsey at the piano with his band, the Wandering Syncopators Orchestra, in 1923.

AP Photo

Thomas dropped out of school at the age of eleven to play piano in movie houses and vaudeville theaters. He later became a blues piano player in Atlanta brothels and clandestine parties. He left Atlanta for Chicago at the age of seventeen and, under the name Georgia Tom, eventually made a reputation for himself accompanying blues singers such as Ma Rainey and Bessie Smith.

Throughout the course of Dorsey's early life as a blues pianist, he developed a soft style of playing in order to avoid uninvited police attention from disturbing the peace in after-hours house (or rent) parties. At one point as a Chicago blues musician, Dorsey dabbled in writing sacred music. His first gospel composition was actually included in the second edition of the hymn book *Gospel Pearls*, published by the National Baptist Convention in 1921. This was the first collection of songs published by a black congregation describing them as gospel songs. Dorsey attempted to leave the world of secular music to use his talent in the Baptist church, but facing rejection of his music by most conservative black churches, he returned to playing secular blues music until he experienced a crisis in his life and gave up the blues in favor of gospel forever. Dorsey, however, had been influenced not only by blues artists but by Dr. Charles A. Tindley (1851–1933), of Philadelphia, a composer and publisher of early gospel music.

It is important to note that although gospel music was essentially a creative synthesis of musical forms associated with secular blues songs and religious lyrics, this new type of music was not immediately accepted in the mainline black churches. Many within the well-established northern Baptist and Methodist churches were very conservative in their opinions about what type of music was most appropriate in the context of the worship service. Frequently, pastors of these congregations rejected Dorsey's gospel songs because the music sounded too much like that heard in nightclubs and bars—places their church members were not supposed to be. Indeed, some of the songs that have come to be seen as traditional gospel songs (such as the highly successful "Move On Up a Little Higher," recorded by Mahalia Jackson) sound very much like blues or other kinds of secular music played and heard during their original era.

Thomas A. Dorsey is recognized as the father of gospel music for first synthesizing his secular blues piano musical style and sensibility with lyrics that spoke of faith in God and redemption from the trouble of the world. He is credited with having written more than 400 gospel songs, many of which have become classics not only within the African American community but in American culture at large. One such example is the song "Precious Lord, Take My Hand," written in response to the tragic death of his beloved wife Nettie and their son in childbirth in 1932, which has become virtually an American classic, even among some non–African Americans.

The Twentieth-Century Institutionalization of Gospel Music

Thomas A. Dorsey is not only an important figure as gospel music's creator but also because he was responsible for several important ways of distributing this new music and institutionalizing it to allow it to endure long beyond his and his colleagues' initial efforts. Beyond authorship of particular songs, Dorsey's influence can also be seen in the way gospel music was marketed to the masses. He first set up a sheet music publishing company that not only published musical notation but the lyrics as well. His partner in this venture (the first publishing company featuring this new music) was gospel singer Sallie Martin (1896–1988). Raised as a member of the Church of God in Christ, Martin came to Chicago from Pittsville, Georgia, in order to work with Dorsey. She accompanied him as they traveled to local churches, introducing the music by performing gospel songs for the congregation. Dorsey also established a series of concerts in which gospel music was heard and the sheet music was sold to individuals. The songs were sold individually rather than requiring consumers to purchase a hymnal or entire song book in order to obtain particular pieces they wanted.

Along with musician Kenneth Morris, a talented musician, arranger, and transcriber, Sallie Martin later went on to form another publishing company, the Martin and Morris Music Studio. The company was different from others in that it sold not only its own published gospel songs but those of other publishing houses as well. Within a relatively short time, theirs became the top publisher of gospel music in the country. Martin also formed the Sallie Martin Singers, a group that toured the country singing gospel music. Morris is the person responsible for introducing the Hammond organ into gospel music along with the piano, thus producing a distinctive sound that remained an essential part of the music for decades.

The importance of Dorsey, Martin, and Morris to the development of gospel music extended far beyond the creative acts of composition and performance; they were also instrumental in establishing it as an industry at its earliest stages. In 1932 Dorsey and Martin organized the National Association of Gospel Choirs and Choruses (NAGCC) as a national institutional structure—it became an important network that allowed Dorsey to promote new work and teach it to performers from around the country. Dorsey's national choir association set the stage by providing an institutional example and structure for James Cleveland to come along with the Gospel Music Workshop of America (GMWA); Cleveland was greatly influenced by Roberta Martin, another important figure in the history of this music. Later, along with Shirley Caesar, Cleveland recorded the first live gospel album in 1962 (Savoy Records), the first gospel music artist to receive a star on Hollywood's Walk of Fame. Cleveland had worked with Dorsey in Chicago as a young man.

EARLY GOSPEL STARS

Another prominent gospel music performer to emerge during this period was Sister Rosetta Tharpe, whose church affiliation was also with the Church of God in Christ. Sister Rosetta, as she was commonly known, became the first gospel music star during the 1940s and 1950s, signing a recording contract with a secular label. Her story illustrates some important dimensions of gospel music's relationship to the Church. Sister Rosetta was one of gospel music's first crossover artists, achieving success playing in secular settings in addition to recording and playing for church-based audiences. But her secular successes were at times seen as problematic by people within the church, who felt she should make a choice and sing either secular music to secular audiences or gospel music to the church.[8]

Another of Dorsey's contemporaries was William Herbert Brewster (1897–1987), of the East Trigg Baptist Church in Memphis, Tennessee. Brewster also wrote some of the most popular gospel songs, including "Surely, God Is Able" and "Move On Up a Little Higher"—the latter of

Mahalia Jackson

Library of Congress

which was recorded by Mahalia Jackson (1911–1972), the Queen of Gospel, becoming the first gospel recording to sell more than a million copies.

GOSPEL'S GOLDEN AGE AND FURTHER INFLUENCE

Choirs and quartets dominated during the period between the 1940s and the 1960s as gospel music became an increasingly popular part of religious as well as secular radio airplay. Some of the most famous of these were the Clara Ward Singers, the Caravans, and the Soul Stirrers (led by Sam Cooke). With the coming of doo-wop, many groups that had originally been gospel singers switched over to secular R&B and soul music. Some of the most well-respected and influential performers in twentieth-century

American popular cultural history, such as Little Richard, Aretha Franklin, Sam Cooke, Patti Labelle, Gladys Knight, Dionne Warwick, and her younger cousin, Whitney Houston, all had their beginnings singing gospel music either as part of church choirs or touring groups. The influence of black gospel music and performance styles on America and the world can also be seen and heard in the work of successful musicians the world over, including the Beatles, Jerry Lee Lewis, the Rolling Stones, and Elvis Presley (still considered by some to be the King of Rock and Roll).

African American Sacred Music in the Struggle for Civil Rights

The main argument of this essay has been that black sacred music gave voice to certain aspects of African American consciousness and carried multiple meanings and uses that ranged from religious to political. One final example of the adaptation of this sacred music into a political context can be found in the Civil Rights movement, beginning with the 1955 Montgomery [Alabama] Bus Boycott. Through the network of church leaders formed through the Southern Christian Leadership Conference (SCLC), the black churches that participated in the movement provided not only a communications network, a meeting place, and economic resources but also called on their religious faith and that of their followers for inspiration, using it as the basis for moral right-standing in the fight. The music that helped encourage and inspire nonviolent civil action was made up of songs adapted from spirituals and gospel music. Thus these religious songs were transformed into freedom songs that helped to galvanize situations and people and to provide ultimate meaning to political struggle.[9]

Most notably, the song "We Shall Overcome" was adapted from the gospel song "I Shall Overcome"; "Keep Your Hand on the Plow" was transformed into "Keep Your Eyes on the Prize"; and "Ain't Gonna Let Nobody Turn Me Around" became an anthem sung by marchers and protesters across the South. The sacred music of African Americans was once again appropriated and adapted to new, nonreligious purposes while still retaining its central themes of freedom, critique of inequality, and commentary on the world around them.

Contemporary Gospel Music

Several larger categories are used in the recording industry to define the boundaries of contemporary Christian music. Traditional gospel is one of these. Work within this category generally represents recordings by choirs—frequently but not exclusively church based—and their style and repertoire tends to be more heavily weighted toward the more or less standard gospel songs and hymns, perhaps reinterpreted with limited

CeCe, left, and BeBe Winans perform during the Dream Concert at Radio City Music Hall in 2007.

AP Photo/Jason DeCrow

contemporary alteration. Groups within this category include John P. Kee (and the New Light Community Choir), Hezekiah Walker (and the Love Fellowship Choir), and Andraé Crouch.

Contemporary gospel pop artists include CeCe Winans, Yolanda Adams, Donnie McClurkin, Karen Clark Sheard, and Israel and New Breed. Quartets continue to be a strong presence within gospel music with acts such as the Williams Brothers, the Blind Boys of Alabama, and the Mighty Clouds of Joy. Urban gospel includes Kirk Franklin (and God's Property), Fred Hammond (and Radical for Christ), Donald Lawrence (and the Tri-City Singers), the duo MaryMary, Tye Tribbet, and Kierra "KiKi" Sheard. Other fusions of Christian lyrical content with popular musical idioms commonly associated with (or having their origins in) the black/African American experience include rap/hip-hop acts (such as KJ-52, Grits, the Gospel Gangstaz, T-Bone, and BBJ) and reggae acts (such as Papa San, Avion Blackman [formerly of the reggae group Christafari], and Sherwin Gardner).

Gospel music has become an extremely large and profitable industry. Several record labels, such as Verity, Gospo-Centric, and EMI–Gospel are at the forefront of producing acts whose music presents a Christian message. Across the country, certain markets, such as Chicago, Detroit, New York, Houston, and Atlanta, have radio stations dedicated to the gospel music format. Numerous gospel lifestyle and industry magazines such as *Gospel Today, Gospel Industry Today,* and *Gospel Flava,* as well as a multitude of Internet sites such as *GospelCity* continue to promote artists and publish news and commentary about the industry.

African American Sacred Music and the Church: Tension and Coexistence

Although the church and the form of African American sacred music that came to be known as gospel music are very closely linked, their relationship has not always been without serious tension. Lyrical content that expresses African American spiritual sensibilities and longings has always made some feel that the connection between this music and its numerous secular counterparts—from blues to hip-hop—has been far too close to serve the purpose of delivering the good news, or the gospel of salvation through belief in Christ. The life and career of gospel singer and musician Sister Rosetta Tharpe continues to provide an illustrative example of this philosophical divide as concerns the performance of African American sacred music. Sister Rosetta is often referred to as gospel music's first crossover star because of the popularity of her music outside Christian circles. She sang with both gospel and secular artists, appeared on early television variety shows, and played in nightclubs throughout the country, to the great dismay of those in her home church. Apparently, Sister Rosetta was unwilling to choose between performing within either a strictly religious or a secular entertainment context, rather preferring to be able to move freely between the two in what is sometimes referred to as straddling the fence. With her great success in the larger world of popular entertainment came the opprobrium of some of her fellow Christians—thus she never attained the stature of her contemporary Mahalia Jackson, who is still considered the queen of gospel music by many.

On the other side of this debate is the conviction that it is outside of the walls of the church—where so many people may never venture— that the message of salvation must be carried in order to bring into the fold the unchurched or those who have left fellowship for one reason or another. For this reason many of today's most successful performers of African American sacred music, although they may be subjected to some degree of disapproval, enjoy much more freedom to cross over and to achieve recognition and acclaim in the secular music industry. In many respects they are encouraged to do so as a way of creating musical forms having broad appeal because of their similarity to R&B or other forms of secular music but that express a Christian theological outlook (or at least an inspirational message of encouragement for hearers). Some of contemporary Christian music's most successful artists include those who continue to be among the best-selling artists on secular ratings charts and among secular audiences. Such artists as Kirk Franklin, Yolanda Adams, the duo MaryMary, Donnie McClurkin, and BeBe and CeCe Winans are among this group of gospel artists who have enjoyed great crossover success.[10]

Not only are gospel music artists enjoying success beyond the bounds of the black Christian community, but some of them are also gaining access to the center of American popular cultural production more broadly. Most notable in this respect is the artist Kirk Franklin, who became the first gospel music artist to score a mainstream feature film (2001). Along with the sister duo MaryMary, Franklin was depicted on the cover of a subsequent issue of *Gospel Today* magazine with the question "Have They Gone Too Far?"—an indication that there remain limits for which the black Christian community considers acceptable levels of success and mere self-promotion in the form of selling out the Christian message for secular success and personal gain. Recent years have seen a number of high-profile leaders of large African American megachurch congregations become heads of their own record labels, a move that allows them to shift their relationship to the music from one of consumer to that of producer.

In conclusion, African American sacred music—just like African American religion and religious institutions—has had to serve purposes that go far beyond expressing and ministering to the spiritual needs of the community. This music expressed and continues to express African American sensibilities, using and adapting existing musical idioms while simultaneously creating new ones. This music also had political purposes. Through songs such as "Didn't My Lord Deliver Daniel?" or "Everybody Talkin' 'Bout Heaven Ain't Goin' There," African Americans voiced their critique of ongoing systematic domination in the United States. Civil Rights leaders adapted traditional gospel and spiritual songs into freedom songs that encouraged and helped mobilize the masses of African Americans to challenge and ultimately defeat the Jim Crow system of the American South. Even today, African American sacred music continues to have multiple meanings and uses, and its influence extends far beyond the walls of the church.

NOTES

1. C. Eric Lincoln and Lawrence H. Mamiya, *The Black Church in the African American Experience* (Durham, NC: Duke, 1990).

2. Eileen Southern, *The Music of Black Americans* (New York: W. W. Norton, 1997); Horace Clarence Boyer, *How Sweet the Sound: The Golden Age of Gospel* (Washington, D.C.: Elliott & Clark, 1995).

3. Albert J. Raboteau, *Slave Religion: The "Invisible Institution" in the Antebellum South* (New York: Oxford, 1980).

4. Lawrence W. Levine, *Black Culture and Black Consciousness* (New York: Oxford, 1977).

5. Eugene D. Genovese, *Roll, Jordan, Roll: The World the Slaves Made* (New York: Pantheon Books, 1974).

6. Boyer, *How Sweet the Sound*; Anthony Heilbut, *The Gospel Sound: Good News and Bad Times* (New York: Limelight Editions, 1997); Robert Darden, *People Get Ready! A New History of Black Gospel Music* (New York: Continuum, 2004).

7. Michael W. Harris, *The Rise of Gospel Blues: The Music of Thomas Andrew Dorsey in the Urban Church* (New York: Oxford, 1992).

8. Jerma A. Jackson, *Singing in My Soul: Black Gospel Music in a Secular Age* (Chapel Hill: University of North Carolina Press, 2004); Gayle Wald, *Shout, Sister, Shout! The Untold Story of Rock-and-Roll Trailblazer Sister Rosetta Tharpe* (Boston: Beacon Press, 2007).

9. Don Cusic, *The Sound of Light: A History of Gospel Music* (Bowling Green, OH: Bowling Green State University Popular Press, 1990).

10. Darden, *People Get Ready!*

FURTHER READING

Boyer, Horace Clarence. *How Sweet the Sound: The Golden Age of Gospel.* Washington, D.C.: Elliott & Clark, 1995.

Cusic, Don. *The Sound of Light: A History of Gospel Music.* Bowling Green, OH: Bowling Green State University Popular Press 1990.

Darden, Robert. *People Get Ready! A New History of Black Gospel Music.* New York: Continuum, 2004.

Genovese, Eugene D. *Roll, Jordan, Roll: The World the Slaves Made.* New York: Pantheon Books, 1974.

Harris, Michael W. *The Rise of Gospel Blues: The Music of Thomas Andrew Dorsey in the Urban Church.* New York: Oxford, 1992.

Heilbut, Anthony. *The Gospel Sound: Good News and Bad Times.* New York: Limelight Editions, 1997.

Jackson, Jerma A. *Singing in My Soul : Black Gospel Music in a Secular Age.* Chapel Hill: University of North Carolina Press, 2004.

Levine, Lawrence W. *Black Culture and Black Consciousness.* New York: Oxford, 1977.

Lincoln, C. Eric, and Lawrence H. Mamiya. *The Black Church in the African American Experience.* Durham, NC: Duke, 1990.

Raboteau, Albert J. *Slave Religion: The "Invisible Institution" in the Antebellum South.* New York: Oxford, 1980.

Southern, Eileen. *The Music of Black Americans.* New York: W.W. Norton, 1997.

Wald, Gayle. *Shout, Sister, Shout! The Untold Story of Rock-and-Roll Trailblazer Sister Rosetta Tharpe.* Boston: Beacon Press, 2007.

3

African Americans and Rock 'n' Roll

Maureen Mahon

Rock 'n' roll is a quintessentially American musical product, the result of African American and European American crossings and borrowings. Rock 'n' roll has a long list of black progenitors and an early history as a form played by and for black people under the name rhythm and blues in the 1940s and 1950s. Over the years, however, rock 'n' roll has come to be viewed as white music for white people, a result of its association with white performers and audiences. Black musicians who strike out in the white-dominated rock 'n' roll terrain are in the peculiar position of looking like anomalies in a genre created by black people. Rock 'n' roll's first performers were predominantly poor, black, and Southern. Over the years, this initial association with the nation's outsiders and its appeal to youth who were resisting elements of mainstream society helped rock 'n' roll develop an image as an antiestablishment art form driven by the quest for rebellion, liberation, and unreserved self-expression, including the expression of sexuality, a taboo in mainstream America. The idealized story of rock 'n' roll is of openness and experimentation, a musical embodiment of the American dream of self-fashioning through a quest for a new sound and a better beat. Telling a more accurate story requires historicizing the black American presence in and contribution to rock 'n' roll, addressing the challenges that its black practitioners have experienced.

The major limitation for black Americans in rock 'n' roll is the racially defined labeling and marketing systems that the recording industry has always used for popular music. Assessing the findings of its 1987 study of the industry, the NAACP concluded, "No other industry in America so openly classifies its operations on a racial basis. At every level of the industry, beginning with the separation of black artists into a special category, barriers exist that severely limit opportunities for blacks."[1] These barriers are long-standing, as evidenced by *Billboard* magazine's early decision to use a separate chart to track the sales of music targeted to black audiences. Since 1942 the chart has been called Harlem Hit Parade, Race, Rhythm and Blues, Soul, Black, Hip Hop, and Urban.[2] These names distinguish music made for black audiences from music made for white audiences, exemplifying and perpetuating segregationist belief and practice. Commenting on the impact of this mentality on music categories, music critic Robert Palmer observed:

> By the sixties, "rock and roll" carried such "white" connotations that writers began referring to the new, rhythm-oriented styles in black popular music first as "soul," then "funk." By the time rap and hip-hop came along, many younger artists took pains to differentiate their music from "rock and roll" altogether.[3]

Segregation is one of the cornerstones of popular music marketing. It dominates the industry's approach to signing and promoting artists, restricting the type of music they perform and the audiences they reach. This article discusses the effect of segregation and racially defined marketing practices on key African American figures in the history of rock 'n' roll and charts their contributions to the form even in the face of these limitations. It also traces how, in the years since the emergence of rock 'n' roll, black Americans have been distanced from the form but have continued to participate in it. Success as a professional musician depends on talent, drive, and luck—but, as this article demonstrates, for African Americans in the field of rock 'n' roll, the ability to express one's musical vision also requires negotiating the additional burden of race.

FROM RHYTHM AND BLUES TO ROCK 'N' ROLL

In 1949, in an effort to find a more palatable term, *Billboard* magazine changed the name of its black music chart from "race" music to "rhythm and blues."[4] Rhythm and blues (R&B) encompassed a spectrum of music linked by the blackness of its performers and audiences. Aesthetic factors also connected music in the R&B category: "honking" or "screaming" saxophones, propulsive piano, loud drums, vocals shouted over instrumentation, and danceable boogie-woogie rhythms that presaged the importance of the beat in rock 'n' roll. R&B began to gain radio exposure as a small coterie of white disc jockeys programmed it on their shows. AM radio signals were wide reaching, and the black music played on stations such as Nashville's WLAC could be heard in the Caribbean and Canada and as far west as the Rocky Mountains.[5] These shows reached young white listeners as well as their intended black audiences.

In June 1951, Cleveland disc jockey Alan Freed began calling his R&B radio show *Moondog's Rock'n'Roll Party*.[6] He hoped the new term would downplay the blackness that R&B indexed and ease the crossing over of the

Little Richard in *Mister Rock and Roll,* 1957.

Paramount Pictures/Photofest

music. *Rock'n'roll* indicated "music that was black ('R&B') in style but not necessarily made by black artists or aimed at black audiences."[7] Freed's new label was a colloquial term for *sex* in the black community, but rocking and rolling also meant dancing, and sanctified churchgoers "rocked" when the spirit took them. The convergence of the sexual, physical, and spiritual in the term *rock 'n' roll* is fitting, given the fusion of these features in the music. Changing R&B's name to package black music for white audiences is significant in light of the form's history of simultaneous dependence on and erasure of black people, a contradictory relationship to blackness that is at the heart of the form and the challenges that African Americans face in it.

It is impossible to isolate a single moment when rhythm and blues transformed into rock 'n' roll, but *Rocket 88*, released in 1951, is often identified as the first rock 'n' roll record.[8] Credited to Jackie Brenston and His Delta Cats, the song was recorded by Brenston and guitarist Ike Turner and his Kings of Rhythm at Sun Studios. The song has many of the features associated with rock 'n' roll: a lyric about a car, a prominent boogie rhythm, and well-amplified, distorted guitar. Sam Phillips, the owner of Sun Studios and the record's producer, asserted that *Rocket 88* paved the way for rock 'n' roll, encouraging "young white males and females . . . to get even more interested in rhythm and blues or black music."[9] Phillips, a white Southerner, had opened his studio to record the blues and R&B of black musicians such as Brenston and Turner, but he soon recognized the limits that black artists faced in a segregated nation. He began to search for white musicians who could play with what he called "the Negro sound and the Negro feel," certain he could profit if he did.[10] Eventually, he discovered and recorded Elvis Presley, Carl Perkins, and Jerry Lee Lewis, white Southerners who had learned the Negro sound and feel from black musicians.

Before the arrival of these performers, black R&B artists such as Ruth Brown and Fats Domino were charting with songs that shaped rock 'n' roll. Brown signed to the independent R&B label Atlantic Records, where she was directed to approach music with a new rhythm. Her first hit, "Teardrops From My Eyes" (1950) stayed on the R&B charts for 11 weeks.[11] Other releases, including "5-10-15 Hours" (1952) and "Mama, He Treats Your Daughter Mean" (1953), were similarly successful. Known for a vocal squeak that influenced Little Richard, Brown was dubbed Miss Rhythm in recognition of her facility with a new beat that went on to shape rock 'n' roll. Brown, like many other R&B artists, saw little difference between R&B and the more lucrative crossover form called rock 'n' roll. She explained:

> When they called it rock 'n' roll it was only rhythm and blues now being done by white kids and accepted and danced to and being played on the Top 100 and the Top 10 stations. . . . Like Fats Domino said, "I had been singing rock 'n' roll 15 years before they started calling it that."[12]

Born in New Orleans, Antoine "Fats" Domino Jr. played boogie-woogie piano but sang with a country twang. Domino is one of rock 'n' roll's best-selling performers; with the exception of Elvis Presley and the Beatles, he achieved more gold records than any artist working in rock 'n' roll's first decades.[13] A stout man who often wore a smile, Domino had a calm sound and warm, laid-back delivery. Never overtly sexual, Domino was a "safe" black performer, a fact that may have eased his acceptance by white audiences who were enticed by the "clean arrangements, simple melodies, casual feels, and catchy lyrics" that characterized his music.[14] Having started his career at the beginning of the 1950s, Domino was the R&B artist who most successfully crossed over to the rock 'n' roll audience, producing hits like "Ain't That a Shame" (1955), "Blueberry Hill" (1956), "I'm Walkin'" (1957), and "Walking to New Orleans" (1960).[15]

Although at first *rock 'n' roll* was a term for R&B being promoted to white listeners, "the change in name induced a change in the music itself."[16] To engage its teenage audience, rock 'n' roll's producers simplified R&B's rhythm, accenting the backbeat, and narrowed its lyrical references to teen themes.[17] Rock 'n' roll was a young person's music and seasoned R&B artists, with their adult voices and adult lyrical content, had a difficult time crossing over to young white audiences.[18] In contrast, black rock'n'rollers conveyed youthful energy, sang about young people's concerns, and developed unusual visual styles that helped to sell their new rhythms. Along with Fats Domino, the black artists who were most successful in the early years of rock 'n' roll—Little Richard, Bo Diddley, and Chuck Berry—popularized an aesthetic and attitude that laid the groundwork for future generations of rock'n'rollers.

Commenting on his contribution to the genre, Little Richard (born Richard Wayne Penniman) proclaimed, "I'm the innovator, I'm the emancipator, I'm the originator, I'm the architect of rock 'n' roll."[19] Little Richard's effervescent flash and over-the-top enthusiasm drew fans to the genre while providing a primer on how to rock and roll. Little Richard had a remarkable visual style: an outrageously high pompadour, pancake make-up and eyeliner, and sharp suits. He played the piano with ferocity and sometimes stood on his instrument. Mixing boogie-woogie and blues, Little Richard performed in traveling carnivals, medicine shows, and the black clubs that made up the chitlin circuit. His creative and commercial breakthrough came with the song "Tutti Frutti" (1955). Little Richard recalled the recording as being a result of an attempt to distinguish himself from other R&B singers at a session: "I started singing 'Tutti Frutti' as loud as I can. 'A Womp-Bomp-a-Loo-Momp Alop-Bomp-Bomp! Woooo!' Just screaming. And people said, 'Oh, he's gone crazy.'"[20] "Tutti Frutti" was a risqué ditty that Little Richard sang in clubs.[21] Once his production team decided that the song could be a hit, they enlisted the help of Dorothy La Bostrie, a New Orleans songwriter, to clean up the lyrics. "Tutti Frutti" sold 500,000 units and was successful on both the R&B and pop music charts; later releases such as "Rip It Up" (1956), "Long Tall Sally" (1956), and "Good Golly, Miss Molly" (1958) also faired well. Black and white teenagers were attracted to his infectious songs and ecstatic vocal blend of "sighs, moans, screams, whoos and breathless panting" that later generations of rock 'n' roll singers emulated.[22]

As a teenager, Bo Diddley (born Ellas Otha Bates McDaniel) shifted from violin to guitar and began experimenting with rhythm. He explained, "I couldn't play like Muddy Waters or John Lee Hooker, Jimmy Reed and Howlin' Wolf and all these people so I had to go back in the corner and try and develop a style of my own and I stumbled upon that rhythm and that's the rhythm that I made my first record with."[23] Taking fragments of children's rhymes and fusing them to a Latin rhythm, Bo Diddley created what has come to be called the Bo Diddley Beat, a shuffling rhythm that turns up repeatedly in rock 'n' roll. Bo Diddley's search for a new sound is typical of musical innovators in all genres: he was looking for a unique form of expression. He explained, "I mainly play chords and stuff like that and rhythm. I'm a rhythm fanatic. I played the guitar as if I were playing drums. That's the thing that makes my music so different. I do licks on the guitar that a drummer would do."[24] Like the other early rock 'n' rollers, Diddley telegraphed his musical difference visually. Although he and his band members were neatly attired, the group looked a bit peculiar. The square and V-shaped bodies of Diddley's guitars (which he designed and built himself) were futuristic and cartoonish.[25] The traditional bass, drum, and guitar ensemble was supplemented by an electric violin and maracas. He also made the unconventional decision to feature women instrumentalists in his band, a vivid sign that this new music was upsetting a tradition.

As a guitarist, singer, songwriter, and performer, Chuck Berry (born Charles Edward Anderson Berry) is rock 'n' roll's most influential early performer. His pithy lyrics, filled with internal rhymes and wordplay and delivered with a rapid fluency, are models of masterful storytelling. Beatle John Lennon called Chuck Berry "the greatest rock 'n' roll poet," and Rolling Stones guitarist Keith Richards, on whom Berry's influence is clear, described him as having "the whole sound—rhythm, lyrics—the sound" of rock 'n' roll.[26] In spite of his stature as a rock 'n' roll pioneer, Berry is modest when describing the development of his classic rhythm:

> The first time I heard that was in one of Carl Hogan's riffs in Louis Jordan's band . . . I love T-Bone Walker: slurs and it's bluesy. So, put a little Carl Hogan and a little T-Bone Walker and a little Charlie Christian, the guitarist in Tommy Dorsey's band, together: Look what a span of people that you will please. And that's what I did . . . And making it simple is another important factor, I think, that resulted in a lot of the artists understanding and being able to play my music. If you can call it "my music." But there's nothing new under the sun.[27]

Aware of the commercial limitations of R&B, he made musical and lyrical choices that he hoped would help him reach as broad an audience as possible. He overlaid his R&B derived riffs with country-inflected vocals that featured lyrics about school, cars, and love, subject matter with which young rock 'n' roll fans could identify. Starting with "Maybellene" in 1955, Berry released a string of hits now recognized as rock 'n' roll classics: "Roll Over, Beethoven" (1956), "Rock and Roll Music" (1957), "Johnny B. Goode" (1958), "Sweet Little Sixteen" (1958), and "Almost Grown" (1959). Delivering these songs live, Berry put on a show intended to maintain audience attention, dropping down into a "duckwalk" while playing the guitar. His signature moves, along with his sound, solidified Berry's place in the rock 'n' roll canon. The racial ambiguity of Berry's hillbilly-inflected music and a vocal twang that did not "sound black" eased his acceptance by white audiences but also created confusion when people who had heard his records saw him play. They expected a white man to step on stage. Berry's effort to gain a white audience was successful, but in pitching his music to white teens, Berry and his music were distanced from black audiences.

ROCK 'N' ROLL REPERCUSSIONS

Rock 'n' roll developed alongside the growing Civil Rights movement. Although rock'n'rollers were not political activists, they were at the forefront of integration. Their milieu was not lunch counters or public schools, but the concert halls, clubs, television programs, and movie theaters where they performed to mixed and majority white audiences. Low-budget rock 'n' roll films including *Rock, Rock, Rock* (1956) and *Mr. Rock & Roll* (1957) featured black rock'n'rollers such as Frankie Lymon and the Teenagers, Chuck Berry, and LaVern Baker performing for approving white teenagers. The rock 'n' roll tours that brought the music to communities across the country were integrated. White artists such as Buddy Holly and the Everly Brothers performed alongside Fats Domino and Chuck Berry, touring for months at a time and sometimes playing several shows a day. These tours were difficult for black artists whose experience on the road—especially in the South—included police harassment, refusal of service at white-owned eateries, and often futile quests for accommodations that would accept black patrons. In some cases, they had to play one show for black people and one for white people to appease club owners who didn't want "race mixing" at their venues; in these cases, they usually received payment for only one show.[28] Describing a run-in with the police while touring in Georgia, Bo Diddley recalled:

> I was made to get out of the car, me and my band, and because we didn't have no liquor . . . they pulled out the gun and said, "Since you all are musicians, entertainers, you all entertain us and we'll let you go." . . . They made us take off the [doo-] rags and dance . . . With a .38 in your face and a shotgun, you'll do flips and everything. In order to deliver the music, we went through some terrible ordeals to continue, to get to where it has come now. We built a hell of a highway.[29]

The major problem was that rock 'n' roll exposed white people to black culture, upsetting an entrenched preference for denying the significance of African Americans. Rock 'n' roll's distinguishing features contributed to the frenzied embrace of the form among youth and the impassioned negative response from their elders. Guardians of propriety regarded the music's sound and its performers' antics as threats to decency. Moreover, they routinely characterized rock 'n' roll as "jungle music" and "primitive," attacking the form at its black roots. Sometimes they attacked the performers physically. Little Richard remembered, "I had police take me off the stage in Augusta, Georgia . . . and beat me with blackjacks, but I had so much energy I just bounced off them. . . . 'You're down there singing all this nigger music to these white kids.' That's what they said."[30] Producer Sam Phillips noted that white rock'n'rollers were also harassed: "They accused us of causing white people to love 'niggers.' They accused us of mutilating music by trying to integrate and trying to copy and just totally destroy all that was good in music. Believe me, the resistance on this was absolutely incredible."[31]

Involvement in rock 'n' roll, it seemed, could compromise the morals of white youth, especially young white women who were often featured—on television and in photographs—screaming enthusiastic responses to the performances of black male rock'n'rollers. The specter of miscegenation conjured by these images led some white adults affiliated with white citizens' groups to organize against what they called "vulgar animalistic nigger rock and roll bop."[32] Rock 'n' roll's revolutionary fusing of black musical style and white teenage frustration was potent and presumed dangerous. Blackness and sexuality bubbled in the music and in the hip-swinging performances of its leading artists. Rock 'n' roll's connection to these taboos fueled white youths' interest. Not only did rock 'n' roll have a great beat, it also irritated their parents. Rock 'n' roll's image as a form of youthful rebellion grew out of these tensions.

The moral panics stirred by rock 'n' roll did not suppress the music, but the actions of the mainstream recording industry limited some of its artists. When rock 'n' roll first emerged, major label executives assumed it was a fad. They had long ignored black rhythm and blues—both forms were recorded on independent labels—and saw no reason to embrace the fledgling offshoot. The majors gambled that they could ride out rock 'n' roll's popularity by using the white pop artists they had under contract to compete with genuine rock'n'rollers recording on independent labels. Their white acts would cover songs originated by black artists, allowing the labels to tap into the rock 'n' roll market without having to commit to it. This approach not only made economic sense but fit long-standing white American resistance to black American advancement. Little Richard, whose songs "Tutti Frutti" and "Long Tall Sally" were covered by white pop singer Pat Boone, argued, "They didn't want the white kids looking up at this big ol' greasy black guy out of Georgia, out of Mississippi, out of Chicago. They wanted their kids to see a little smooth white boy looking pretty and on duty."[33] Covers submerged the vibrant energy of musical blackness and circumscribed the career possibilities of black people.

Major labels released their cover versions soon after the originals and used their considerable influence on radio stations and distributors to flood the market with their artists' work. This made it almost impossible for the black artists' original versions to receive the kind of radio exposure that generated sales. This was the case for Etta James, the dyed-blonde vocalist who recorded an answer song to the racy Hank Ballard and the Midnighters tune "Work With Me, Annie" in 1955. Changing James's original song title "Roll With Me, Henry" to the tamer "The Wallflower" seemed like a good way for James to get radio airplay, but white pop singer Georgia Gibbs covered the song before James's version had a chance at the charts. Describing her outrage at Gibbs's "Suzy Creamcheese version," James observed:

> [Gibbs] turned "Roll With Me, Henry" into "Dance With Me, Henry." Now if you listen to the original version, I really was talking about dancing. . . . It's just that the word *roll* had a sexual suggestiveness prudes couldn't handle. Georgia's cutesy-pie do-over went over big. My version went underground and continued to sell while Georgia's whitewash went through the roof. Her Henry became a million seller. I was happy to have any success, but I was enraged to see Georgia singing the song on *The Ed Sullivan Show* while I was singing it in some funky dive in Watts.[34]

James's comments indicate the importance of double entendre in R&B and the way that covers proffered a single, safe meaning. Her use of the term *whitewash* for this process is apt: it was not a simple "cleaning up" but an actual whitening that occurred when a white singer copied a black artist's song. Performers whose work was covered had no legal protection; no law prohibited copying an arrangement. Independent labels reaped financial rewards for licensing songs to the majors, but the artists who originated the songs received nothing. As teens became more educated consumers, they demanded the black originals—but covers undercut black performers and enabled major labels to profit from black creativity without compensating black people.

White covers of black R&B and the growing number of white rock'n'rollers put a wedge between black performers and rock 'n' roll so that, as Bo Diddley noted, "R&B became what we was doing and rock 'n' roll became what the white kids was doing."[35] Racialized definitions of musical categories, covers, and the racism that limited black opportunity in the United States marginalized the black pioneers of rock 'n' roll from the form they had created. By the 1980s, it became apparent that they had also lost out on the financial side when Ruth Brown, famous in her heyday for a vocal squeak, became a "squeaky wheel" about the economic exploitation of early R&B artists. Brown's label, Atlantic Records, was known as "The House That Ruth Brown Built" with her consistent chart success in the 1950s, but Brown herself received little financial benefit from her labor. Working with a tenacious legal team on behalf of several R&B artists, Brown went public with a battle for royalties. Testifying before Congress and commenting in the media, she revealed industry practices that contributed to the precarious financial position that many R&B artists were in as they approached retirement age. Most artists in the 1950s were paid a flat rate to record—Brown received $69 per side—and recouped little in terms of royalties.[36] In fact, Brown had received no royalty payments between 1964 and 1983, even though her records sold throughout this period.[37] The case demonstrated that record labels often went to great lengths to avoid paying royalties.[38] With public exposure and legal decisions, Brown and other artists began to receive back royalties. To further assist R&B pioneers, Brown helped start the Rhythm and Blues Foundation in 1988, using seed money from the labels to provide financial and medical assistance to the black forebears of rock 'n' roll.

ROCK 'N' ROLL VOCAL GROUPS

By the end of the 1950s, the artists most identified with rock 'n' roll had vanished from the scene: Little Richard returned to the Church, Elvis Presley had joined the army, Jerry Lee Lewis was ostracized for his marriage to his thirteen-year-old cousin, and Chuck Berry was entangled in legal proceedings stemming from charges that he violated the Mann Act. In spite of these setbacks, rock 'n' roll did not disappear. It shifted form as vocal groups took center stage. Rooted in the harmonized singing of black gospel groups and secular street corner singing, doo-wop had found a place on the R&B and pop charts during the 1950s. This rock 'n' roll vocal style, performed by black artists, was named for the nonsense phrase sometimes used in its background vocals.[39] Among the most popular groups were the Coasters, Frankie Lymon and the Teenagers, and the Platters, whose single "The Great Pretender" (1955) was the first doo-wop record to top the pop charts.[40] Many vocal group recordings resulted from the collaboration of white songwriters and producers and black vocalists. For example, the white songwriting team of Jerry Leiber and Mike Stoller penned the rock 'n' roll classic "Hound Dog" (1953) for black R&B singer Willie Mae "Big Mama" Thornton (Elvis Presley covered it in 1956), "There Goes My Baby" (1959) for The Drifters, and humorous scenarios of teen life such as "Young Blood" (1957), "Yakety Yak" (1958), and "Charlie Brown" (1959) for the Coasters.

The vocal group tradition changed as all-female groups (known as "girl groups" because of the youth of the performers) became prominent in the early 1960s. Performing songs written by professional songwriters, the Shirelles, the Chiffons, the Chantels, the Crystals, the Marvelettes, and the Ronettes introduced a new style of rock 'n' roll. The girl groups continued rock 'n' roll's focus on teen love, but from a female perspective. The Shirelles' "Will You Love Me Tomorrow" (1960), written by Carole King and Jerry Goffin, for example, articulates a concern many young women struggled with: the consequences of giving in to a boyfriend's pleas for intimacy. Although both black and white girl groups recorded, the leaders of the movement were young African American women, prompting songwriter Jerry Goffin to observe, "In the 1960s, God was a black girl who could sing."[41] With few exceptions, however, the writers and producers were white. Among the most influential was Phil Spector, who created "the wall of sound." For his recording sessions, Spector would assemble an enormous orchestra—two pianos, two drum kits, as many as five guitars, and three basses, as well as large horn and string sections—whose sheer size produced a loud, echoing sonic wall. The singers on these recordings had brash vocal power, but they received little individual credit for their work. Darlene Love, one of his primary vocalists, contributed lead and backing vocals to numerous Spector recordings that were released under other artists' names. The lead singer of the Ronettes, Veronica Bennett (known as Ronnie Spector once she married Phil Spector), managed to forge an individual identity. She had the ideal rock 'n' roll voice: an emotional catch in the throat accompanied by stuttered "oh, oh, ohs" that conveyed the passion and frustration of adolescence. Her sound and sultry appearance helped her become an early rock 'n' roll sex symbol. Phil Spector's greatest chart successes came through his work with black girl groups in songs such as "He's a Rebel" (1962) and "Da Doo Ron Ron" (1963) by the Crystals and "Be My Baby" (1963) and "Walking in the Rain" (1964) by the Ronettes.

Another major contributor to the vocal group sound was Berry Gordy Jr., a jazz-loving independent record producer who founded Motown Records in Detroit in 1960. Gordy hired African American songwriters, producers, singers, and musicians, making the label an exception to the white producer/black artist model that dominated the era's rock 'n' roll production. Gordy wanted his label's music to have appeal and sales beyond the black community, and his staff mastered the art of mining and modulating musical blackness to create a listener-friendly sound that meshed with popular tastes. Motown's records blended black gospel and white pop into songs replete with catchy hooks, memorable key phrases, and danceable rhythms. At "Hitsville, USA," as Gordy nicknamed his label, staff members applied the assembly line practices of their hometown's automobile industry to music production. Company songwriters such as William "Smokey" Robinson Jr., Norman Whitfield, and the team of Eddie

Holland, Lamont Dozier, and Brian Holland were encouraged to find and use formulas that produced hit records. Performers followed company dictates about the material they recorded and the way they recorded it. A band of former jazz musicians, known as the Funk Brothers, played on most of the tracks, helping to give the label its sound.

Attention to quality control was intense, and the public image of the artists was a concern. Motown artists trained with Maxine Powell, whose "finishing school" taught the mostly working-class Motown singers the rules of etiquette and self-presentation. Choreographer Cholly Atkins provided dance moves and body postures that rocked—but in a tasteful way. This type of polishing was in keeping with Gordy's desire to go beyond the chitlin circuit, presenting his acts in elite venues, including on television. It also prompted the charge that Motown artists were so carefully handled to meet the presumed preferences of white audiences that they compromised their blackness. Motown's middle-class striving and pursuit of crossover reveal Gordy's investment in the Civil Rights movement's goals of integration and resulted in the label becoming one of the most profitable black-owned businesses in U.S. history. Over the years, Motown released an unprecedented number of pop chart hits by the Miracles (featuring Smokey Robinson), Martha and the Vandellas, the Marvelettes, Mary Wells, the Four Tops, the Temptations, Marvin Gaye, "Little" Stevie Wonder, the Supremes (featuring Diana Ross), Gladys Knight and the Pips, and the Jackson Five. Holland–Dozier–Holland alone penned twenty-eight songs that became Top 20 pop hits.[42] During the 1960s, the Motown staff created what Gordy had dubbed "The Sound of Young America," a body of music that made an indelible imprint on rock 'n' roll and U.S. culture.

African American vocal groups promoting their music in the early 1960s probably could not have imagined that their primary competitors would be white British bands playing black American blues, R&B, and rock 'n' roll. Not even the members of the Beatles, the English band that started this shift, expected to succeed in the United States. They assumed that American audiences would prefer the black American artists who originated the type of music they played. Industry professionals also had low expectations; in fact, no major label would take on the stateside release of the Beatles' first single, leaving Vee-Jay, an independent, black-owned label to issue the first American copies of "She Loves You" (1964).[43] As it turned out, the English band took the U.S. teenage record-buying public by storm and launched the British Invasion of the American pop market. The success of bands such as the Beatles, the Rolling Stones, and the Animals confirmed Sam Phillips's supposition that white people with "the Negro sound and feel" would be able to sell black music. The success of British bands precipitated the disappearance of many black vocal groups from the pop charts. Racial commonality mattered and white American kids, it turned out, were happy to see other white kids perform the black music that they had begun to embrace as their own.

1960s ROCK

By the late 1960s, rock 'n' roll was a central part of youth culture. The sound and attitude of rock 'n' roll were changing, and fans began to call their music "rock." Performers began to write their own material, and the subject matter expanded as references to cars and love were complemented by poetic commentaries on politics and everyday life. Musicians began focusing on producing albums intended to make conceptual and

Jimi Hendrix

Photofest

artistic statements, and rock became a site of authentic self-expression. The standard of dress changed as both performers and audiences followed the era's casual approach to self-presentation. White artists and fans dominated the scene, and the majority of young African Americans focused on soul music. Still, black American musicians were involved in rock: the most prominent were musical giants Sly Stone and Jimi Hendrix and psychedelic cult figure Arthur Lee.

Working in Los Angeles, Arthur Lee formed a band with Johnny Echols, a black guitarist, and Bryan Maclean, a white guitarist and songwriter. Inspired by the sound of folk rock and the British Invasion, they set aside the R&B covers they had previously felt obligated to play and began to write their own material in 1965. Lee explained, "I realized I could sound like the Byrds and the Beatles, and I said, 'Hey, *this* is you. Stop trying to be an imitator' [of R&B acts]."[44] Maclean, steeped in the music of Broadway and Tin Pan Alley, and Lee, immersed in the British sound, composed songs that meshed classic American pop with a garage band's grit: jangly guitars ringing out against lushly orchestrated strings and brass. Taking the name Love, the band appropriated one of the words most associated with the burgeoning hippie movement, or Love Generation. Lee was a proud part of this counterculture and often lamented that his friend Jimi Hendrix got credit for being the first black hippie.[45] As Love's front man, Lee wrote and sang surreal lyrics, contributing to a style of writing that evoked the imagery and emotions unleashed in the "acid trips" made possible by the ingestion of LSD, the counterculture's drug of choice.

Love performed in the major rock 'n' roll venues in Los Angeles, becoming the top band on the circuit. Commenting on Love's profile in the scene, Doors keyboardist Ray Manzarek observed, "Arthur Lee and Love, they were in charge. We would see them play the Whisky A Go-Go and think that one day we wanted to be like Love."[46] The first rock band to sign to the Elektra label, Love released its first and eponymous album in 1966, featuring a cover of "Hey Joe," a song later made famous by Jimi Hendrix. In 1967, with more original material under its belt, Love released the albums *Da Capo* and *Forever Changes*. The latter is widely considered to be a rock 'n' roll masterpiece. Replete with arcane titles such as "Maybe the People Would Be the Times or Between Clark and Hilldale," the album's beautifully arranged songscapes jostle against images of decay and mutation that indexed the visual and emotional effects of the Vietnam War.[47] Lee's resistance to touring stymied Love's ability to break out beyond the Los Angeles scene, and Love disbanded in 1972. Their music circulated on record, however, and took hold in Great Britain, where fans and musicians celebrated Arthur Lee as an influential innovator and the "prince of orchestral acid pop."[48]

Arthur Lee's low profile contrasts with the fame of Sly and the Family Stone, who burst onto the airwaves in 1968 with the infectious song

"Dance to the Music." Formed two years earlier, the seven-member band was the brainchild of San Francisco Bay–area resident Sylvester Stewart, a disc jockey and record producer known as Sly Stone. With Freddie Stone, his brother, on guitar, his sister Rose Stone on keyboards, Cynthia Robinson on trumpet, Jerry Martini on saxophone, Larry Graham on bass, and Greg Errico on drums, Sly Stone (on electric organ) founded an interracial, mixed-gender band. A rare example of black and white men and women making music together, the band played a vibrant fusion of soul and rock and seemed to embody Love Generation and Civil Rights–era ideals of positive energy and racial harmony.[49] Their songs featured soul horn blasts, gospel inspired vocals, and the prominent bass riffs of Graham, who expanded the rhythmic territory of funk that James Brown was exploring. Unlike bands with a single lead singer, the members of the Family Stone shared vocal duties, incorporating a range of vocal timbres into a song. Songs such as "Everyday People" (1968), "Sing a Simple Song" (1968), "Stand!" (1969), and "Everybody Is a Star" (1970) tapped popular catchphrases and childhood chants and conveyed life-affirming messages to a nation facing serious political challenges, notably the Vietnam War and the 1968 assassinations of Martin Luther King Jr. and Robert F. Kennedy.

Significantly, Sly and the Family Stone was a predominantly black band, but they were marketed to the white rock 'n' roll audience, an approach Sly Stone had insisted on when he signed his contract with CBS Records.[50] In spite of the label executives' concern that a white audience would not "get" the band, it became a favorite on the rock circuit. They were among the few black performers invited to Woodstock, the 1969 concert that was the counterculture's most important gathering. Sly and the Family Stone's profile changed with the 1971 release of *There's A Riot Going On.* The joyous chants were replaced with a starker sound and vision. These tendencies were present in the acerbic "Don't Call Me Nigger, Whitey" (1969), and *Riot* marked a complete shift. Spare with muted and distorted vocals, the songs stretched beyond radio-friendly length. A breakthrough album, *Riot's* content was too black and too bleak for some white listeners.[51] Exacerbated by the erratic behavior of Stone, the album precipitated a break with the mainstream audience that the group's more accessible follow-up, *Fresh* (1973), could not heal. By 1975, Sly and the Family Stone had disbanded, leaving behind an extraordinary body of music.

Guitarist Jimi Hendrix is rock's most recognized black star. Born in Seattle, Hendrix began playing guitar when he was thirteen. By the time he was in his early twenties, he was touring as a sideman on the R&B circuit, playing in black clubs before black audiences with artists such as Little Richard and the Isley Brothers. Hendrix settled down in New York City in the mid-1960s and performed in Greenwich Village's predominantly white rock 'n' roll clubs.

His break came when Chas Chandler, a former member of the British Invasion band the Animals, convinced Hendrix that his music would connect with the white British bands and fans of black American blues and R&B. In 1966, Hendrix relocated to England, changing the spelling of his name from Jimmy to Jimi on the way. Chandler assembled a band for his protégé—Noel Redding on bass and Mitch Mitchell on drums—and the trio began recording. Their first release, *Are You Experienced* (1967), sold well in England, and the songs "Purple Haze" and "Hey Joe" established Hendrix as an artist worth watching.

The Jimi Hendrix Experience made its unforgettable U.S. debut at the 1967 Monterey Pop Festival. Using the showmanship he learned on the chitlin circuit, Hendrix performed with an arresting, sexually suggestive style. In addition to playing his guitar behind his back and with his teeth, he made metaphoric love to the instrument before concluding the show by setting it on fire. Some critics worried that his performance pandered to white stereotypes of black male sexuality, but others were enthusiastic about his inventive playing. The bottom line was that Hendrix had captured the American rock 'n' roll community's attention. He released *Axis: Bold As Love* (1967) and *Electric Ladyland* (1968), critical and popular successes, and became one of the highest-paid performers of the era, reigning at the top of the scene until his untimely death in 1970. Hendrix's influence reverberates in rock 'n' roll. His use of volume, distortion, feedback, and electronic effects define how rock guitar should sound, and his blend of technical wizardry and passionate playing set the standard for the guitarists who have followed him.

Hendrix's relationship to black and white mainstreams demonstrates the challenges faced by a black artist in the rock milieu.[52] Hendrix was not marketed to black audiences; although he had black fans, his audience was predominantly white. In an era of increasing black cultural consciousness, Hendrix's association with his white band mates and the white hippie counterculture, coupled with the sound of his high-volume, blues-derived guitar playing, marginalized him from the mainstream of black American culture.[53] Explaining the reason black Americans accepted the black rock 'n' roll of Sly Stone, but rejected that of Hendrix, music historian Nelson George notes, "Hendrix drew from a style blacks had already disposed of; Sly shrewdly stayed just a few steps ahead of the crowd."[54] And, as cultural critic Greg Tate observes, "Hendrix wasn't just a racial-political heretic but a musical one as well."[55] The voice, Tate argues, was the most important instrument to black audiences, and Hendrix's vocals were far from the powerful soul man's voice that appealed to mainstream African Americans.[56]

In the late 1960s, Hendrix began to leave behind his showy entertainer persona and focus on musicianship. He also seemed to assert the blackness that had been muted and questioned, splitting off from his white band mates and working with black musicians. In 1970, he released *Band of Gypsys*, the self-titled document of his new all-black band with drummer Buddy Miles and bass player Billy Cox. As with Stone's *Riot*, the "blacker" sound of the Band of Gypsys did not sit well with some of Hendrix's white fans. Up to that point, they could erase or ignore his race, characterizing him as someone who "didn't seem black." This allowed them to account for the presence of a black man in their midst without disrupting notions of "normal" black behavior or questioning the general absence of black people in their scene. It also explained the appeal of someone from a reviled demographic. Rock critic Charles Shaar Murray sees Hendrix's "whitening" as a response to a long standing conundrum: "the central thrust of twentieth century American popular music [is] the need to separate black music (which, by and large, white Americans love) from black people (who, by and large, they don't)."[57] The usual approach to the dilemma is to celebrate white performers who possess "the Negro sound and feel," but the process took a different form with Hendrix. His white fans separated him from his black identity and proclaimed his "raceless" musical brilliance.

As a black man in the white counterculture, Hendrix was hypervisible. Another experience for African Americans in rock is invisibility. For example, few people—black or white—comment on the fact that one of the producers who helped usher in the folk-rock movement was black. Tom Wilson produced Bob Dylan's first electric album—*Bringing It All Back Home* (1965), a rock 'n' roll landmark—as well as Dylan's biggest hit single, "Like a Rolling Stone" (1965).[58] In 1966, Wilson produced *Wednesday Morning, 3 A.M.*, Simon and Garfunkel's debut album. It was his idea to add an electric guitar, bass, and drums to the duo's acoustic hit "The Sounds of Silence"—and the new version went to number one.[59] Wilson also signed experimental rockers Frank Zappa and the Velvet Underground to recording contracts and produced some of their early tracks. Sometimes visible and always audible were the numerous black women who provided background vocal support to many of the best-known white artists of the era.[60] Black women vocalists such as Darlene Love, Minnie Riperton, Chaka Khan, Patti Austin, Claudia Lennear, Venetta Fields, Madeline Bell, and Merry Clayton lent their vocal talents to the recordings of artists such as Joe Cocker, Rod Stewart, the Rolling Stones, Pink Floyd, Steely Dan, and Dusty Springfield. White British artists in particular were passionate about black music and, in addition to styling their vocals in ways that "sounded black," they drew on the vocal resources of black women to lend more musical authenticity to their projects. The list of artists with whom Merry Clayton recorded indicates the pervasive presence of black women in rock. Clayton sang on the Rolling Stones' *Let It Bleed* (1969), Carole King's *Tapestry* (1971), and Joe Cocker's *With a Little Help from My Friends* (1970), as well as on recordings by Buffalo Springfield, Leon Russell, Jerry Garcia, Lynyrd Skynyrd, Neil

Young, Paul Butterfield Blues Band, Phil Ochs, and Rare Earth. Clayton is best known for her riveting vocals on the Rolling Stones' single "Gimme Shelter" (1969).

BLACK ROCK 'N' ROLL IN THE 1970s

The crossover success of Sly and the Family Stone, Hendrix, and Motown, as well as the strong sales of the soul produced on independent labels such as Stax and Atlantic convinced major labels of the profitability of music by African American artists. In the early 1970s, they launched black music departments to produce and promote this music. Although this meant expanded opportunities for black artists, few of whom had been signed to major labels until then, the labels maintained a racially defined approach. By the end of the 1960s, rock was in place as a white youth-oriented form distinct from its parent rock 'n' roll. With few exceptions, black men and women were confined to the clearly demarcated field of black music. Still, in spite of labeling practices that separated black people from rock, the early 1970s saw a new breed of black rock'n'rollers such as the Isley Brothers, Parliament, Funkadelic, Labelle, the Ohio Players, Mandrill, Rufus (featuring Chaka Khan), War, Mother's Finest, and Betty Davis. These artists were inspired by the artistry of Stone, Hendrix, and James Brown and were influenced by the sonic and visual impact of the rock counterculture.

Usually, these bands were large, with seven, eight, or nine members—double the size of most white rock bands—and featured keyboards, horns, and percussion alongside bass, drums, and guitars. The black rock groups' "funk" rhythm, pioneered by James Brown in the late 1960s, placed the emphasis on the first beat of the measure. In funk, the bass was prominent and the polyrhythmic interplay between instruments was central. This music was confusing to a segregated marketplace. Although audible blackness in backing vocals and the efforts of white lead vocalists to sound black were common parts of rock production, the actual blackness of a lead singer and band members, coupled with the mixing of rock, soul, and Latin styles, led to black rock groups' categorization outside of rock. These bands were often "too black" and bass-heavy to fit comfortably on album-oriented rock (AOR) radio and "too rock" and raucous for black stations. Indeed, many of these black self-contained bands muted the guitar and sweetened their sound to secure airplay on black radio.[61] Although sometimes referred to as "black rock," the music produced by black bands during this period is usually categorized as funk, a label that maintained the racially segregated process of naming and selling music.[62]

The rock 'n' roll impulses of high volume, pleasurable revelry, and challenging the mainstream, however, were very much a part of the performance aesthetic of funk as exemplified by bandleader George Clinton's Funkadelic and Parliament. During the 1960s, the Parliaments had met the expectations of the vocal group era, performing doo-wop harmonies and wearing matching uniforms and processed hair. Working on the periphery of Motown, the group had one hit, "(I Wanna) Testify" in 1967. Not long after this, Hendrix and Sly Stone captured Clinton's attention, and he set about transforming his group. He called his new band Funkadelic, a merging of funk and psychedelic, the musical genres his band was exploring. By the mid-1970s, Clinton was also leading a band with the resuscitated name Parliament. The two bands shared personnel and became known as an ever-expanding collective that included the classically trained keyboard-player Bernie Worrell and William "Bootsy" Collins, a young bass player who had cut his professional teeth in James Brown's band. With Funkadelic, Clinton developed his version of rock 'n' roll. He mined the unmentionable and celebrated the life force through irreverent references to sex and partying, while addressing threats to good times. The band played gigs with the Stooges and the MC5, white Detroit bands known for their garage rock sound. Funkadelic was similarly testing the limits of volume, distortion, and feedback; its early recordings *Funkadelic* (1970), *Free Your Mind . . . and Your Ass Will Follow* (1970), and *Maggot Brain* (1971) feature the guitar pyrotechnics of Tawl Ross and Eddie Hazel in multidimensional songs that owed as much to Pink Floyd, the English psychedelic band, as they did to Hendrix.

Funkadelic resisted the strictures of soul performance and stretched out with epic rock jams and irreverent stage antics. Band members wore oversized hats, enormous platform boots, and sparkling capes, and used stage props such as the Mothership, a spaceship that the band beckoned down to the stage with its funky riffs. These visual markers were part of the black science-fiction-meets-comic-book cosmology that Parliament-Funkadelic wove. For all their irreverence, the band also slipped in social commentary in quips such as "Think! It ain't illegal yet!" and the album title *America Eats Its Young* (1972). Funkadelic did not enjoy much chart success, but it did have cult credibility. Parliament, developed with a greater commercial focus in mind, garnered hits for the collective. In 1978, Clinton hit the jackpot with two R&B number one songs: "Flash Light" by Parliament and "One Nation under a Groove" by Funkadelic.[63] The music Clinton made with Parliament-Funkadelic is among the most sampled in hip-hop, and its breadth and experimental vitality inspired the next generation of black rock musicians, white funk rockers (such as the Red Hot Chili Peppers), and rap iconoclasts Outkast.

PUNK AND ROCK IN THE 1980s

The musicians who emerged in the 1980s were the first generation to be raised with the sound of rock 'n' roll as a given and the first to come of age in a period when rights for African Americans were legally protected. As members of the post-Civil Rights generation, many of these black musicians had grown up in integrated contexts and expected to have the same rights and access as white Americans.[64] They were fans of black musicians such as Jimi Hendrix, Sly Stone, James Brown, Miles Davis, and George Clinton, as well as of white bands such as Led Zeppelin. They were also paying attention to a significant change in music that had started in the mid-1970s when a coterie of musicians that had wearied of the excesses of corporate rock responded with a stripped down sound. Eventually called punk, the new music featured simple three-chord songs that expressed the rage and disillusion of the young people who performed it. Punk bands such as London's Sex Pistols and New York's Ramones inspired a new generation of youth to pick up instruments and form bands of their own.

Among them were the young black men who formed Bad Brains, a leading band in the Washington, D.C., homegrown punk rock scene. Raised in the Maryland suburbs of the nation's capitol, Dr. Know (born Gary Miller) on guitar, Darryl Jenifer on bass, Earl Hudson on drums, and his brother H. R. (born Paul Hudson) on vocals started their band in the late 1970s. They began as a fusion band but changed their focus after hearing an album by the punk band the Dead Boys and seeing reggae artist Bob Marley.[65] The resulting link between punk rock energy and Rastafarian philosophy changed the sound of punk. Taking advantage of the musicianship they had developed when playing fusion, Bad Brains perfected the high-speed playing, rapid-fire lyrics, dramatic pauses, and performance intensity that characterized hardcore, the new style of punk that the quartet helped create. The band included straight-up reggae songs in their performances and recordings, and their versatility and musicianship were unusual in a scene that celebrated amateurism. Working far outside the mainstream recording industry, Bad Brains followed punk's Do It Yourself ethos and made their first recordings at local studios that were supporting the work of musicians in Washington's burgeoning punk rock scene. Their song "Pay to Cum" (1980) is often identified as hardcore's first single; their albums *I Against I* (1986) and *Attitude: The ROIR Sessions* (1989), a collection of early singles, are indispensable punk documents. The members of Bad Brains embraced Rastafarianism and sported long dreadlocks, choices that indexed their blackness. Still, although Bad Brains had black fans (many of whom went on to form bands of their own), the band stood out for being an all-black band in the white punk rock context. They were a fixture at Washington's 9:30 Club and then moved to Manhattan, where they made their name at CBGB, the birthplace of punk in the United States. Bad Brains influenced black rockers such as Fishbone and Living Colour and also hard-rocking guitar bands such as punk's Minor Threat, metal's Metallica, and indie rock's Nirvana.[66]

As the 1970s wound down, another major black rock 'n' roll artist emerged. Multi-instrumentalist, singer, and songwriter Prince (born Prince

Rogers Nelson) launched his eclectic career with two fairly standard R&B albums. *For You* (1978) and *Prince* (1980) displayed his musical promise and yielded "I Wanna Be Your Lover" (1979), a song that reached the pop Top 20 and hit number one on the R&B charts. With his first albums, Prince acceded to the recording industry's standard approach for handling black artists: he created music that proved successful in the R&B market before being actively marketed to the mainstream. He started to express his broad musical vision with *Dirty Mind* (1980) and *Controversy* (1981), albums on which he connected sexual and social liberation and treated the spiritual and the erotic as two sides of an enticing coin. Mining the history of black rock 'n' roll, Prince meshed hard rock, funk, and soul impulses and produced music with exemplary guitar playing, vocal expressiveness, and rhythmic energy. He performed with James Brown–style screams and spins and was a clear musical descendent of Jimi Hendrix and Sly Stone. He embraced the sound of a fiery lead guitar and a vision of multiracial unity, forming a mixed-race, mixed-gender band. Prince grabbed attention through sexually evocative song titles such as "Head" and "Soft and Wet" and a stage presentation in which he wore black bikini underwear and high-heeled boots. His

Prince (as The Kid) in Albert Magnoli's 1984 film *Purple Rain*.

Warner Bros./Photofest

glossy pompadour, sexual ambiguity, and transgressive lyrics recalled Little Richard and continued the rock 'n' roll spirit of rebellion on albums such as *1999* (1982), *Purple Rain* (1984), and *Sign o' the Times* (1987).

Although Prince received a great deal of exposure on MTV, the 24-hour music-only cable television station, access to the network was not a given for black artists. Launched in 1981, when the majority of cable television subscribers were suburban whites, MTV used a format that it presumed would appeal to its white, middle-class, and under-twenty-five target audience.[67] Music by black performers was rarely programmed. In MTV's first year and a half, the station played 750 videos, fewer than twenty-four of which featured black artists. In 1983, funk rock guitarist Rick James was among the first to publicly charge the station with racism: his album *Street Songs* (1981) had sold three million copies, but he could not get MTV airplay. Industry executives worried that absence from MTV would deny black artists the improved sales that were almost guaranteed for artists played on MTV. Ultimately, it took pressure from CBS/Epic Records to convince MTV to program black artists. The label threatened to withhold all of its artists' videos unless the station put Michael Jackson's video for the song "Billie Jean," from his album *Thriller* (1982), into rotation. The popularity of Jackson's video helped make *Thriller* a blockbuster and paved the way for black musicians such as Prince, Lionel Richie, Donna Summer, and rock 'n' roll survivor Tina Turner on MTV.

Tina Turner's arrival on MTV was the final phase of a hard-fought comeback. Born Anna Mae Bullock, Turner started her career in the mid-1950s, when Ike Turner hired her to sing with his R&B band. Ike changed her name to Tina to help create a more exotic image.[68] Recording as the Ike and Tina Turner Revue even before they were married, they scored an R&B hit in 1960 with "Fool in Love" and toured tirelessly during the 1960s and early 1970s. Tina Turner was revered for her powerful voice, exuberant dancing, and shapely legs. The undisputed Queen of Rock, she appeared on the cover of the second issue of *Rolling Stone*, the counterculture's premier magazine.[69] After divorcing Ike in 1976, Tina started over professionally, performing in small clubs and building a show as a solo artist. She received assistance in her endeavor from white British musicians who were longtime fans. Both Rod Stewart and the Rolling Stones invited her to perform with them in 1981, giving her access to their audiences. Before long, she had secured a record deal. On *Private Dancer* (1984), Turner left behind the rough edges of R&B for a slicker sound rooted in the commercial pop of the era. It was a remarkably successful move. With the help of heavy MTV rotation of the single "What's Love Got to Do With It?," *Private Dancer* sold ten million copies. The Top 5 album had three Top 10 singles and garnered Grammy awards for Turner who, after almost three decades in the business, finally got her commercial due.[70]

Tina Turner in 1985

Photofest

THE POLITICS OF BLACK ROCK

Turner's story notwithstanding, commercial success was hardly guaranteed for black rock musicians. Fishbone's trajectory exemplifies the dilemmas faced by many black rockers. The Los Angeles band made jubilant musical leaps from ska to punk to funk to metal and developed a reputation for live performances infused with frenzied energy. Formed as a sextet when they were in junior high school, Fishbone's original members were Angelo Moore on vocals and saxophone, Walt Kibby on vocals and trumpet, Kendall Jones on guitar, Chris Dowd on keyboard and trombone, and brothers John Norwood Fisher and Phillip "Fish" Fisher on bass and drums, respectively. The band's promising first single, "Party at Ground Zero" (1985), was a euphoric, ska-inflected dance number, but its releases on Columbia Records, which included *Truth & Soul* (1988), *The Reality of My Surroundings* (1991), and *Give a Monkey a Brain* (1993), did not achieve significant chart success in spite of critical praise, consistent positive response to live shows, and inclusion in high-profile rock events such as the inaugural Lollapalooza traveling rock music festival in 1991. One common explanation was that their eclectic sound caused them to fall through the cracks, not quite right either for rock radio or for black radio. The irony was that the Red Hot Chili Peppers and Jane's Addiction, white bands that had come out of the same genre-blending Los Angeles scene as Fishbone, were commercially successful.

It seemed that racial barriers were at least partly to blame for Fishbone's situation. In spite of rock 'n' roll's countercultural image, the industry that sold the music followed the American tradition of segregation. By the mid-1980s, the recording industry had been operating with race-based assumptions about music taste for a long time: rock music was made by and for white people; black people were only interested in R&B and dance music. In 1985, a collective of New York–based African American musicians, artists, and music industry professionals formed an organization to respond to this situation. Led by cofounders Vernon Reid (a guitarist), Greg Tate (a writer), and Konda Mason (an artist manager), the Black Rock Coalition (BRC) addressed the racial segregation of music in the recording industry and provided a support network for black rock musicians playing outside the industry-dictated confines of black music. Founded during the conservative Reagan era, when Civil Rights–era gains were being eroded at the federal level, the BRC drew attention to the fact that racism was still an issue. So was historical amnesia. BRC members asserted that contrary to the dominant image of rock music as white music, the form derived from black music and was developed through the innovations of black artists.

Reclaiming the black contribution to rock 'n' roll was also a way for BRC members to justify their musical taste in the face of the common charge that black people who played rock were trying to be white. On the contrary, their argument went, they were engaged in a black cultural practice that white people had appropriated. The BRC stressed that black and white Americans alike needed to acknowledge the black roots of rock 'n' roll. Claiming that "rock and roll is black music and we are its heirs," the BRC critiqued recording industry practices that limited black musicians to only a few forms of musical expression.[71] Using the language of expressive freedom so valued in the rock community and of rights so important to African American political organizing, the BRC declared the musical independence of black musicians and united artists who played punk, funk, fusion, hard rock, and metal. The organization presented concerts showcasing black rock bands and tribute shows celebrating black rock forebears. The BRC also sponsored panel discussions and released recordings that compiled the music of member bands. Over the years, artists who have affiliated with the organization include Jean Paul Bourelly, Burnt Sugar, the Bus Boys, Don Byron, the Family Stand, Dave Fiuczynski, Nona Hendryx, Kelvyn Bell, Michael Hill's Blues Mob, Meshell Ndegeocello, Sekou Sundiata, 24-7 Spyz, and Living Colour, the most commercially successful act to emerge from the BRC.

It was Living Colour guitarist Vernon Reid's frustration with the contradictory reception his all-black rock band was receiving in the mid-1980s that led him to call the meetings that started the BRC. Living Colour had

Living Colour, circa 1980s. Shown from left: Will Calhoun, Vernon Reid, Corey Glover, Muzz Skillings.

Photofest

a reputation as one of New York City's best unsigned bands, but the major label executives Reid met with were not prepared to sign a black rock band. Although the publicity that the BRC generated may have helped, the band's big break came when Rolling Stone Mick Jagger became a supporter of the band and financed some of the band's early demos. Living Colour finally got a deal—with Epic Records—and released its first album, *Vivid*, in 1988 with Reid on guitar, Corey Glover on vocals, Muzz Skillings on bass, and William Calhoun on drums. Living Colour was unquestionably a rock band. Influenced by the volume, distortion, and guitar-centered arrangements of Jimi Hendrix, Led Zeppelin, and Carlos Santana as well as the propulsive rhythms of funk, the band forged a distinctive, heavy sound. The band's visibility was raised when it opened for the Rolling Stones on their 1989 Steel Wheels tour and when "Cult of Personality," a single from *Vivid*, was placed into heavy rotation on MTV. *Vivid* went platinum, and the band won Grammy awards in the rock category, an unprecedented achievement for an all-black band. The band continued its genre-crossing on follow-up albums *Time's Up* (1990) and *Stain* (1993)—Doug Wimbish replaced Skillings on the latter. Living Colour disbanded in 1995 and regrouped in 2000.

The members of Living Colour and the Black Rock Coalition made critiquing the segregated recording industry part of their mission. Other black rock 'n' roll artists who were their contemporaries eschewed this type of direct engagement while producing work that also did not fit into the black music category. In 1988, Tracy Chapman surprised the recording industry with the success of her self-titled debut album. An acoustic guitarist, singer, and songwriter, Chapman had a stripped down, folk-informed sound. Her rich alto voice and spare songs captured the imagination of a broad base of fans both black and white, male and female. Her Top 10 single "Fast Car" and the song "Talkin' Bout a Revolution" presented vignettes about people on the margins who longed for better lives. *Tracy Chapman*, a multiplatinum album, helped her garner a Best New Artist Grammy. A year later, rocker Lenny Kravitz released his debut *Let Love Rule* (1989). Like Chapman, he produced a record that returned to the aesthetic of an earlier era, drawing on Hendrix and the Beatles. Once signed to a major label, Kravitz was marketed, like Hendrix and Sly and the Family Stone, to a rock audience and, like Living Colour and Chapman, never received much airplay on black radio stations. Kravitz has received multiple Grammy awards and his albums *Are You Gonna Go My Way* (1993) and *Greatest Hits* (2000) achieved multiplatinum sales. Above all, he has enjoyed a long, commercially successful career—a rarity for black rock musicians.[72]

During the 1990s and 2000s, a critical mass of black rock musicians emerged. Along with Kravitz, Chapman, Living Colour, and Fishbone came Terence Trent D'Arby, Dionne Farris, Marc Anthony Thompson (who performed under the name Chocolate Genius), Toshi Reagon, Ben Harper, Stew (born Mark Stewart) of the Negro Problem, Meshell Ndegeocello, Cody ChesnuTT, Faith, Tamar-kali, the Veldt, Apollo Heights the Family Stand; Follow for Now; Weapon of Choice; Earl Greyhound, and TV on the Radio. In spite of their growing number, most of these artists had to explain their engagement in rock and nonparticipation in rap and R&B. When rapper Mos Def formed his all-black rock group Black Jack Johnson in the early 2000s, he fielded so many questions that he told a reporter, "This is the most I've had to explain myself about any project. And if I was [sic] a White boy doing it, I wouldn't be going through this questioning. I'm treated like I'm approaching something that's foreign to me. My artistic pockets are being patted down because I want to do rock 'n' roll."[73] Indeed, in the new millennium, the presence of black people in rock 'n' roll was still unusual enough to warrant coverage from media outlets looking for a good story. Articles discussed the latest wave of black rockers, noting their persistent attachment to a genre in which black people were at once foundational and marginal.[74]

The turn of the millennium also saw the arrival of books and films documenting the experiences of African Americans in rock 'n' roll.[75] James Spooner's self-produced, low-budget documentary *Afro-Punk* helped black punk rock fans across the United States build a sense of community through the Internet, film screenings, and concerts at local clubs. The Do It Yourself mode of production that Spooner used to make and distribute his film had long been a part of punk rock. As the new century began, musicians of all races were beginning to use the independent model. Increasingly accessible technology—low-cost, professional-quality studio equipment and computer programs for mixing music—enabled artists to produce, promote, and distribute their music on their own. The Internet facilitated the promotion of this music on artists' Web sites and through social networking sites such as Myspace.com. The online environment enabled the sale of music in digital format, challenging the primacy of compact discs as people in their teens and twenties—a crucial demographic—revealed a preference for this option. This approach allowed artists to avoid the pitfalls of major label deals (really production loans repaid by artists) and gave them greater creative control over their products. Instead of waiting to be discovered, artists could make their music on their own terms.

For African American artists who had witnessed in frustration the ineffective ways major labels promoted black rock artists such as Fishbone and who were tired of being told to play a more marketable style of black music, independent production offered an opportunity for self-determination and a respite from the racism that festered in the mainstream recording industry. In fact, the major label deal that had so preoccupied BRC members and most fledgling rock bands in the previous decade became somewhat less important. Although a major label still offered the broadest distribution possibilities, the independent approach to making and circulating music was viable.

Limitations remain, but these technological shifts offer ways for contemporary black rock'n'rollers to circumvent old problems embedded in an industry that has historically resisted their presence and impeded their progress. A commitment to rock music puts African American musicians in the position of having to negotiate the demands and expectations of a racially segregated professional environment while following their creative preference for artistic integration. They have been involved in this struggle since the beginning of rock 'n' roll, and in the new millennium, they are still rocking, still striving for access and success.

NOTES

1. National Association for the Advancement of Colored People, *The Discordant Sound of Music (A Report on the Record Industry)* (Bethesda, MD: NAACP Press, 1987), 16–17.

2. Joel Whitburn, *Joel Whitburn Presents Top R&B Singles 1942–1999* (Menomonee Falls, WI: Record Research, 2000), vii–viii.

3. Robert Palmer, *Dancing in the Street: A Rock and Roll History* (London: BBC Books, 1996), 8.

4. Ibid.

5. Charlie Gillett, *The Sound of the City: The Rise of Rock and Roll* (New York: Pantheon Books, 1983), 39.

6. Ibid., 13.

7. Palmer, *Dancing in the Street*, 8.

8. Single and album release dates and chart positions for this chapter are from Anthony DeCurtis and James Henke, with Holly George-Warren, eds., *The Rolling Stone Illustrated History of Rock & Roll* (New York: Random House, 1992), and from Dave Thompson, *Funk* (San Francisco: Backbeat Books, 2001).

9. Sam Phillips quoted in Episode 1, "Renegades," in *Rock & Roll*, VHS, senior producer David Espar, (South Burlington, VT: WGBH-TV, 1995).

10. Peter Guralnick, *Last Train to Memphis: The Rise of Elvis Presley* (Boston: Little, Brown), 96.

11. Ruth Brown with Andrew Yule, *Miss Rhythm* (New York: Donald Fine Books, 1996), 62.

12. Brown quoted in *That Rhythm . . . Those Blues*, director George T. Nierenberg (Boston, MA: WGBH-TV, 1988).

13. Peter Guralnick, "Fats Domino," in *Rolling Stone Illustrated History*, 48.

14. Ibid., 50.

15. Gillett, *Sound of the City*, 138–139.

16. Ibid., 22.

17. Ibid.,167.

18. Gillett, *Sound of the City*, 129–130.

19. Little Richard, quoted in "Renegades," in *Rock & Roll*.

20. Ibid.

21. Charles White, *The Life and Times of Little Richard: The Quasar of Rock* (New York: Da Capo Press, 1984), 55.

22. Langdon Winner, "Little Richard," in *Rolling Stone Illustrated History*, 52.

23. Diddley, quoted in "Creators—Bo Diddley," *Hail! Rock'n'Roll*, DVD, director Taylor Hackford (Santa Monica, CA: Universal Music, 2006).

24. Diddley, quoted in "Renegades," in *Rock & Roll*.

25. Palmer, *Dancing in the Street*, 73.

26. Lennon and Richards, quoted in *Hail! Rock'n'Roll*.

27. Berry, quoted in *Hail! Rock'n'Roll*.

28. Bruce Pegg, *Brown Eyed Handsome Man: The Life and Hard Times of Chuck Berry* (New York: Routledge, 2002), 50.

29. Diddley, quoted in "Creators—Little Richard, et. al.," in *Hail! Rock'n'Roll*. (A doo-rag is a cloth tied around the head to protect a processed hairdo.)

30. Little Richard, quoted in Ibid.

31. Sam Phillips, quoted in "Renegades," in *Rock & Roll*.

32. Palmer, *Dancing in the Street*, 28.

33. Little Richard, quoted in "Creators—Little Richard, et. al," in *Hail! Rock'n'Roll*.

34. Etta James and David Ritz, *Rage to Survive* (New York: Da Capo Press, 1998), 49–50.

35. Diddley, quoted in *Hail! Hail! Rock'n'Roll*.

36. Brown with Yule, *Miss Rhythm*, 197.

37. Ibid., 219.

38. Ibid., 217.

39. Barry Hansen, "Doo-Wop," *Rolling Stone Illustrated History*, 92.

40. Ibid., 98.

41. Goffin, quoted in Palmer, *Dancing in the Street*, 35.

42. Joe McEwen and Jim Miller, "Motown," in *Rolling Stone Illustrated History*, 280.

43. Nelson George, *The Death of Rhythm and Blues* (New York: Plume, 1988), 84.

44. Lee, quoted with original emphasis, in Andrew Sandoval, CD liner notes, *Love Story: 1966–1972* (Los Angeles: Rhino Records, 1995), 9.

45. Barney Hoskyns, "Paint Me White: Bad Days, Black Rock, and Arthur Lee's Love Story," in *Rip It Up: The Black Experience in Rock'n'Roll*, ed. K. Crazy Horse (New York: Palgrave Macmillan, 2004), 11.

46. Ray Manzarek, quoted in Richard Cromelin, "In Bloom Again," *Los Angeles Times*, May 1, 2002, F5.

47. Hoskyns, "Paint Me White," 19.

48. Ibid., 21.

49. Dalton Anthony, "A.K.A. Sly Stone: The Rise and Fall of Sylvester Stewart," in *Rip It Up*, 46.

50. George, *Rhythm and Blues*, 109.

51. Rickey Vincent, *Funk: The Music, the People, and the Rhythm of the One* (New York: St. Martin's Griffin, 1996), 96.

52. Maureen Mahon, *Right to Rock: The Black Rock Coalition and the Cultural Politics of Race* (Durham, NC: Duke University Press, 2004), 231–256.

53. George, *Rhythm and Blues*, 109.

54. Ibid., 108.

55. Greg Tate, *Midnight Lightning: Jimi Hendrix and the Black Experience* (Chicago: Lawrence Hill Books, 2003), 14.

56. Ibid.

57. Charles Shaar Murray, *Crosstown Traffic: Jimi Hendrix and the Post-War Rock'n'Roll Revolution* (New York: St. Martin's Press, 1991), 86.

58. "Tom Wilson," Wikipedia, http://en.wikipedia.org/wiki/Tom_Wilson (accessed January 20, 2007).

59. Stephen Holmes, "Paul Simon," in *Rolling Stone Illustrated History*, 320.

60. Maureen Mahon, "Women in African American Music: Rock," in *African American Music: An Introduction*, eds. M. Burnim and P. Maultsby (New York: Routledge, 2006), 571–573.

61. Vincent, *Funk*, 119.

62. Ibid.

63. Ibid., 89.

64. Mahon, *Right to Rock*.

65. Greg Tate, CD liner notes, *Banned in D.C.: Bad Brains Greatest Riffs*, (New York: Caroline Records, 2003).

66. Tate, *Banned in D.C.*

67. Mahon, *Right To Rock*, 167–169.

68. Tina Turner and Kurt Loder, *I, Tina* (New York: Avon Books, 1987), 75.

69. Gillian G. Gaar, *She's a Rebel: The History of Women in Rock & Roll* (New York: Seal Press, 2002), 83.

70. Turner and Loder, *I, Tina*, 221.

71. BRC Manifesto, quoted in Mahon, *Right To Rock*, 89.

72. Greg Tate, "Rock Steady," *Vibe* (December 2001): 126.

73. Mos Def, quoted in Darrell M. McNeill, "Rock, Racism, and Retailing 101: A Blueprint for Cultural Theft," in *Rip It Up*, 146.

74. Jon Caramanica, "Electric Warriors," *Vibe* (February 2002): 85–90, and Jon Pareles, "Black Musicians Reclaim Hard Rock," *New York Times*, August 4, 2001, sec. A, p. 20.

75. Crazy Horse, *Rip It Up*; Mahon, *Right to Rock*; Tate, *Midnight Lightning*; *Afro-Punk: The Rock'n'Roll Nigger Experience*, DVD, directed by James Spooner (Brooklyn, NY: High Yellow Productions, 2003); *Electric Purgatory: The Fate of the Black Rocker*, VHS, director Raymond Gayle (Houston, TX: Payback Productions, 2005).

4

Hip-hop Moguls

Christopher Holmes Smith

During the waning years of the Clinton administration, and at the peak of the dot-com stock market bubble, black entertainer-cum-entrepreneurs such as Russell Simmons, Sean "Diddy" Combs, Percy "Master P" Miller, Damon Dash, and Shawn "Jay-Z" Carter reached a new threshold of public recognition and acclaim for their ability to legitimize and diversify hip-hop's commercial appeal. In a time of imminent technological dislocation in the recording industry, all these men became famous for turning the relatively segmented market for urban music into a sprawling mainstream empire of lifestyle-based merchandise spanning fashion, restaurants, soft drinks, film and theatrical production, and personal services. Under their leadership—seemingly overnight—it became possible for the business of hip-hop culture to become a defining feature of the culture itself. This trend represented a profoundly new direction within the hip-hop tradition.

Throughout the late 1970s, 1980s, and early to mid-1990s, rappers had regularly rendered lyrical compositions that reflected a deep-seated "double-consciousness" toward the music industry. On the one hand, songs such as EPMD's "Please Listen to My Demo" expresses the ardent desire every unknown MC had to be discovered by a record label's A&R representative and summarily signed to a deal that would signal the beginning of a long and lucrative career.[1] Conversely, songs such as A Tribe Called Quest's "Show Business" depicts record companies and their executive leadership as nothing more than duplicitous and opportunistic hucksters intent on peddling a watered-down version of rap music and hip-hop culture to the mainstream audience for a fast profit.[2] Rappers' pronounced level of mistrust for big business in general, and music industry managerial practice specifically, stemmed from popular memory of how black artists and musicians had been exploited in the early days of rhythm and blues.[3] Throughout black America, impressions of record label procedures were significantly influenced by grassroots "stories of chart-topping

Left to right: P. Diddy Combs, Jay Z, and Russell Simmons during the Zac Posen Fall 2005 Collection, New York.

AP Photo/Jennifer Graylock

black artists who died penniless because they didn't have the financial wherewithal to own their own product or the ability to compete with mainstream record labels."⁴ Neither the significant precedents of African American ownership established in the 1960s, 1970s, and 1980s by record label heads such as Berry Gordy and Clarence Avant nor the mainstream taste-making acumen so ably demonstrated by market-moving impresarios such as Quincy Jones completely revised the abiding black social common sense about the more dubious aspects of the recording business.

   Against this historical legacy of limited industry enfranchisement, the emergence and rise to power of visionary young black entrepreneurs such as Simmons, Combs, Miller, Dash, and Carter captivated the attention of music fans, industry critics, the popular press, and the broader creative community. The hugely influential HBO cable TV series *The Sopranos* even featured a veritable "hip-hop mogul" as the central protagonist in an episode during its premier season in 1999. The episode, entitled "A Hit Is a Hit," presented the story of a wealthy rap entrepreneur named "Massive Genius" (Bookeem Woodbine) who confronts a Jewish mobster affiliated with the Soprano mafia family in order to collect unpaid royalties for a distant relative who had scored a hit record in the doo-wop era. In this respect, the rap mogul resembles a capitalist avenger whose wealth represents not only individual gain but also a moral claim for material reparations on behalf of his racial fellows.

Simmons, known as the Godfather of Hip-hop because of his pioneering efforts to grow hip-hop as both entertainment and a lifestyle, began his career as a local rap promoter in New York City during the late 1970s. In 1984, he partnered with Rick Rubin, a white college student who was running a record label out of his dormitory at New York University. Together the two men created Def Jam Records, a seminal rap imprint that went on to launch some of the most influential rap acts in history, including Run-D.M.C., LL Cool J, and Public Enemy. In 1999, Simmons sold his stake in Def Jam to Seagram Universal Music Group for $100 million. In 2004, Simmons also sold his Phat Fashions clothing line to the Kellwood Company for $140 million. Currently, as CEO of Rush Communications, Simmons oversees a wide variety of ventures, including television, theater, and film production, finance, mobile telephony, and philanthropy.

Miller is the founder and CEO of No Limit Enterprises, an entertainment and financial conglomerate that became known for a range of influential guerilla marketing techniques. Before Miller's forays into the industry, rap artists had traditionally focused on merely the creative side of the music while shunning the business and financial aspects. All that changed in 1996, when Miller signed a music distribution deal with Priority Records for his No Limit label that enabled Miller to retain 100% ownership of his artists' master recordings and keep 85 percent of their record's sales, Priority obtaining 15 percent of revenues in return for pressing and distribution. Miller subsequently made hundreds of millions of dollars from this deal, and his profitable track record in recordings, in the then-nascent direct-to-video category, and in a diverse array of ancillary products raised the bar for rappers' expectations of professional autonomy.

Combs is CEO of Bad Boy Worldwide Entertainment Group, a holding company that includes the $400 million Sean John clothing and fragrance line in addition to restaurants and a record label. Like many of the other moguls, Combs—who is known for his lavish parties in the Hamptons vacation area of East Long Island, NY—has been extremely successful at leveraging his celebrity as an extension of his business enterprises.

Dash cofounded Roc-A-Fella Records in 1996 with star rapper Shawn "Jay-Z" Carter and Kareem "Biggs" Burke, later helping to found the Rocawear urban fashion brand, which in short order was reportedly grossing $300 million annually. In 2004, Dash sold his interest in Roc-A-Fella to Universal-owned Island Def Jam Records for $10 million. He also sold his stake in Rocawear to Carter for $30 million. He has subsequently founded the Damon Dash Music Group, and his other businesses include America Magazine, Armadale Vodka, Dash Films, Pro Keds sneakers, and Tiret watches, providing financial backing for his wife Rachel Roy's clothing line, nightclubs, and a professional boxing management and promotion company.

Carter exploded on the rap scene in 1996 as Roc-A-Fella Records's signature act. Known for his laid-back vocal delivery and uncanny ability to bring street and pop vernaculars together in his musical productions, Jay-Z went on to garner significant critical acclaim while becoming one of the best-selling rappers in industry history. In December 2004, after having announced his retirement as a performer, Jay-Z was appointed president and chief executive of Def Jam Recordings, Roc-A-Fella's parent company, which prompted bitter buyout negotiations over Roc-A-Fella's music and apparel divisions with his former business partners. While head of Def Jam, Carter reportedly earned $8–10 million in annual compensation. In March of 2007, Jay-Z sold the rights to the Rocawear brand to Iconix Brand Group for $204 million in cash. Currently, Carter is part owner of the New Jersey Nets NBA franchise and the 40/40 Club sports bars and has been instrumental in marketing efforts for brands such as Anheuser-Busch's Budweiser Select and HP's notebook computers. Most recently, in keeping with the rapid state of flux in the industry, Jay-Z broke with Def Jam and signed a 10-year, $150 million deal with the Beverly Hills–based concert giant Live Nation. As CD sales continue to plummet, such "360" deals, encompassing recordings, concerts, and merchandising, are being considered as the most viable near-term business model for the ailing industry.[5] Through all of these ventures, Carter, like Combs, has become a legitimate pop cultural icon as paparazzi chart nearly every move he makes, whether alone, with his entourage, or in the company of his wife, pop and R&B diva Beyoncé Knowles.

The extent to which a wave of financial speculation accompanied the rise of hip-hop moguls to celebrity status in the mainstream press—and the degree to which the mogul phenomenon served as a cultural metaphor for "boom times"—is exceedingly significant.[6] The cultural studies media scholar Stuart Hall suggests that it is crucial to examine the social circumstances that adhere within a specific social discourse at any given time. He calls such examinations the theorization of "articulation." For Hall the concept of articulation presents "both a way of understanding how ideological elements come, under certain conditions, to cohere together within a discourse, and a way of asking how they do or do not become articulated, at specific conjunctures to certain political subjects."[7] In this respect, the emergence of the new "mogul" parlance in regard to rap's executive class should not be seen as a "natural" occurrence that stemmed solely from the self-directed actions of a handful of "great men." Instead, Hall's theory of articulation invites interested observers to consider the "hip-hop mogul" notion as utterly contingent upon how disparate cultural phenomenon gradually became woven into a very particular pattern of interpretation.

Any assessment of the mogul discourse's political effects, therefore, must take serious consideration of the broader social relationships that enabled the discourse itself to coalesce. In line with discursive analysis based on Hall's theory of articulation, it is noteworthy that literature surveys suggest that strong correlations were made in the mainstream, ethnic, and industry press between hip-hop moguls, their collective cultural impact, and the stock market mania that swept the land in the late 1990s.

According to historian Edward Chancellor, speculative manias in the stock market recollect the scenarios prevalent during Renaissance fairs and carnivals in which people's pent-up energy is unleashed and the typical progression of the social hierarchy is temporarily turned upside down. Just as Renaissance carnivals undermined the authority of the Church, speculative manias reverse capitalism's regulatory social values of patience, honesty, thrift, and hard work. [8] As in carnivals, festivals, and fairs, tantalizing conditions of transcendence are imbued within all speculative outbreaks, moments wherein a new dispensation seems in the offing and recourse to "the fundamentals" no longer lays claim to the recognition of value. Indeed, during periods of speculative euphoria, traditional rules of conduct are not nearly as persuasive to social actors as is emulating behavior by the crowd at large. At topsy-turvy moments such as these, when the appropriate calculus for valuation is anyone's guess, conventional wisdom becomes inflected with a populist accent as the abiding utility of once hallowed metrics of discernment and judgment are called into question. During the 1990s bull market, an explosion of entrepreneurial and speculative activity in the technology, media, and telecom sectors—collectively codified as a "New Economy"—triggered a similar paradigm shift in U.S. culture and society.

Between 1980 and 2001—a period when the United States underwent a wrenching transition from a manufacturing to a service basis—the phrase "New Economy" initially functioned in the American press as a way of describing the human devastation wrought by deindustrialization. By the mid-1990s, the phrase was used more often than not to identify the dawning of a technological utopia that synthesized neoliberal philosophies advocating open markets and free trade abroad, a managerial and market-based approach to multicultural diversity at home, and—above all else—perpetual economic growth. The popularization of the Internet was crucial to this national change of disposition toward the new service-oriented economy. As the mainstream press experimented with more accessible ways of reporting its social and industrial effects, the Web became a benign symbol of epochal change that people could understand and embrace; the more comfortable people felt with the technological shifts the Internet represented, the more they felt emboldened to invest in the companies charting its course.

Historians point to the initial public offering for Netscape Communications in August 1995 as the tipping point when average Americans stopped hating the New Economy and learned to love it instead.[9] A week after Netscape's debut, according to the *New York Times*, "investors fell all over one another trying to snap up the first publicly available shares" of the Web-browser manufacturer. What startled the *Times* and many others about the flotation's appeal to investors was that Netscape had "no earnings, hardly any sales and looming competition from [the] big boys."[10] Netscape's cash windfall and stunning defiance of traditional business valuation helped unleash a wave of financial speculation in similarly fledgling operations, many with much worse long-term prospects than Netscape's. Indeed, as news began to spread that the Net offered opportunities to get rich fast, Americans plowed their liquid assets into the stock market at an unprecedented rate, undertaking a feverish quest to find the next upstart technology company whose market capitalization was primed to soar into the stratosphere. Whereas in 1952 only 4 percent of Americans owned common stock, just two years after Netscape's fateful IPO, 40 percent of Americans were in the market.[11] As stock indexes skyrocketed and the speculative mania proliferated, representations of the new synergy between Wall Street and Silicon Valley spread the popular gospel that anyone with a notion, a small amount of cash, and a thimble-full of gumption could play the game of turbo-capitalism and eventually amass a personal fortune. By 1999, the *New York Times* noted that millions of Americans were focusing "on the one thing that most define[d] their lives, the upward and downward ticks of interest rates, the gyrations of their mutual funds, the achingly palpable lure and temptations of wealth."[12] By 2001, the Federal Reserve determined that 52 percent of the nation's citizens had some form of stock ownership. Among registered voters, shareholders outnumbered those not in the market 53 percent to 43 percent.[13]

The respective decisions that average citizens made to join the equity-owning class had tangible benefits. Indeed, the typical American's stock portfolio enjoyed healthy gains during the 1990s, rising in value from $10,800 in 1989 to $25,000 in 1998. Stock holdings across a broader base of American households helped send the net worth per family from $59,700 in 1989 to $71,600 in 1998.[14] More important than any particular quantitative tabulation of relative prosperity, however, was the sheer belief in the popular mind that the Internet would be the apocalyptic battering ram that would finally demolish the barricades separating everyday people from the gilded bastions of the controlling classes. No group figured as prominently on the frontlines of the New Economy's populist assault on the old monetary order as American youth.

When the 1990s began, the most pressing domestic concern was how to reckon with the fact that "for the first time in American history" a generation of young people (Generation X) would not be as wealthy as their parents. This creeping sense of socioeconomic stagnation created a loss of purpose in the psychic life of the nation and paved the way for the election of Bill Clinton in the decade's first presidential election. However, thanks to the Internet, by the decade's close, American youth were no longer seen as economic dropouts and perennial underachievers but as technological wizards, market innovators, social visionaries, and increasingly at the financial vanguard of their ostensibly parent-led households. During the dot-com boom, the press repeatedly proclaimed the arrival of a new class of precocious teens called "The Enfatrepreneurs."[15] Individual members of this new demographic—emboldened by the rhetorical rallying cry "Who Needs a Diploma?"[16]—boldly stepped into suburban living rooms across America with freshly minted dot-com business plans in hand and proudly declared to their submissive, tech-ignorant, and somewhat awed parents: ". . . I'm the boss now."[17]

Some of the hoopla over money's more youthful visage in the Internet Age was upheld by statistical data. According to a survey conducted by the Hartford, CT–based Phoenix Home Life Mutual Insurance Company, for example, the number of U.S. households with a net worth of $1 million grew to 6.7 million in 1998, up from 1.8 million in 1990. The survey also found that in 1998, 45 percent of the country's millionaires were younger than 55, 80 percent of them first-generation millionaires.[18] the *New York Times* reported similar findings, telling readers in a March 2000 article that "5 of every 100 people in the top 1 percent of the wealthiest Americans are 35 years or younger, compared with a fraction of a percent just 17 years ago."[19] This explosive trend in the creation of new wealth—fueled by a speculative mania for dot-com companies on Wall Street—led many to believe that the Internet had indeed changed everything and that a radical new social order was coming into view. Thus, the emergence of the hip-hop mogul class of entertainment executives only seemed to further delineate and reinforce a broader socioeconomic rupture of seismic proportions.

Echoing Chancellor's observation on the carnivalesque aspects of financial speculation, John Seabrook uses the word *Nobrow* to define the historically specific cultural milieu from within which hip-hop moguls emerged in the late 1990s.[20] For Seabrook, Nobrow signals a new synergy between marketing and creativity that gives the judgments and tastes of the masses more influence in cultural affairs than traditional social elites. In Seabrook's estimation, this trend is epitomized best by an inversion of influence whereby purveyors of hypercommercial multiculturalism, such as MTV, have usurped the fortunes of once sacrosanct cultural filters such as the *New Yorker*. Stanford legal historian Lawrence M. Friedman ascribes this global cultural movement to the ability of information technology to accelerate social change and to the ways in which frameworks of social governance are revised accordingly.[21] Nobrow crystallizes these shifting times by identifying how the commercialization of artistic creativity—guided always by the invisible hand of an increasingly consolidated electronic and digital media oligarchy—has set once-fixed assumptions about the nature of cultural value into motion. These conditions of rapid historical change have created new opportunities for everyday people to accumulate the continually emergent forms of cultural capital that can be most easily exchanged for social status in the marketplace of ideas. Culture, in Seabrook's estimation, is now equivalent to a deregulated economy of signs defined by endless flux and reconfiguration, within which modern individuals can affiliate with ideas, experiences, and social groups across local, regional, and national borders in quicksilver fashion. In this vein, social identity becomes the functional equivalent of a "mosh pit" wherein speculative personal investments are constantly allocated and repositioned in a market of contingent cultural values and forms.

Sociologists use the concept of status to explain how everyday acts and perceptions construct a hierarchy of relative social positions. Individuals' locations within that hierarchy shape others' expectations of and actions toward them and thereby determine the opportunities and constraints that they confront. Under the rubric of Nobrow, social status is not the static by-product of one's birthright, but rather the dynamic coupling of charisma—what rappers and athletes call "swagger"—with tactical engagement in the consumer marketplace. The incessant competition for differentiation and distinction, described famously by the French sociologist Pierre Bordieu, still abides, but no longer according to the old cultural rules.[22] The Nobrow metaphor helps identify, therefore, how hip-hop has politicized taste within the cultural field by bringing to the market forms of underground social knowledge that can be exchanged and circulated like economic resources. Quite appropriately, when Jay-Z describes himself as "[t]he Martha Stewart, that's far from Jewish/Far from a Harvard student, just had the balls to do it" on the song "What More Can I Say" from his celebrated *Black Album*,[23] he succinctly summarizes the hip-hop mogul's capacity to shape mainstream taste by leveraging nothing more than large reserves of self-confidence and a willingness to take the initiative.

Indeed, through the boundary-defying powers of the electronic and digital media, socially isolated territories of disreputable cultural knowledge, such as America's inner cities, have become essential to dominant modes of social identity–formation.[24] This unlikely symbolic reversal has been progressive to the extent that, like the ritualized state of disorder in Renaissance carnival, it has shattered the old high-low cultural hierarchy predicated upon "good breeding," "proper schooling," and "aesthetic appreciation," having instead placed the market's consumptive ethos of equal opportunity at the center of the individual's protean capacity for self-definition. However, this trend also threatens to make the great twentieth-century sociologist W. E. B. Du Bois's "Talented Tenth" paradigm for black civic enfranchisement and communal development seem quaint, if not utterly irrelevant.[25] In Du Bois's day, taste, status, and eligibility for social leadership were all predicated upon incontrovertible ideas of truth and knowledge that were to be gleaned from passage through a range of civic institutions, most notably the black colleges and universities that had been founded in the hopeful days of Reconstruction. The standards of judgment accrued during this intellectual and spiritual training regimen represented "blue chip" standards of personal equity. This elitist trajectory of achievement formed the basis of the cultural catholicity that Du Bois formulated as a remedy for the gloomy condition of perpetual indebtedness that the sharecropping system virtually preordained for black freedmen. The seductive mass mediation of Nobrow hegemony, however, has increasingly motivated American cultural consumers to legitimize themselves largely without the imprimatur of traditional knowledge-bearing institutions. As exemplary signs of the New Economy's ability to promote categorical dissolution,[26] many black cultural practitioners—especially those within hip-hop—became widely known as unlikely but ultimately legitimate representatives of late-1990s prosperity, privy to a Shangri-la of mushrooming capital gains and seemingly endless liquidity.

Thus, whether within speculative manias of financial or cultural variety, a reordering of the social hierarchy takes place. Depending on one's standing in the pecking order, such a circumstance may not be such an unfortunate turn of events. A brief passage from F. Scott Fitzgerald's *The Great Gatsby* captures the timeless allure of this proposition while illustrating how race supplements the specifically American notion of speculative symbolic reversal. In it, the reader enters the reverie of the book's narrator, Nick Carraway, as he rides toward the island of Manhattan, the epicenter of carnivalesque possibility during the Jazz Age:

> Over the great bridge, with the sunlight through the girders making a constant flicker upon the moving cars, with the city rising up across the river in white heaps and sugar lumps all built with a wish out of non-olfactory money. The city seen for the first time, in its first wild promise of all the mystery and beauty in the world . . . As we crossed Blackwell's Island a limousine passed us, driven by a white chauffer, in which sat three modish negroes, two bucks and a girl. I laughed aloud as the yolks of their eyeballs rolled toward us in haughty rivalry. 'Anything can happen now that we've slid over this bridge,' I thought; 'anything at all . . .'[27]

The surge of wealth creation on Wall Street during the 1990s New Economy offered everyday people a similar opportunity for protean self-redefinition as hip-hop moguls became racial icons for the bull market's democratic promise of structural inversion.

As perhaps Nobrow's supreme symbolic idiom, hip-hop shifted during the 1990s from being antithetical to the cultivation of aesthetic disposition and leisure preference in mainstream commercial channels to serving as one of the most profitable means toward that end.[28] Though still dogged by intermittent outbreaks of moral panic[29] from mainstream society, hip-hop culture gradually became known as just one innovation among the many that the dot-com economy had wrought, and therefore a more tolerable presence in the United States' millennial celebration of prolonged economic growth. In an article on the hip-hop mogul phenomenon, Tania Padgett conflates post-industrial innovation and cultural marketing in a particularly apt manner, noting how "in the '80s, it was the leveraged buyout; in the '90s, technology. But at the beginning of a new century, it's the selling of 'cool' that is building empires and making moguls . . . millions with what is surely the coolest widget around: hip-hop."[30] This robust market muscle is the function of the new synergy between black cultural producers, white youth, commercial media, and the mainstream consumer market. In previous historical eras, black cultural expression from the bottom of the social hierarchy, and the standards of moral value that they conveyed, functioned as the cultural equivalent of what Harvard Business School professor Clay Christensen calls "disruptive technologies."[31] In this respect, prior to the hip-hop mogul's arrival on the scene, middle managers in most mainstream marketing organizations had only intermittently regarded rap as a cultural sensibility worth embracing. Even many black record company executives did not consider hip-hop a sustainable cultural trend in the idiom's early days.[32] As the 1990s lapsed into the twenty-first century, however, black cultural tastes—especially those stemming from the aspirations and lifestyles fundamental to hip-hop's worldview—became extremely efficient devices for extracting profit from the consumptive habits of America's youth across a broad spectrum of product verticals, from apparel to mobile telephony.

Herein we find the hip-hop mogul's primary business imperative: namely, the effective identification, packaging, and marketing of the politically and socially volatile minority underclass's expressive culture. On a certain level, the use of urban variations on signs of blackness as a wedge for greater market share is nothing new. After all, channeling the experiential abundance of America's multicultural masses into commodity form has been part of the historical project for America's barons of leisure since the days when minstrel sheet music extolled the nefarious exploits of Zip Coon.[33] This endeavor has traditionally employed art and performance to transcend the boundaries of social stratification and enable new modes of interracial and interethnic recombination—no matter how circumscribed and degraded such contact may inevitably have been. What *was* unprecedented in the 1990s, however, was the degree to which the hip-hop mogul's growing importance installed young black men at the helm of America's pop market logic toward social diversity—and gave them an owner's stake in the multimedia bonanza surrounding its circulation. Henry Louis Gates Jr. noted of the new black creative gatekeepers that "for the first time, we have a significant presence of black agents, black editors, [and] black reviewers. Blacks now run and own record labels. . . . With the active recruitment of minorities into the mainstream, blacks have an institutional authority without precedent in American cultural history."[34] With this new influence came a veritable explosion of urban cultural offerings throughout the commercial landscape, spearheaded by the strong growth in rap music sales. In 2000, for example, "the Recording Industry Association of America [estimated] that rap music generated more than $1.8 billion in sales, accounting for 12.9 percent of all music purchases . . . surpass[ing] country music as the nation's second most popular genre after rock and roll."[35] These figures have since softened considerably, mirroring the fundamental deterioration of profit margins in the music industry as a whole, but the fact remains that in the late 1990s hip-hop culture unquestionably solidified itself as a key rampart of the national structure of feeling.[36]

Hip-hop's burgeoning cultural and financial influence enabled the black cultural producers who best embodied mastery of speculation's inherent risks to join the ranks of the corporate celebrity class. Two hip-hop entrepreneurs, Percy Miller and Sean Combs, were listed squarely in the middle of *Fortune* magazine's roster of "America's Forty Richest under 40" at the time. Master P sat directly behind Vinny Smith, chairman and CEO of Quest Software, with a net worth of $293.8 million; Diddy, whose personal fortune came in at a cool $293.7 million, ranked ahead of such luminaries as actress Julia Roberts, the golf wunderkind Tiger Woods, and a slew of technology and software tycoons.[37]

As the 1990s wound to a close, hip-hop's centrality within Nobrow hegemony became more iron-clad than ever. In keeping with the emergence of the new cultural common sense, *Time* defined the last days of the twentieth century as "the age of hip-hop."[38] Given the prevailing contours of the zeitgeist, it was not altogether surprising to see the hip-hop impresario Sean Combs headlining the Metropolitan Museum of Art's annual Costume Institute gala mere weeks before the arrival of Y2K. This was a Nobrow cultural moment par excellence: Within one of the more formidable citadels of Western civilization, and at an end-of-the-century celebration cochaired by *Vogue* editor Anna Wintour and attended by such disparate luminaries as comedian Jerry Seinfeld, billionaire buyout kingpin Ronald Perelman, film producer Harvey Weinstein, former secretary of state Henry Kissinger, actress Gwyneth Paltrow, and socialites Patricia Buckley, Nan Kempner, and Alexandra von Furstenberg, rap, the gruff baritone voice of the ghetto, was anointed as the most appropriate musical keynote with which to "ring out the old and ring in the new."[39]

Ultimately, the mainstream media seemed most keen to observe how aptly hip-hop moguls' spending habits reflected the excesses of the times. Time and again, across a wide range of publications, hip-hop's culture of bling was proclaimed as the hallmark of a self-indulgent decade. Fashion columnist Amy Spindler wrote in the *New York Times*, for instance, that when historians recalled the stylish excesses of the Internet gold rush, they would do so in terms of how hip-hop served as a consumptive bellwether for the champagne and caviar set. "Silicon geeks and dot-comers may earn triple-digit billions," Spindler noted, "but the folks who *really* have the knack for spending—the true nouveau riche, our Carringtons of the new Millennium—are hip-hop impresarios like Puffy Combs."[40] And what sort of bounty did Spindler conflate with Combs's mogul lifestyle? How about the following: a sable vest from Fendi ($18,500), silver stilettos from the red-hot designer Jimmy Choo ($650 a pair), an 18-karat gold Tiffany necklace and matching bracelet, both decked out in diamonds ($33,500 and $27,000, respectively), a bottle of Burgundy at Alain Ducasse's new restaurant at the Essex House on Central Park South ($800), a pound of Crème de la Mer facial lotion designed to spec for NASA ($1,000), and title to the ninetieth-floor penthouse at Trump World Tower at United Nations Plaza ($38 million). It's important to recollect that during the 1990s bull market the spendthrift ways of the wealthiest rappers were hardly socially aberrant. Throughout the long boom, many Americans had their personal fortunes lofted in the updraft of the speculative winning streak, and they rewarded themselves by spending relatively extravagantly in their own right. Indeed, the major symbolic figures of that halcyon age, from celebrity CEOs and upstart technology entrepreneurs to magazine publishers and publicity mavens, were known for spending lavishly to promote their goods, their services, and themselves. Consequently, hip-hop's "wealth effect" spending patterns became inserted rather easily within the New Economy's dominant social and cultural constellation.

The legitimate longing for freedom and equality within such paroxysms of "irrational exuberance" aside, Edward Chancellor's financial history reminds us that "periods of carnival and speculative mania end" and that the latter typically see figureheads of excess "pilloried, stripped of their wealth, and imprisoned."[41] Quite predictably, the dot-com bubble slouched toward posterity amid an intense moral backlash that targeted the New Economy's privileged class, particularly the CEOs, investment bankers, and equity research analysts who appeared to service their greed during the golden years by bilking the masses with phony information. Curiously, despite this call for reformation and redress, the entertainment sector where the hip-hop moguls were ensconced continued to thrive as what one columnist in the *New York Times* called the last "safe haven for ridiculous expenditure."[42] When one considers the enduring good fortune of the mogul cohort, it is well worth noting that unlike many of the corporate icons of Web 1.0, the deflation of the Internet equity bubble did not spell the demise of hip-hop's market for "cool." In addition, figures such as Shawn Carter and Damon Dash escaped the jeremiads against the "fabulous life" of greed and excess that brought the dot-com era to a close because their wealth and consumptive practices were viewed as legitimate products of a strenuous striving to succeed, and representative therefore of an unexpected—almost divinely ordained—social mobility that arose against the grain of public expectation. Generally speaking, social mobility defines the degree to which, in a given society, an individual's social status may change throughout the course of his or her lifetime, much as the hallowed myth of the American Dream suggests that an individual can move from poverty to wealth in one generation. In rap's typical bling narrative "it goes without saying that the squandering protagonist is a rags-to-riches figure who beat overwhelming odds and has every right to the fruits of that success."[43] Furthermore, unlike publicly traded companies that have an obligation to serve the material interests of their shareholders, the type of investments that rap moguls need to make to redeem themselves with their consuming public are almost entirely psychic in nature. Accordingly, the rap moguls' primary duty and obligation is to reinvent themselves as the incarnation of their customers' collective dream for a more abundant life, something radically different from the template of propriety and accountability under which CEOs of publicly traded firms must operate. In the late 1990s, this meant that even as many celebrity CEOs were publicly humiliated for their fiscal imprudence, whether for crimes symbolic or real, rap moguls generally came away from the dot-com collapse unscathed. As the *New York Times* quipped, "Sean Combs was once accused of hitting a record executive with a chair and a Champagne bottle, but at least he has never smacked your 401(k) around."[44]

Nevertheless, politically speaking, hip-hop moguls remain charged cultural figures precisely because of their ability to appeal to various interpretive communities, each possessing very specific stakes vis-à-vis the moguls' rise to economic power and cultural influence. Therefore, even though moguls may not have been directly implicated by mainstream commentators in the dot-com meltdown, in black America their flashy lifestyles were alleged to exemplify a troubling generational shift between the civil rights and hip-hop generations over the market's role as a meaningful referent and basis for the activist-oriented black public sphere.[45] The civil rights political establishment's puritanical restraint regarding commodity consumption stands in contradistinction to the opportunistic demeanor of the hip-hop moguls, who recognized that progressive aspirations can be bought and sold—and the higher the price the better.[46] For many of rap's more populist artists and fans, the emergence of the hip-hop mogul as a visual signifier for the "good life" identified neoliberal forms of social uplift as the "new normal" within black political discourse.

Neoliberalism contends that the best path to social progress runs through the free market. Accordingly, neoliberal political economy strives to intensify and expand market transactions. From the neoliberal perspective, every human being is an entrepreneur managing his or her own life and should act as such. Neoliberals also believe that society and the state should not have fixed goals but should evolve purely through market-based competition; those who do not or cannot participate in the market have failed in some way.[47] Most importantly, in neoliberal political economy, "'risk' represented as potential dangers to be collectively managed is increasingly replaced by 'risk' represented as opportunity or reward for individuals."[48] Nobel-winning economist Amartya Sen frames debates over neoliberalism in terms of an intellectual dividing line between growth-mediated strategies for social progress and support-led communal development. Sen says that a classic support-led initiative "does not operate through fast economic growth, but works through a program of skillful social support of health care, education and other relevant social arrangements." Sen defines growth-mediated development as "working through fast economic growth [with] its success [depending] on the growth process being wide-based and economically broad . . . and . . . utilization of the enhanced economic prosperity to expand the relevant social services, including health care, education, and social security."[49] Tellingly, it is this second part of the growth-mediated equation that neoliberal regimes typically leave out. Indeed, Jay-Z's lyrical argument that "I can't help the poor if I'm one of them/So I got rich and gave back/To me that's the win, win"[50] does not fully convince many fans and critics alike that the hip-hop mogul's ability to represent opulence and aspiration actually enables new modes of development and freedom for communities wherein such enhancements would mean quite a lot.

What is certain is that the representational frameworks depicting rap's upwardly mobile motifs generally have to do with identity-shifting, or, at least, identity "layering." In other words, although rappers—whether moguls or otherwise—never deny their racial and ethnic heritage, they fuse their identities with ethnic and racial others, fashioning odd juxtapositions to symbolically expand the options for social mobility normally afforded blacks and Latinos in postmodern capitalist society.[51] When it comes to riffing on mainstream corporate culture, this means that auditors can frequently hear MCs describe themselves as the "Black Bill Gates," the "Black Warren Buffett," or the "Black [Donald] Trump" as a means of establishing the grandiose level of their riches and the extensive reach of their social fluidity. Similarly, MCs in the later 1990s frequently deployed the trope of ethnic Mafiosi in their lyrical constructions to metaphorically escape the limited place afforded minority men of color in American society. Through the gangster motifs of narcotics, fast cars, fast women, fancy clothing, strong liquor, and a "never say die" attitude, rappers sought to gain greater symbolic fluidity and transcend what Manthia Diawara has called the constraint of racial immanence that hems black people within the immutable realm of the stereotype.[52]

Rappers who exploited the latitude of such lyrical constructions to proliferate new images of urban blackness were described by critics as having converted black identity into the dematerialized cultural equivalent of a financial derivative[53] and subsequently weathered punitive reactions from rival artists and crews within the hip-hop community. For example, in the summer of 1996, at the dawn of mogul representational hegemony, the group De La Soul used its single "Itzsoweezee," from the album *Stakes is High*, to admonish MCs fixated on Mafia-inspired self-portrayals. In one line, the group scolds "pawns of the industry" that "Cubans don't care what y'all niggas do/Colombians ain't never ran with your crew." In another verse, the group pulls back the veneer of the aggrandizement within mafioso reiterations by joking with a hyperconsumptive MC that "the only Italians you know are Ices."[54] The most vocal critics of the moguls' representational strategies were a cadre of rappers who, in the tradition of Hebrew spiritual reformers, appointed themselves as prophetic pedagogues, street-level intellectuals, and storefront theologians committed to leading black youth away from what W. E. B. Du Bois called a "Gospel of Pay" through lyrical constructions that urged auditors to undertake a spiritual conversion. Manthia Diawara says that by definition, conversionist rhetoric deploys

> [n]arratives about the worst sinners to justify the need for transformation . . . whether politicians or religious leaders, [conversionists] build their audiences by blaming the culture of the people that they are trying to convert. They always expect people to achieve a revolutionary consciousness or a spiritual awakening and walk out of their culture, shedding it like a shell or a cracked skin, in order to change the world.[55]

By heeding the rap conversionist's words, black youth would be able to discover the "Truth" of their condition within the neoliberal order and initiate a multipronged campaign for communal revitalization.

   To gird the rank and file at the vanguard of spiritual battle, rap conversionists crafted lyrics that fashioned a seductive blend of Afrocentricity, quasi-Islamic invective, and monitories that advocated the rejection of Euro-derived forms of material culture, the appetite for which the prophet regarded as the source of black spiritual disorientation. For instance, at the beginning of a song called "Ital (Universal Side)" from their album *illadelp halflife,* Black Thought from the Roots and Q-Tip from A Tribe Called Quest identify the politically debilitating generation gap within black America, the anti-intellectual "code of the streets" afflicting its youth, and the apocalyptic infernos of moral collapse looming in the nation's not-too-distant future.[56] Throughout the song, Q-Tip and Black Thought use their rhymes to identify structural and behavioral impediments to the ghetto's spiritual and material rehabilitation. The Roots also used their music video to the single "What They Do," from the *illadelp halflife* album, as a critique of the Moët-drinking, fast-living lifestyle epitomized by such rappers as Jay-Z and Combs. In 1998, Lauryn Hill, then a leading prophetic voice within rap, released a song called "Final Hour," which implores auditors to find a middle road between capital accumulation and spiritual renewal, offering her own spiritual odyssey and successful musical career as a template for ethical action. As the song's title alludes, Hill's ultimate message concerns the ways that excessive preoccupation with capitalist materialism, as well as blatant disregard for social inequality, distracts mankind's attention from the inevitable Day of Judgment. Hill presented herself as a sage, a street-savvy prophet who had come to educate her audience about saving their souls. As she explained succinctly: "I'm about to change the focus/From the richest to the brokest."[57] In 1999, a song by Mos Def called "Fear Not of Man" offers another celebrated example of rap prophecy.[58] In the song's spoken word prelude, Mos Def calls his auditors to order with a quick Islamic chant before broadening his invitation to listen to everyone within earshot, or, as he puts it, "All the continent, Europe, all abroad, international." During his ensuing lyrical bars and measures, Mos Def calls for every individual within hip-hop's global community to reevaluate their personal worth according to metrics not endorsed by the idolatrous conventions of late twentieth-century life, especially the pagan belief that technology could replicate the omnipotence of the Almighty.

   Rap conversionists joined the dissenting voices of other social critics who argued in the late 1990s that the New Economy's intertwined narratives of progress, prosperity, and social cohesion had depended upon the spread of Western capitalism abroad and the legislation of widespread surveillance, incarceration, and social control at home. This vocal opposition argued that despite the hoopla attending the record period of economic growth in the United States, for far too many folks, the boom in the domestic economy sanctioned by globalization had proved to be a bust—resulting in assaults on a wide range of social welfare systems, the resurgence of blame-the-victim explanations for poverty, racism in the name of color blindness, the erosion of democracy, and systematic violations of human rights. Taken as a single element in this broader social discourse, hip-hop's antimogul backlash represented further attempts within the black community to negotiate the competing interests between market-led initiatives and traditional constructions of African American communal safe havens. As an alternative to the more dire forms of rap eschatology and prophetic belief,[59] rap moguls proposed that the vision of mass black opposition to capitalism was no longer tenable and, while not letting white America, the financial power structure, and the police state completely off the hook for their oppressive tendencies, insisted that the abiding goal should be for black individuals to make the most of present conditions however they could.

In a certain sense, the word *nigga* increasingly gained cachet in rap circles throughout the 1990s as the quintessential expletive that inner-city black men used to signify both comradeship and rivalry with those who made a whole way of life from the loud gestures that tried to preempt and short-circuit the disciplinary mechanisms that society deployed to thwart their struggle for broader social mobility and enhanced self-esteem.[60] "Niggas" were continually idealized in rap poetics as those men continually willing to take the heat for their brazen social pageantry and able to pay the ultimate price to escape the abject locales to which they had been relegated. According to rap's "bad man" mythology,[61] if the nigga lived long enough to realize recompense for his initiative and was savvy enough to leverage his gains within and against his immediate surroundings, then he could graduate from relative obscurity and move up to the more elevated plane occupied by the moguls and their handpicked superstars. When this happened, he could join the esteemed ranks of men such as Curtis James "50 Cent" Jackson, who had made a similar ascent up from the anonymity of the street corner.[62] Tellingly, even as niggas were jousting to establish their self-worth and prove themselves in a hostile environment, moguls possessed the sense of entitlement required to begin speculating on the value of the surrounding world.

Given that black disenfranchisement has been predicated upon making black people the objects rather than the subjects of capitalist speculation, even critics noted that there was much to be said for the mogul's display of nerve.[63] In fact, it is this gumption that still makes moguls worthy of celebrity status and mass mediation. However, in a regressive manner, moguls achieved their version of utopia via social isolation from, and antagonism toward, less successful ghetto residents—even as they claimed, paradoxically, to represent and inspire their aspirations for greater glory. Whether or not they portrayed themselves as gangsters, above all else, the mogul calibrated the distance between the lowly member of the hoi polloi that he once was and the elite persona to which he could lay claim via recourse to money, jewels, automobiles, VIP parties, exotic travel, and an abundance of willing sexual partners.[64] In short, the mogul stood out as "a self-made aristocrat, a former member of the underclass [who'd] raised himself up from its ranks and seized his chance to 'shine.'"[65] Because of his largesse, the mogul loomed large as an elect member of the ghetto community and regarded himself as an activist of sorts, an example to others of what they could make of their lives if they would simply seize the right opportunity when the time came. For the rap mogul, in true neoliberal fashion, success for individual strivers in the hip-hop nation was as simple as learning how to "Do, You!"[66]

Like all neoliberals, moguls despise government regulation and attempts to nullify asymmetrical outcomes of individual achievement via social engineering, the chief difference being that rappers frequently couch neoliberal dogma in colloquial terms befitting their derring-do in the risk-laden underworld of crack cocaine.[67] As moguls go about making their case for greater liberty, they may lament the plight of the black masses and may simulate reference to these constituencies in the name of authenticity, but they don't sacrifice their own quest for the American good life on others' behalf. Rather, the mogul's vision of gilded glory is as socially-competitive and exclusive as it is opulent. As the prototypical mogul anthem "Hate Me Now" attests, moguls and their talented minions flaunt their rise from among the ranks of the downtrodden by making public displays of their newly acquired wealth.[68] For moguls, jealousy, envy, and hatred from onlookers are merely rites of passage; to be the object of such "hatred" merely serves to crystallize their essential charisma and mark them as among God's chosen few. As self-made people, moguls are not inclined to wait around for social intervention but spot available opportunities for material advancement and seize them as best they can. They simply want people to get out of their way and let them handle their business. When those whom they have left behind betray their envy and become "playa-haters," that simply lets moguls know that they have done the "right thing," further reinforcing their solipsistic moral code. [69]

Combs, for example, who made a cameo appearance on Nas's "Hate Me Now," released a song of his own called "P.E. 2000," in which he sulked about what a dreary life being a well-connected multimillionaire by the age of thirty had turned out to be. Like the tragic bewilderment of Fitzgerald's Jay Gatsby, whose childlike faith in wealth's ability to beget unconditional adoration from those around him shattered upon the shoals of an unyielding adulthood, Combs's "P.E. 2000" was a classic capitalist lament penned by a frustrated yet doggedly optimistic dreamer. Like most mogul figures, Combs suggested that his protestation be understood as a spur to the motivations of others. The mobilization Combs sought to incite was completely different, however, from the mobilization in previous moments in rap's history. As the *New York Times* reported at the time,

> "P.E. 2000," a remake of Public Enemy's 1987 classic "Public Enemy No. 1" . . . replaces the original's political militancy with [Combs's] trademark blend of self-aggrandizement and self-pity. Where "Public Enemy No. 1" spoke for the man on the street, "P.E. 2000" invites rap fans to identify with the man cruising in the silver Bentley and brooding over the astonishing fact that money and power do not inevitably bring peace of mind."[70]

This form of spiteful self-absorption that poses as neighborliness is typically at the root of all capitalist-derived notions of community and is deemed to be one of the more regrettable elements of the postwar consumptive consensus that has infiltrated the ghetto's childhood dream of what it wants to be when it grows up. Nevertheless, the *New York Times* article noted that despite the relative tedium of the mogul's message, "rap fans continue[d] to find vicarious enjoyment in the . . . fantasy, in which being hated is the inevitable price for being one of the few who makes it in a world that otherwise guarantees anonymity and poverty for most."[71] Again, in this respect, the most economically privileged rappers were completely in sync with the mainstream attitude and outlook. During the late 1990s, the prevailing social obsession with relative social position meant that among the privileged, often there was "not a thought given to public service."[72] Anyone who dissented from this new consensus regarding the desirability of material excess became labeled as a "lifestyle scold" and a whining member of "The Indulgence Police."[73] People were told not to worry about widening socioeconomic outcomes but rather to rejoice in the fact that America guaranteed equal opportunity. Indeed, it became an open question by decade's close as to whether inequality even mattered at all.

Still, symbolically speaking, moguls should not be understood solely as figures of ideological alienation, for they can never be too discursively disconnected from the spectacle of the black masses; it is the volatile energy of the crowd that gives them creative impulses to channel, package, and sell. In this respect, moguls are figures who attain celebrity through their mastery of what has been called the ghetto sublime.[74] In other words, they can grant audiences thrilling proximity to a form of social danger of truly epic proportions while simultaneously providing safe remove from the object of collective fascination. Moguls, therefore, are intrepid prospectors for underground creative expression whose daring enables them to extract valuable jewels from the yawning ghetto maw for the benefit of broader society—their efforts simultaneously registering inclusion within and resistance toward mainstream capitalism.[75] There is always a political dimension to moguls' balancing acts as regards the symbolic multitudes of everyday folk. Hip-hop culture, whether under the auspices of moguls or not, always needs periodically to resurrect the black masses as the foundational thematic element from its own hallowed past. Indeed, if moguls cannot claim to understand the volatile energies of the street and possess the eminent capacity to tap them, they will cease to exist as viable figures of commercial and cultural enterprise. In this regard, moguls are the epitome of utopian double consciousness as regards the masses.

> [The mogul] is the man of the crowd: at once immanent and transcendent, at once an insider and an outsider, at once everyman and the exceptional individual who provides the masses with a singular identity, a singular face, a mirror image of a sovereign collectivity that is now always in motion. . . . Fully swept up in the multicolored and polyphonic waves of modern revolution, he is able to channel their tidal fury towards higher and nobler ends: national sovereignty, liberty, empire, progress.[76]

Thus, for all of his upwardly mobile pretensions, hip-hop moguls need the spectacle of the more impoverished masses, for they give them the raw material, the literal human canvas, for and upon which their ascent can be made emblematic.

Yet, socioeconomic trends suggest that it may be more difficult for moguls to achieve this structural balance. Harvard professor Henry Louis Gates Jr. notes that the radical divergence of life chances for the affluent and the poor represents one of the more perplexing and troubling phenomena within contemporary black American experience.[77] During the prosperous 1990s, the black upper-middle class developed rapidly. According to the U.S. Census Bureau, in 1988, a little over 220,000 black households earned at least $100,000 per year. By 1998, that figure had almost doubled to slightly over 414,000 households.[78] Unfortunately, the inordinate numbers of blacks warehoused in the nation's prisons made the otherwise bright interpretation of the New Economy's "tight labor market" much cloudier. The *Wall Street Journal* reported on the contradictions:

> The strong economy has pushed U.S. joblessness to the lowest levels in three decades. But a grim factor is also helping the numbers: a record 1.7 million people are currently imprisoned in the U.S. Prisoners are excluded from unemployment calculations. And since most inmates are economically disadvantaged and unskilled, jailing so many people has effectively taken a big block of the nation's least-employable citizens out of the equation. The proportion of the

population behind bars has doubled since 1985, note labor economists Lawrence Katz and Alan Kreuger. If the incarceration rate had
held steady over that period, they suggest, the current 4.1% unemployment rate would be a less-robust 4.3%. And because minorities
are jailed at a much higher rate, black unemployment—currently a
historically low 7.9%—would likely be as high as 9.4%, says Harvard's
Dr. Katz.[79]

Presumably, the numbers that the economists uncovered would have
been even higher for black men between the ages of eighteen and thirty-
five—the prime constituency for hip-hop's "nation within the nation."
Black women increasingly became part of the New Economy's prison
industrial complex, as well.[80] Furthermore, a raft of recent academic studies demonstrate that since the 1990s, the prospects for the black disadvan-
taged—particularly for young black men—have worsened.[81]

Figures also reveal that aggregate gains in household wealth during the
late 1990s masked growing discrepancies between white and black households. Indeed, statistics indicat that although the median net worth of
whites rose seventeen percent in 2001 to $120,900, it fell by 4.5 percent, to
$17,000, for minorities. The underparticipation of African Americans in
equity ownership seemed to at least partially explain the durability and
increase in the wealth gap. Surveys revealed that even at the height of dot-
com mania, the majority of African Americans did not enlist in the emerging class of "citizen capitalists." A survey conducted in 2000, for example,
found that blacks accounted "for just 5% of stock investors."[82]

The explosive economic growth of Dot.com era also did not make the
nation less segregated. In fact, the *Financial Times* recounted that

> [r]esults of the 2000 US census indicate neighborhoods are still sur-
> prisingly segregated by race. Although Hispanics and Asians have
> increasingly integrated with the rest of society, blacks and whites still
> tend to go their separate ways. In a recent analysis of 2000 US Cen-
> sus data, the State University of New York (SUNY) at Albany showed
> the typical white person living near a metropolitan centre is in a
> neighborhood that is 80 percent white and just 7 percent black. A
> typical African-American lives in an area that is 33 percent white and
> 51 percent black. The numbers have barely changed from a decade
> ago—the last time the census was taken.[83]

Disturbingly, the aforementioned figures suggest that despite the widespread mythology of industrious individualism, and despite the average
American's very real ambitions for monetary wealth—and despite the
explosion of new millionaires during the decade—the fruits of prosperity

during the 1990s were even more heavily skewed toward the already rich than they had been in prior booms. By the decade's close, the richest 1 percent of the nation held 35 percent of the nation's wealth. Yet the top five percent of households in 1998—those making $132,199 or more— held just over 21 percent of all income. In 1967, this group represented only 17.5 percent of the national income pie.[84] Nevertheless, "like the diversity myth, America clings to a 'mobility myth' that states that as long as one works hard and has the good luck that follows being prepared, one will always be on an upwardly mobile track."[85] Because of this belief that the poor always get richer from one generation to the next, America continues to largely ignore widening wealth and income inequality. It seems likely that this ideological bent helps enable such minority celebrity figures as the hip-hop moguls to assume such grand representational proportions by simulating communal wealth in the guise of individual achievement.

From one historical era to the next, lack of financial aptitude continually hampers the efforts of young American minorities to share in the nation's economic good fortune when capital investment cycles turn favorable. As former Federal Reserve chairman Alan Greenspan argued soon after the dot-com bubble's collapse, "improving basic financial education . . . is essential to help young people avoid poor financial decisions that can take years to overcome."[86] Efforts to use the allure of celebrity figures such as hip-hop moguls for such pedagogical imperatives are increasingly being explored and pursued. For example, the record label magnate Russell Simmons and longtime Civil Rights activist Dr. Benjamin Chavis have formed the Get Your Money Right Hip-Hop Summit on Financial Empowerment, which travels to urban centers across North America with one overarching theme: teaching financial literacy to at-risk youth. At each Get Your Money Right event, rappers and black financial professionals deliver lessons in personal banking, vehicle financing, repairing bad credit, understanding credit scores, and learning basic savings techniques. In the United States, where the Get Your Money Right tour originated, an estimated twelve million households do not have bank accounts—a demographic called the "unbanked" by the financial industry. Empowerment campaigns such as Get Your Money Right and Sean Combs's Vote or Die! voter registration initiative build upon recent attempts by black leadership, as in Jesse Jackson's Wall Street Project, to consider growth-mediated and celebrity-driven approaches to communal development. These projects defy the conventional wisdom of the left-wing political establishment, which is typically slow to consider growth-mediated paths out of disenfranchisement for black Americans,[87] and have taken on even greater urgency in the wake of the harrowing human tragedy suffered by the black poor in the aftermath of Hurricane Katrina in August 2005.

At the very least, the ascension of the hip-hop mogul has gone a long way toward opening up space in working-class and poor minority communities in which to view mainstream corporate enterprise with more than absolute suspicion and disdain. These openings may enable emergent progressive coalitions to advance their social empowerment agendas without being hamstrung by the class-based friction that has typically plagued the hip-hop generation from within.[88] Charting how this process takes shape in the new millennium will provide much insight on the evolution of black political struggle as well as the nation's general orientation toward shaping a more inclusive form of economic democracy.

NOTES

1. EPMD, "Please Listen to My Demo," *Unfinished Business* (Priority, 1989).

2. A Tribe Called Quest, "Show Business," *Low-End Theory* (Jive, 1991).

3. Reebee Garofalo, "Crossing Over: From Black Rhythm & Blues to White Rock 'n' Roll," in *Rhythm and Business: The Political Economy of Black Music*, ed. Norman Kelley (NY: Akashic Books, 2002).

4. Tania Padgett, "Hip Hop Moguls Livin' Large and in Charge," *New York Newsday*, October 13, 2004, http://www.newsday.com/entertainment/music/nyc-etmogul1013,0,790305,print.story?coll= (accessed April 1, 2007).

5. Jeff Leeds, "In Rapper's Deal, a New Model for Music Business," *New York Times*, April 3, 2008.

6. Christopher Holmes Smith, "'I Don't Like to Dream About Getting Paid': Representations of Social Mobility and the Emergence of the Hip-Hop Mogul," *Social Text* 77 (2003): 69–97.

7. Stuart Hall, "On Postmodernism and Articulation," in *Stuart Hall: Critical Dialogues in Cultural Studies*, eds. David Morley and Kuan-Hsing Chen (London & New York: Routledge, 1996).

8. Edward Chancellor, *Devil Take the Hindmost: A History of Financial Speculation* (New York: Plume, 2000).

9. John Cassidy, *Dot.con: How America Lost its Mind and Money in the Internet Era* (New York: HarperCollins, 2002).

10. Leslie Eaton, "Netscape Fever: Will It Spread?" *New York Times*, August 13, 1995, 3.

11. Irwin M. Stelzer, "Crash or Boom? On the Future of the New Economy," *Commentary*, October 2000, 26.

12. Peter Applebome, "Where Money's a Mantra Greed's a New Creed," *New York Times*, February 28, 1999, 5.

13. Jacob Weisberg, "United Shareholders of America," *New York Times Magazine*, January 25, 1998, 29.

14. Richard W. Stevenson, "Fed Reports Family Gains from Economy," *New York Times*, January 19, 2000.

15. Evgenia Peretz, "The Enfatrepreneurs," *Vanity Fair*, September 2000, 248–262.

16. Mark Wallace, "Who Needs A Diploma?" *New York Times Magazine*, March 5, 2000, 76–78.

17. Katie Hafner, "Mother, I'm the Boss Now," *New York Times*, July 4, 2000, 1.

18. "A Snapshot of the Wealthy," *Journal of Financial Planning*, August 1, 2000.

19. Laura M. Holson, "Nothing Left to Buy?" *New York Times*, March 3, 2000, C17.

20. John Seabrook, *Nobrow: The Culture of Marketing and the Marketing of Culture* (New York: Vintage, 2000).

21. Lawrence M. Friedman, *The Horizontal Society* (New Haven, CT: Yale University Press, 1999).

22. Pierre Bourdieu, *Distinction* (Cambridge, MA: Harvard University Press, 1984).

23. Jay-Z, "What More Can I Say," *The Black Album* (Def Jam, 2003).

24. Cora Daniels, *Ghettonation: A Journey Into the Land of Bling and Home of the Shameless* (New York: Doubleday, 2007).

25. W. E. B. Du Bois, *The Souls of Black Folk* (New York: Library of America, 1990).

26. Orlando Patterson, *Rituals of Blood* (Washington, D.C.: Civitas, 1998).

27. F. Scott Fitzgerald, *The Great Gatsby* (New York: Charles Scribner's Sons, 1925, 1953).

28. Stuart Elliott, "Advertising," *New York Times*, November 19, 1999.

29. Jeffrey O. G. Ogbar, "Slouching Toward Bork: Race, Culture Wars and Self-Criticism in Hip-Hop," *Journal of Black Studies* 29 (1999): 164–183.

30. Padgett, "*Hip Hop Moguls*," 2004.

31. Clayton Christensen, *The Innovator's Dilemma* (Boston: Harvard Business School Press, 1997).

32. Nelson George, *Hip Hop America* (New York: Penguin, 1998).

33. John Strausbaugh, *Black like You: Blackface, Whiteface, Insult & Imitation in American Popular Culture* (New York: John P. Tarcher/Penguin, 2006).

34. Henry Louis Gates Jr., "Parable of the Talents," in *The Future of the Race*, eds. H. L. Gates Jr. and Cornel West (New York: Knopf, 1996).

35. Kelefa Sanneh, "Gettin' Paid," *New Yorker*, August 20–27, 2001, 60.

36. Just days before the release of Eminem's hit film *8 Mile* in November 2002, the *New York Times* reported that "after more than two decades of growth, hip-hop album sales hit a wall in [2001], declining about 15 percent to 89 million . . . from a peak of 105 million the previous year, according to the Nielsen SoundScan company, which tracks sales figures. Album sales for the music industry were down overall, but less—3 percent in 2001—reflecting both the recession and the growth of free Internet file-sharing services. For the first six months of 2002, sales of hip-hop albums were down almost 20 percent from the same period [in 2001], compared with a general industry drop of 13 percent." Lola Ogunnaike, Laura Holson, and John Leland, "Feuding for Profit," *New York Times*, November 3, 2002.

37. *Fortune*, September 16, 2002, www.fortune.com/fortune/40under40/.

38. Christopher John Farley, "Hip-Hop Nation," *Time*, February 8, 1999, 54–57.

39. Frank DiGiacomo, "It's the Last Party of the Century," *New York Observer*, December 23, 1999, 3–8.

40. Amy M. Spindler, "Character Development," *New York Times Magazine*, July 23, 2000, 54.

41. Chancellor, *Devil Take the Hindmost*, 28.

42. Rob Walker, "When Diamonds and Escalades are O.K.," *New York Times*, January 19, 2003, 16.

43. Ibid., 17.

44. Ibid.

45. Todd Boyd, *The New H.N.I.C.: The Death of Civil Rights and the Reign of Hip Hop* (New York: NYU Press, 2004).

46. David Brooks, "The Triumph of Hope over Self-Interest," *New York Times*, January 12, 2003.

47. Jean Comaroff and John L. Comaroff, "Millennial Capitalism: First Thoughts on a Second Coming," *Public Culture* 12 (2000): 291–343.

48. Paul Langley, "The Making of Investor Subjects in Anglo-American Pensions, *Environment and Planning D: Society and Space* 24 (2006): 919–934.

49. Amartya Sen, *Development as Freedom* (New York: Knopf, 1999).

50. Jay-Z, "Moment of Clarity," *The Black Album* (Def Jam, 2004).

51. Christopher Holmes Smith, "Method in the Madness: Exploring the Boundaries of Identity in Hip-Hop Performativity," *Social Identities* 3, no. 3 (October 1997): 345–374; also Robert Jay Lifton, *The Protean Self: Human Resilience in an Age of Fragmentation* (Chicago & London: University of Chicago Press, 1993).

52. Manthia Diawara, *In Search of Africa* (Cambridge, MA: Harvard University Press, 1998).

53. Thomas C. Holt, *The Problem of Race in the Twenty-first Century* (Cambridge, MA: Harvard University Press, 2001).

54. De La Soul, "Itzsoweezee," *Stakes is High* (Tommy Boy, 1996).

55. Manthia Diawara, "Situation III: Malcolm X," *In Search of Africa* (Cambridge, MA, and London: Harvard University Press, 1998).

56. The Roots, "Ital," *illadelph halflife* (Geffen Records, 1996).

57. Lauryn Hill, "Final Hour," *The Miseducation of Lauryn Hill* (Sony, 1998).

58. Mos Def, "Fear Not of Man," *Black on Both Sides* (Priority, 1999).

59. John Fiske and Christopher Holmes Smith, "Naming the Illuminati," in *Music and the Racial Imagination*, eds. Ronald Radano and Philip V. Bohlman (Chicago and London: University of Chicago Press, 2000): 605–621.

60. Todd Boyd, *Am I Black Enough for You? Popular Culture from the 'Hood and Beyond* (Bloomington: Indiana University Press, 1997).

61. Eithne Quinn, *Nuthin' but a "G" Thang: The Culture and Commerce of Gangsta Rap* (New York: Columbia University Press, 2004).

62. 50 Cent and Kris Ex, *From Pieces to Weight: Once Upon a Time in Southside Queens* (New York: MTV Books, 2005).

63. Mark Anthony Neal, "Diddy-cized," Seeing Black, http://www.seeingblack.com/2004/x061404/diddy.shtml.

64. Eric Robinson, "It's a Wonderful World," *Rap Pages*, February 1999, 96.

65. Simon Reynolds, "It Isn't Easy Being Superman," *New York Times*, October 10, 1999, 29.

66. DMX/Funkmaster Flex, "Do You," *The Mix Tape Vol. 4* (Relativity, 2000); also Russell Simmons and Chris Morrow, *Do You!: 12 Laws to Access the Power in You to Achieve Happiness and Success* (New York: Gotham, 2007).

67. Jeff Chang, "Moving On Up," *The Nation*, January 4, 2007.

68. Nas, "Hate Me Now," *I Am* (Sony, 1999).

69. Clarence Page, "Hating," *Newshour with Jim Lehrer* (PBS, July 12, 2004).

70. Simon Reynolds, "It Isn't Easy Being Superman," *New York Times*, October 10, 1999, 29.

71. Reynolds, "It Isn't Easy Being Superman."

72. Ralph Gardner Jr., "Class Struggle on Park Avenue," *New York*, June 14, 1999, 24.

73. Daniel Askt, "The Indulgence Police," *Wall Street Journal*, October 29, 1999, W17.

74. Smith, "I Don't Want to Dream About Getting Paid . . ."

75. Jackson Lears, "Luck and Pluck in American Culture," *Chronicle of Higher Education*, January 24, 2003, B15.

76. Jeffrey T. Schnapp, "The Mass Panorama," *Modernism/modernity* 9 (2002): 243–281.

77. Henry Louis Gates Jr., "America Beyond the Color Line" (PBS DVD, 2004).

78. Monte Williams, "Is There a Black Upper Class?" *New York Times*, March 7, 1999, 1.

79. "Work Week: Full Prisons Make Unemployment Look Rosier," *Wall Street Journal*, February 1, 2000, 1.

80. Mary Frances Berry, "The Forgotten Prisoners of a Disastrous War," *Essence*, October 1999, 194.

81. Bob Herbert, "The Danger Zone," *New York Times*, March 15, 2006; also Erik Echolm, "Plight Deepens for Black Men, Studies Warn," *New York Times*, March 20, 2006.

82. Ianthe Jeanne Dugan, "Broken Trust," *Wall Street Journal*, September 12, 2000, 1.

83. Victoria Griffith, "Still a Case of Black and White, Even in Liberal America," *Financial Times*, May 3, 2001, 24.

84. Sarah Lueck et al., "Charting the Pain Behind the Gain," *Wall Street Journal*, October 1, 1999, B1.

85. Michael M. Weinstein, "America's Rags-to-Riches Myth," *New York Times*, February 18, 2000, A28.

86. "Greenspan Urges Better Money Sense," *New York Times*, April 7, 2001.

87. George Packer, "Trickle-Down Civil Rights," *New York Times Magazine*, December 12, 1999, 76.

88. Henry Louis Gates Jr., "Must Buppiehood Cost Homeboy His Soul?" *New York Times*, March 1, 1992.

5

The Roots and Aesthetic Foundation of Hip-hop Culture

Cheryl L. Keyes

Hip-hop can be defined as a youth arts mass cultural movement that evolved in New York City during the 1970s. Hip-hop is identified by its four elements—breakdancing (b-boy/b-girl), graffiti (writers), disc jockeying (DJing) and emceeing (MCing)—and is expressed by its adherents as language, gestures, and a form of dress that all embody an urban street consciousness.[1] Although many credit the Bronx, New York, as the mecca of hip-hop culture, it is regarded more broadly as part of the global landscape of contemporary urban youth culture. Its roots extend much farther, however. As one scholar observed, "hip-hop culture grew out of the cross-fertilization of African American vernacular cultures with their Caribbean equivalents."[2] Afrika Bambaataa, the Godfather of Hip-hop, also asserts that although hip-hop started in the Bronx, where African American and West Indian cultures intersected, one of its elements, rap, is likened to "a chanting style which goes back to Africa."[3] Veteran hip-hop artists contend that there is a strong connection between the West African griot (storyteller) and the rapper. The West African bardic tradition comprises mainly a storyteller, known popularly as a *griot* or *jeli*, self-accompanied by a musical or string instrument called the kora. This style of storytelling is structured in a poetic narrative form and delivered in a chant-like fashion over the repetitive musical lines played on the kora. Griots are essentially praise poets and serve as oral historians or keepers of the nation's history and cultural mores. Although the bard seemingly gives credence to the historical roots of rap's poetic performance, this aspect is not confined to the African continent alone but is rather idiosyncratic to oral traditions throughout the African diaspora.[4]

Another semblance of an African-derived aesthetic expressed in hip-hop arts is most apparent in the art of b-boy/b-girl dance, known popularly to the masses as breakdancing. The dance movements of this element of hip-hop

Afrika Bambaataa

Tommy Boy/Photofest

consist of angular turns, stylized twists, sweeps, spins, squats, hip or pelvis gyrations, and upper torso movements. Often recognized by dance scholars as a "Kongo-influence," that is, "breaking the beat," or an improvisational dance interlude by which a dancer incorporates an array of the aforementioned movements, it serves, nonetheless, as a template for hip-hop dance styles as well as for other black cultural forms including double-dutch, cheerleading, basketball court moves, and hip-hop's Brazilian cousin, capoeira.[5] Additionally, African art historian Robert Farris Thompson recognizes the element of movement common to sub-Saharan art that he perceives as "danced art," unlike the more linear and symmetric style common in the conception of European art. In graffiti, movement defines its lettering style as "bubbled letters or peppermint-stick letters to highly evolved and complex wildstyle, an energetic interlocking construction of letters with arrows and other forms that signify movement and direction."[6]

Although hip-hop is often assumed to be the result of intercultural borrowings as evident with black and Latino youth engagement particularly during its formative years, the making of a hip-hop aesthetic and performance practice evolve intraculturally among persons of African descent from South and North America and the Caribbean. Hip-hop stands as testimony of this intracultural nexus when tracing its sources from Jamaican dancehall or sound-system culture to African American signifyin' jive. But, moreover, hip-hop performance practice resonates with what I refer to as cultural reversioning, the foregrounding (consciously and unconsciously) of African-centered concepts.[7]

The history shared by people of African descent in the New World is slavery. Conditions of servitude, despite their inhumanity, forced enslaved Africans to react creatively to their new realities in the New World, where their artistic expressions would serve as historical mirrors. When Africans were transported from West and Central Africa via the trans-Atlantic slave trade routes to the Americas, as early as the fifteenth century, their cultural memory was not shattered. Among the first places in the Americas to which enslaved Africans were brought were the Caribbean (e.g., Cuba and Haiti) and certain parts of South America, such as Brazil. In colonial America, however, Africans were initially positioned in society as indentured servants until the 1650s. After witnessing the success of black slavery in the Caribbean, white colonists gave serious thought about replicating a similar system. By the 1660s, slavery had evolved into an institution in colonial America. Although slavery in the North was somewhat more limited, slaves living as parts of smaller households, slavery existed on a much larger scale in the Southern colonies. By the 1790s, slavery had slowly dwindled in the North. Owing to the longer southern summer months, conducive to growing crops, the South became an agricultural empire whose economic subsistence depended heavily upon a black labor force.

Although slavery was an institution throughout the South, it became, nonetheless, a reservoir of Africanisms.[8] At times, the black populace outnumbered the white. Similar demographics existed in the Caribbean and parts of South America. But the interaction between European settlers and Africans in the New World yielded distinct African diasporic experiences— African Americans of the United States or African Caribbeans, for instance, of Barbados, Trinidad (known collectively as West Indians). Slavery became the crucible out of which African peoples in the Americas forged a distinct culture, music, and language system. Hip-hop is undoubtedly a continuum of African-based expression and thus symbolic of diasporic bonding, the cross-fertilization of African American and Caribbean vernacular cultures.

Living in close confines, for instance, on large plantations or in maroon areas, contributed to the maintenance, continuity, and transformation of African expressive culture as well. These black expressive forms include locution through storytelling, toasting, and verbal play (via veiled/coded speech or signifying), intoned speech patterns (a continuum of African tonal language speaking patterns), dance/movement and music (as interrelated arts or inseparable entities), and art for utilitarian purposes.

Social conditions continued to have a bearing on the evolution of forms that predate hip-hop but no doubt serve as its antecedents. The blues, for example, which developed roughly post-Reconstruction, was a direct outgrowth of the "Jim Crow" South, where slavery was reinvented as sharecropping, a peonage system dominated by African American farmers and their families. Although music scholars often state that the work songs and field hollers that date back to slavery were precursors of the blues, blues emerged as a musical form that echoed the conditions of servitude during the late 1880s and early twentieth century. The blues was traditionally delivered in a sing-songy manner and oftentimes performed as a poetic utterance or lyrical poetic with an AAB rhyme scheme, as illustrated by an excerpt from "Special Rider Blues," by the Mississippi bluesman Son House:

Well look here honey, I won't be your dog no mo'.
Well, look here honey, I won't be your dog no mo'.
Excuse me honey for knockin' on your do'.[9]

Although the musical accompaniment for early or rural blues varied, the guitar was, nevertheless, most common. Most important, the blues artists rendered statements about current conditions or issues of the day affecting community (or simply personal) reflections about a condition, representing a metaphysical state of mind.

Other precursors of hip-hop musical culture include the African American–performed sermon, likened in style to that of an West African griot performance, or the toast, a long narrative poem rendered in rhyming couplets that celebrate the victory and the defeat of opposing characters, a continuum of the African epic poetic tradition.[10] Verbal play common to the toast include repetition, mimicry, metaphor, boasting, exaggeration, formulaic expression, humor, and above all, signification, commonly called "signifyin'" among black vernacular speakers. Signifyin' is a verbal form that is used to refer to a person or situation through the use of indirection, in which meaning is suggestive, or direction, in which meaning is explicit in references toward a family member—namely the mother. The latter device is popularly called "the dozens" or "snaps" and is performed in rhyming couplets. Among the most celebrated toasts is "The Signifying Monkey," made popular via audio recordings by comedian Rudy Ray Moore, also known as Dolemite, in the 1960s black action films. One popular version of the traditional "Signifying Monkey" clearly illustrates features and verbal forms including the dozens and signifyin'. It begins with a lion and a monkey engaging in a verbal tussle after the lion has literally stepped on the monkey's toes. The monkey is forced to hide, however, when the lion begins to exercise his superior force, and soon a regular practice is established whereby the monkey "bullshits" from his tree and the lion "kicks his ass" in return. Eventually, the monkey, resolving to use his wits to level the playing field, tells the lion, "There's a big bad muthafucka comin' yo way./He talked about yo' people 'til my hair turned gray."[11] More personal insults about the lion's family follow, all attributed to this fictional slanderist who is alleged to have escaped from the circus. The rhyming couplet structure of a toast, as in the above, is considered a forerunner of lyrical structure found in rap music.

Facial expressions, body gestures, and movement enhance the effectiveness of the toast or other vernacular forms. Hence, the employment of body movements integrated with song via kinetic oral channels—as expressed in work songs, black girls' play songs, or boys or men on the street corner doing the hambone—is maintained through hip-hop performance.[12] Even the asymmetric designs in material art such as quilting, created by taking scraps of cloths discarded by family members that are interlocked by stitches, regardless of shapes and colors, parallels a similar process for creating beats by hip-hop DJs. In a spiritual sense, hip-hop, like early black musical forms, incorporates elements of spirituality from "crossroads" as heard in the bluesman Roberts Johnson's "Cross Road Blues" and Bone Thugs-N-Harmony's "Tha Crossroads" to themes germane to the folk or "Negro" spirituals about heaven with songs such as "I'll Fly Away," performed by Faith Evans in her eulogy to The Notorious B.I.G. in "I'll Be Missing You," to Richie Rich's eulogy to Tupac in "Do G's Get to Go to Heaven."

BLACK EXPRESSIVE CULTURE IN URBAN TRANSITION

In the 1920s, African Americans transported Southern traditions to the urban North during the massive migration period. These traditions were soon transformed in the new context. For example, the Southern jook joint became the street-corner cavern or speakeasy club, and the old wooden shotgun-structured church was replaced by the urban storefront church. In this new urban context, African American dance emerged as an art form no longer confined to jook joints but also present in urban arenas such as dancehalls and theatrical stages. Dances such as tap, the Lindy hop, and the Big Apple simultaneously superimposed a variety of movements ranging from angular turns, stylized twists, and sweeps to pelvis gyrations and upper torso movements, performed as couple dances or as solos, all with a personal sense of style and attitude.[13] Southern vernacularisms, too, evolved as urban ways of speaking characteristic of reassigning alternative meanings to English words and creating nonstandardized or new vocabulary in constant flux, known commonly among the urban black masses as jive talk. Some of the Harlem Renaissance writers, such as Langston Hughes, capitalized on urban jive and blues forms in their works as urban jive talk became the parlance of jazz culture. By the late 1940s, two black Chicagoan radio jockeys, Al Benson of WGES and Holmes "Daddy-O Daylie" of WAIT radio, introduced jive talk over the airwaves as a way to communicate with their urban black listeners. It was the latter, however, along with Lavada Durst, known to his audience as Doc Hep Cat, of KVET in Austin, Texas, who exploited rhymin' in jive to their audiences. A typical Doc Hep Cat radio rhyme follows:

> I'm hip to the tip, and bop to the top.
> I'm long time coming and I just won't stop.
> It's a real gone deal that I'm gonna reel,
> So stay tuned while I pad your skulls.[14]

Possessing the power of the word exalted these radio disc jockeys as heroes in their respective 'hoods. Black personality jocks' vernacular speech styles were imitated by other jockeys both black or white—such as Lavada "Doc Hep-Cat" Durst of KVET in Austin, Hunter Hancock of KFVD and KGFJ in Los Angeles, Jack "the Rapper" Gibson of WERD in Atlanta, Martha Jean "the Queen" Steinberg and Rufus Thomas of WDIA in Memphis, and Tommy "Dr. Jive" Smalls of WWRL of New York—just to name a few. In addition to their artful use of jive and rhyme, black radio DJs employed "talking through" and "riding gain": in the former, the DJ lowers the volume of the music and continues to talk as it plays; riding gain, on the other hand, occurs when the disc jockey boosts or lowers the volume on the audio board in order to accent various parts of a record.[15]

Although black comedians such as Redd Foxx, Moms Mabley, and Pigmeat Markham were by no means secondary to the use of jive and rhyme in their performances, one athlete who deserves mention in this regard is Muhammad Ali (formerly Cassius Clay). Ali's signature tactic by which to taunt his opponents was with rhyming couplets about his athletic prowess. To one of his challengers, Ernie Terrell, Ali said

> Clay swings with a left, Clay swing with a right.
> Just look at young Cassius carry the fight.

Terrell keeps backing but there's not enough room.
It's a matter of time until Clay lowers the broom.
Then Clay lands with a right—what a beautiful swing.
And the punch raised Terrell clear out the ring . . .
Who on earth thought when they came to the fight
That they would witness the launching of a human satellite?[16]

THE SETTING OF HIP-HOP CULTURE

Many of the above forms of black vernacular expressive culture are products of orality, transmitted and disseminated via oral or aural channels. Although hip-hop culture is no doubt a composite of past traditions, it would be remiss to ignore the impact of high-technology culture on its development and mediation. In observing the oral transmission of the spoken word by means of mediated channels from television and radio to telephone, Walter Ong finds that this type of transmission shifts from primary orality, by word of mouth [or by ear], to secondary orality, by technological means.[17] On the other hand, hip-hop depends on the applicability of technology in its creation and transmission. As such, several secondary oral/aural technological channels affected the development of hip-hop art and served as its creative impetus: (1) Jamaican sound-system or dancehall music of the 1950s to the 1970s, (2) the Black Arts Movement of the 1960s, and (3) the advent of funk and disco music in the 1970s with its stylistic complement to shaping of hip-hop dance. Hip-hop musicians also frequently recognize Jamaican popular tradition as a source. The late Lumumba "Professor X" Carson noted in an interview that "Blacks growing up in the Caribbean . . . call rap toasting. . . . A lot of toasters [came] out of Kingston."[18] Hip-hop's godfather, Afrika Bambaataa listed a legion of Jamaican toasters—Yellowman, I-Roy, U-Roy, Big Youth—whom he calls "rappers over there like you have over here."[19] However, Bambaataa discerned a difference between the two: "[Jamaican toasters] rap over or use reggae rhythms and dubs."[20] Grandmaster Melle Mel further observed the toasting tradition as rhymes sung in Jamaica.[21]

This toasting tradition directly corollates with the dancehall or sound-system culture of Jamaica. Jamaican sound-system culture evolved in earnest around the 1950s, when many Jamaicans immigrated to Great Britain. After World War II, Britain passed the British Nationality Act of 1948, conferring citizenship upon subjects of the Commonwealth in the West Indies. This exodus affected the musical scene in urban areas such as Kingston, Jamaica, with its thriving swing band scene (modeled after American-style "big band" music). The primary context for this music was in rented-out lodges called dancehalls. "Given this open-door policy, Jamaicans and other West Indians left home 'seeking greener pastures.'"[22]

In search of a musical alternative, local DJs were hired to spin records at the dancehalls. With the booming DJ culture came powerful amplifiers for sound systems, or public address (PA) systems—first rented for use at political rallies in Jamaica. Jamaican Hedley Jones was credited with building the first PA system. PA-system—soon to be called sound system or dancehall—culture was pivotal to the creation and dissemination of Jamaican-style popular music.

The dancehall scene became a phenomenon among Kingston's black working class. The repertory or record list of dancehall DJs consisted mainly of American popular music or rhythm 'n' blues played over the Jamaican airwaves. Moreover, competition was steep among dancehall DJs. Not only were DJs expected to spin the latest or hottest radio hits desired by their dance audiences, but their popularity was predicated on having the largest sound systems. The most competitive and popular dancehall DJs possessed sound systems with huge amplifiers and several speakers equipped booming bass projectors. Dancehall DJs abounded as two-to-three member crews throughout Kingston's black working-class communities. Names of each crew signified their uniqueness, such as Sir Coxsone's Downbeat, Duke Reid's Trojan, Tom Wong, or Tom the Great Sebastian, and Count Matchukie, a major innovator of using the microphone to rhyme to the music in patois, called toasting.

By the late 1950s, Jamaican DJs shifted their musical tastes from American-style popular music to a more indigenous sound. Among the forerunners of Jamaica's most popular genre reggae are ska and rocksteady. The rhythmic accents of ska fall on the "and" of beats 1, 2, 3, 4 and make use of the saxophone and trombone—a precursor of reggae-styled rhythms—but rocksteady made little to no use of horns. Rocksteady, futhermore, was slower and more bassy in sound—a common stylistic marker of reggae and its contemporary styles. Among popular ska artists were the Vikings, Prince Buster, Delroy Wislon, Alton Ellis, and the Vendors, ranked as top rocksteady performers in Jamaica.

With the increase of violence at dancehalls, DJs sought out alternative contexts in recording studios. This change was marked by Jamaica's shift in political power from being a commonwealth of Britain to independence and economic recession as a consequence—or price—of independence. During the 1960s, movements such as that of the Rastafarians complemented the hybridization of ska and rocksteady to produce Jamaican reggae, popularized by Bob Marley and the Wailers. Although dancehall or sound-system culture remained closely linked to Jamaica's black working class, it was soon responsive to a discontented youth (sub)culture known as rudies or rude boys.

Rudies, emblematic of Jamaica's youth gang culture, adamantly expressed disenchantment with Jamaica's economic conditions. They hung out on Kingston's ghetto street corners, sporting handguns and knives and wearing certain trademark clothing including "very short green serge trousers, leather or gangster-style jackets, and . . . .shades [sunglasses]."[23] During the first political election after Jamaica's independence, rudies were divided along political party lines, reflective of a vicious political rivalry between prime minister candidates Michael Manley of the People's National Party (PNP) and Edward Seaga of Jamaica Labour Party (JLP). As one scholar and critic observed, "[t]he city of Kingston was divided like a checkerboard into political garrisons controlled by the gangs under the patronage of party leadership."[24]

When gang activity invaded the dancehall scene, DJs retreated to recording studios. Important in the production of dancehall studio-produced music was Osbourne "King Tubby" Ruddock. While mixing tracks for Sir Coxsone, King Tubby discovered a way to fade out the vocal and instrumental parts or to alter them to create several varied versions called dubs. Additionally, King Tubby advanced the dub concept by creating rhythmic reggae grooves consisting of distinct bass lines called riddims. King Tubby's inventions made use of toasting as used in the recent past, but by the 1970s, U-Roy, a known toaster, popularized toasting over dub versions called talk overs, a template for rhymin' to the beats or tracks created or produced by a DJ. Following in U-Roy's path were Big Youth, I-Roy, and Yellowman, among many others.[25]

The Jamaican sound system, dubs, reggae rhythms, talk overs, or toasting concepts were transmitted to the United States by West Indian immigrants during the 1960s. Although West Indians had immigrated to the United States before the 1960s, a large influx of West Indians occurred in the 1960s, when Britain terminated the Commonwealth Immigrants Act in 1962, followed by the independence of Jamaica and Trinidad and Tobago from England and the independence of Guyana and Barbados in 1966. Accordingly, "[t]he U.S. Census reported 171,525 immigrants from the West Indies in New York City [which] represented 73 percent of all West Indian immigrants in the United States, 48 percent of whom arrived between 1965 and 1970."[26] New York City comprised the largest West Indian immigrant community during this period. Among Jamaican immigrants was a young Clive Campbell, soon to be known in hip-hop as Kool "DJ" Herc. Hip-hop DJs Afrika Bambaataa and Joseph "Grandmaster Flash" Sadler are also of West Indian parentage.

Additionally, setting the stage for a rappin' style are those artists of the Black Nationalist movement in the 1960s. Many African Americans have contributed to the shift from jive talk to rap, including the black nationalist figure and Black Panther Hubert or H "Rap" Brown (also known as Jamil Abdullah Al-Amin), whose moniker distinguishes his skill at street jive. In Brown's autobiography, *Die Nigger Die* (1969), he writes in the chapter

"Street Smarts" that he acquired his nickname Rap because of his extraordinary ability at "playin' the dozens" or "snaps" in rhyming couplets—a game he mastered during his adolescent years, which he learned from the streets. Brown distinguishes the dozens as more brutal in tone, directed toward someone's mother. Signifyin', he asserts, is more subtle yet gentler when talking about someone or a situation (in)directly. Below is (a) a typical dozen and (b) a signifyin' example cited by Brown:

(a)
I fucked your mama/ Till she went blind.
Her breath smells bad/But she sure can grind.

I fucked your mama/For a solid hour.
Baby came out Screaming, Black Power.

Elephant and the Baboon/Learning to screw.
Baby came out looking/Like Spiro Agnew.[27]

(b)
If you're white,/You're all right.
If you're brown, Stick around.

But if you're black, Get back, get back.[28]

It is most apparent that Brown's style of speaking and use of dozens (snaps) or signifyin' is typical in language play of rap music lyrics. More important, Brown's signature style of speaking in rhymin' couplets during his tenure as a member of the Black Panther Party—"if America don't come around, America will be burnt down"—gained popular acceptance among black youth in the 1960s, who in turn, renamed "jive talk" as "rap."

A by-product of black nationalism is the Black Arts Movement of the 1960s. The Black Arts Movement (BAM) began during the wake of the assassination of Malcolm X (also known as El-Hadj Malik El-Shabazz) in 1965. Pivotal to the BAM is the poet and playwright Leroi Jones, who later adopted the name Imamu Amiri Baraka, meaning "Blessed Priest and Warrior."[29] After the death of Malcolm X, Baraka sent a letter to black artists summoning them to create art for revolutionary purposes and to use their art to create change in their respective communities. Soon young black artists shifted from using a European canon while creating works of art to an African-based one. Art became, in this sense, community based and functional, and more importantly, it resonated with real-life experiences of African Americans. Black artists realized Baraka's vision via Afrocentric and black nationalist themes and Islamic ideology. As such, many black artists changed their anglicized names to African and Asiatic ones, wore African attire, adopted natural hairstyles (such as braids and Afros), and used certain gestures that signified black pride and culture. During this period, expressions central to African American culture emerged, including the Kwanzaa Holiday.

Art forms, including dance, music, film, and visual art, were reshaped to suit the vision of the new black aesthetic. However, poetry became the centerpiece by which to express the sentiments of black nationalism. Poets of the BAM honed their skills in writer's workshops established in various urban areas, such as the Watts Writers Workshop in Watts or the Umbra Writers Workshop in Greenwich Village. Poetry was not judged merely on the basis of ability to rhyme per se but on skill at articulating themes relevant to African American urban life. Through poetic recitation, black poets made use of repetition, alliteration, breath cadences, heightened speech, intoned speech, and occasional use of expletives, written using stylized indentation, and noncapitalization of *I* (as *i*). Among these poets were Nikki Giovanni, Don Lee, Larry Neal, Ishmael Reed, and Sonia Sanchez, just to name a few. There were poets who experimented with poetry performed to a musical accompaniment, mainly percussion or small rhythm sections. The most popular poets of this style, among the first recognized via their spoken word tours and sound recordings, are the Last Poets (*The Last Poets*, 1970), Gil Scot-Heron (*A New Black Poet: Small Talk at 125th and Lenox*, 1970), and Nikki Giovanni (*Truth Is on Its Way*, 1971). For this reason, hip-hop artists recognized these poets as "the first or original style rappers."[30] Of the three, the Last Poets member Jalal "Lightnin' Rod" Uridin recorded a solo album called *Hustler's Convention* in 1973. Unlike the politically toned poetry of the Last Poets, Lightnin' Rod spins toast-like tales about the exploits of two urban characters: Sport, or The Gambler, and his sidekick Spoon. Because of its close association with street lore, black hypermasculinity, and jive talk, *Hustler's Convention* is recognized by veteran hip-hop emcees such as Grandmaster Caz as a prototype of gangsta or reality rap. Grandmaster Caz of the Cold Crush Brothers said, "I knew the entire Hustler's Convention by heart. That was rap, but we didn't know it at the time."[31]

By the late 1960s, Stax Records songwriter and artist Isaac Hayes incorporated the rappin' concept over music with his solo project *Hot Buttered Soul* (1969). Hayes introduced certain song classics as "By the Time I Get to Phoenix" or "Walk On By" with rappin' monologues detailing a love affair gone sour. Similar raps followed suit with other artists, including Millie Jackson and Barry White and funkster George Clinton, with his rappin' monologues over funk music grooves.

The 1970s ushered in a new era of black popular music in the United States. Drawing from and expanding on musical concepts associated with past styles of jazz, blues, gospel, rhythm and blues, black rock 'n' roll, and soul, black artists created new and diverse forms of contemporary black popular music.[32] The three most distinct styles of black popular music to emerge in the 1970s were funk, disco, and rap. Funk and disco, in particular, were instrumental to the development of rap music as a distinct popular music style.

Black artists, whose musical style comprised soul vocals and a rhythm section surrounded by an orchestral sound, initiated disco. Seminal figures of the disco sound were Barry White of 20th Century Records and groups such as the O'Jays, McFadden, and Whitehead, an in-house orchestra MFSB on the black-owned record label Philadelphia International Records (PIR), started by Kenny Gamble and Leon Huff. The musical basis for the disco sound was soul or gospel style vocals, an orchestral arrangement supported by punctuating horn lines, and a driving rhythm section with bass-drum rhythm accenting all four beats, subdivided by the hi-hat cymbals.

The disco concept was advanced in dance clubs that employed disc jockeys whose sole purpose was to spin records continuously. To facilitate the continuous play model, the 12-inch vinyl record was invented by Tom Moulton, which extended or doubled the playing time of a single 45 rpm. The 12-inch record became a staple in the vinyl collection of early hip-hop disc jockeys.

By the mid-1970s, disco was monopolized by European producers, who reshaped its sound by structuring its bass lines as an eighth-note bass-line figure outlining the notes of a chord or in octave skips, highlighting the bass drum on all four beats, and sustaining orchestral or string lines, with less emphasis on punctuating horn lines, occasionally increasing its tempo. In maintaining a black aesthetic edge, European producers such as Pete Bellotte and Giorgio Moroder featured an upfront African American female vocalist performing in a soulful or quasi-gospel style. Additionally, popular culture cashed in on disco's growing popularity in the mainstream with films such as *Saturday Night Fever* (1977), featuring actor John Travolta and the music of the Bee Gees. Popular music critic Nelson George notes the sudden change toward disco in the American mainstream:

> Disco movers and shakers were not record executives but club deejays. Most were gay men with a singular attitude toward American culture, black as well as white. They elevated female vocalists like [Donna] Summer, Gloria Gaynor, Diana Ross, Loleatta Holloway, Melba Moore, and Grace Jones to diva status, while black male singers were essentially shunned. Funk, which in the late 70s was enjoying great popularity in the South and Midwest, was rarely on their playlists. It was too raw and unsophisticated, and one thing dear to the hearts of disco fans, gay and straight, was a feeling of pseudosophistication.[33]

Alongside the disco craze came funk. The pioneering of the funk music concept can be credited to the late James Brown. As a progenitor, Brown advanced what he refers to as an "on the one feel" and a more earthy, gritty, sound characterized by interlocking horn and rhythm section groove lines peppered with Brown's preachy vocals and grunts. James Brown's songs soon bore the word *funk* in their titles, including "Ain't It Funky Now" (1969), "Funky Drummer" (1970), "Funky President" (1974), and "It's Too Funky in Here" (1979). Glimpses of Brown's sound could be heard in the popularizers of 1970s funk, such as George Clinton (with Brown's former instrumentalists, including Bootsy Collins on bass), and in the music of Larry Graham, a former bass player for Sly and the Family Stone. Clinton's and Graham's collectives, Parliament–Funkadelic and Graham Central Station, placed much emphasis on the pulling-popping-and-slapping bass techniques and soulful background vocals, distinguished by each group's use of keyboards— Hammond B-3 organ by Graham Central Station and keyboard synthesizers by Parliament-Funkadelic. Other artists who followed in the styles of Clinton and Graham, or combined them, were the Ohio Players, Zapp, Brothers Johnson, Kool and the Gang, Dazz, and George Duke. Many listeners of funk describe this music as a party music that adhered more to an earthy blues-based foundation without yielding to the crossover demands of the mainstream music industry. As George Clinton explains, "We just speeded blues up and called it 'funk.'"[34] Brown's and Clinton's music are among the most widely sampled in hip-hop.[35] Funk music was a vital part of the Los Angeles underground dance culture, providing the beat to pop and lock moves, setting the stage for breakdancing. According to producer, director, historian, and former dancer Thomas Guzman-Sanchez, the forerunner of breakdancing emerged in the clubs or party jams in Los Angeles. Don Campbell stands out as a seminal player in creating the robotic locking dance technique that accompanies the funk sound as popularized by his dance collective, Campbellock Dancers, or the Lockers.[36] The Lockers introduced their locking-robotic-jerky movements to the masses via the national syndicated television dance show *Soul Train* as well as on *Saturday Night Live* and the *Carol Burnett Show*. The Lockers' dance style was advanced by the Guzman-Sanchez Chain Reaction dancers and further varied by the Electric Boogaloo Lockers of Fresno, California, who perfected a more robotic locking style called popping in the early 1980s.[37] Hip-hop film classics *Breakin'* (1984) and *Breakin' 2: Electric Boogaloo* (1984) introduced popping and locking dance moves to mainstream viewers. Soon popping and locking would be fundamental moves in b-boy/b-girl dance culture.

The preference for funk music over disco was more evident among inner-city youth of New York City, who witnessed the exploitation of dance music by a predominant white middle- to upper-class following. Bill Adler, hip-hop music critic, observed:

In New York City in the mid-70s, the dominant black popular music was disco as it was every place else. The difference about New York was that kids were funk fiends who weren't getting their vitamins from disco music. It was "too nervous," in their terminology, which meant too fast. It was too gay. It was something, but it just didn't move them, and so they were thrown back into their own resources, and what happened was that they started to . . . play a lot of James Brown. . . . His old records were staples, and Kool and the Gang, and heavy funk like that developed. I mean, part of it just had to do with there being a lot of neighborhood parks in New York City . . . and what kind of music was played in those parks by the disc jockeys there.[38]

A SOCIOCULTURAL OVERVIEW OF HIP-HOP CULTURE: FROM PAST TO PRESENT

Although the overcommercialization of disco did set the stage for hip-hop dance and music, so did other geopolitical factors (such as the disruption of rent-control communities in the Bronx with the construction of the Cross Bronx Expressway), postindustrial conditions (including the replacement of industrial factories with information service corporations), and the eventual dwindling of funds from inner-city and public arts programs. In the 1970s, federal monies allocated to inner-city infrastructure were now redirected to build suburban areas. In the phenomenon known as "white flight," these areas had now become a refuge for whites fleeing the neglected inner cities home, to a burgeoning poor black and Latino working class. Thus "modest blocks were bulldozed flat in the name of social progress, and the promise of these high-rise projects rapidly soured" in areas such as the Bronx. Between 1970 and 1975, there were 68,456 fires in the Bronx—more than thirty-three each night.[39] Some observers believe that these fires were the result of two factors: disgruntled residents who devised schemes to force the government to provide alternative housing, and avaricious slum landlords who intentionally arranged to have their housing complexes burned in order to collect insurance payoffs.

As conditions worsened, crime escalated. Most affected were the youth. As a consequence of their environment, some took matters in their own hands by setting up neighborhood patrols against outsiders. Eventually, the style of protection gave way to gang territorial turf wars. Accordingly, 1973 statistics revealed that New York City gangs totaled 315, with over nineteen thousand members.[40] Gang culture eventually spilled over from the streets into the neighborhood clubs, reminiscent of what happened to the Jamaican dancehall scene. Soon, music providers, the DJs, left the indoor club scene and, as an alternative, set up their sound systems in local neighborhood parks or at block parties, creating an outdoor discothèque. As the Real Roxanne observed:

People used to do jams outside in the schoolyard or handball court. Someone used to bring their two turntables out and plug them into the lamp post outside and that's how they got their power. People would listen and dance to music out in the streets."[41]

DJs garnered reputations in their immediate areas. For instance, Brooklyn was home to Maboya and DJ Flowers, and Harlem had DJ Hollywood and Pete "With the Funky Beat 'DJ'" Jones. A legion of these DJs, however, traveled from borough to borough or location to location as street, or itinerant, DJs. DJs were judged at that time on the size of their sound systems—including speakers—and, of course, their repertoire. The street DJ who provided a shift from the latter style of spinning records to the art of mixing beats or break beats was Jamaican-born Clive Campbell of the Bronx, better known as Kool "DJ" Herc. Patterning after the dancehall DJs in Jamaica, Herc, introduced the break-beats (beats) or breaks concept. Rather than play a record in its entirety followed by a fade into the next record as the discotheque DJs did, Herc blended musical fragments or beats from one record to the next by using a cross-fader lever between the two turntables. He also added electronic sound effects—"echoing and reverbing back and forth between the vocal and instrumental track [while manipulating] the treble and bass knobs"—a trademark of King Tubby.[42] Herc's beats consisted of styles from reggae to funk, but there were certain parts of these records that he highlighted, such as the percussion section groove (including bongos/congas, drums, and bass), called the break section. The term *break* also became a catch-all name specific to hip-hop dancers, called breakdancers, who, during the break section, executed stylized moves. Abbreviated from *breakdancers*, male dancers were called b-boys and female breakers b-girls. The insertion of a break section became a trademark of early hip-hop music recordings.

Kool "DJ" Herc's innovation was perfected by Bronx DJ Joseph "Grandmaster Flash" Sadler. Flash realized that during Herc's performances, there was a tendency to skip a beat when shifting from one beat to the next. Flash figured out a way to perfect the mixing of break beats by creating first a one-ear headphone and then a gadget on his turntable unit that allowed him to hear the music playing on one turntable while pre-cueing the next recording on the other turntable without missing a beat. Flash standardized hip-hop DJ turntable techniques, among them backspinning and punch-phrasing, and his protégé, Grand Wizard Theodore, created scratching, popularized in the Herbie Hancock recording, "Rockit" (1983), featuring Grandmixer D.ST.

Another DJ from the Bronx, Afrika Bambaataa (né Kevin Donovan) dubbed Master of Records, possessed an incredible ear for finding beats. "He blended tracks from Germany, Jamaica, the Philippines, California, and the South Bronx into a beautiful collage called hip-hop jams in the park and created a movement that turned into a world-wide musical and cultural revolution, as well as a billion dollar industry. His parties lifted the dancer into a spiritual state of euphoria based on his overstanding of vibrations, rhythms, cadence, tone, melody and mood."[43] DJs such as Bambaataa, along with others such as his cousin Jazzy Jay, Davy DMX, Whiz Kid, Charlie Chase, Disco Wiz, Disco King Mario, DJ Tex, and female DJ RD Smiley, were accompanied by aspiring DJs or apprentices, forming master-student relationships as surrogate father-son associations. For example, Afrika Islam was considered a Son of Bambaataa, and Funkmaster Flex was recognized as the Son of DJ Chuck Chillout.

Another important thing about Bambaataa was his vision to stop street gang violence in his immediate 'hood, the Bronx River housing project in the South Bronx. In a move similar to that of so many other youths, Bambaataa joined a notorious street gang, the Black Spades. However, by the early 1970s, he redirected his energy by performing as a DJ at local venues. He was later attracted to the philosophy of the Nation of Islam (NOI) and its teachings of the Honorable Elijah Muhammad and Malcolm X as well as to the black nationalist themes of pride and respect espoused in James Brown's "Say It Loud, I'm Black and I'm Proud," among others. In an effort to stop street gang violence in his 'hood, Bambaataa incorporated a philosophy of self-help, self-sufficiency, self-respect, and self-esteem and established the Youth Organization at the South River in 1973, which he eventually renamed the Zulu Nation. He describes this nonsectarian organization as "a huge young adult and youth organization which incorporates people that are into [street arts]: breakdancing, DJing, and graffiti. I had them to battle against each other in a nonviolent way, like rapper against rapper rather than knife against knife."[44] Membership in the Zulu Nation extended to black as well as Latino members. To its membership abroad, the Zulu Nation is known as the Universal Zulu Nation (UZN). Furthermore, Bambaataa's Zulu Nation laid the foundation for hip-hop not only as an arts movement but as a youth (sub)culture recognized around the globe. When asked about the etymology of *hip-hop*, Bambaataa traces it to Lovebug Starski, a DJ from the South Bronx. He stated how at Starski's parties, he was known to say, "'hip hop you don't stop that makes your body rock.' So I coined a word myself and started using the word 'hip-hop' to name this type of culture and it caught on."[45]

During the formative years of hip-hop, neighborhood parties or jams incorporated all four elements of hip-hop as recalled in the hip-hop film cult classic *Wild Style* (1983). The film's title derives from a graffiti-writer term meaning "a complicated construction of interlocking letters."[46] Graffiti is perhaps the oldest of the four elements. Although some critics note that graffiti dates to World War II (or even earlier), its recognition among New York City youth dates back to the 1950s, during the onslaught of gangs who "tagged" their names on neighborhood street walls to mark territory. In 1971, the *New York Times* featured a story of a writer of Greek origin, Taki 183, whose name was tagged throughout the city. Although city officials viewed graffiti as a crime, its writers perceived graffiti as an art, treating subway trains, walls, and even popular landscapes as concrete canvases on which to showcase their art.[47] Graffiti writers prefer to use various spray paints (such as Krylon) and magic markers to create larger works in the form of murals. Writers often produce smaller sketches of art ideas in their sketch pads prior to producing them on a large public canvas. Organizations such as United Graffiti Artist (UGA) and Nation of Graffiti Artists (NOGA) were established in order to provide graffiti artists with certain venues or places, including art galleries or designated neighborhood wall/concrete canvases to exhibit their works. However, docudramas such as *Style Wars* (2005) and *Infamy* (2007) best capture the insider perspectives of graf writers and their relentless efforts to establish graffiti as a legitimate art.

As hip-hop evolved in the Bronx and eventually throughout New York City, street DJs were accompanied by dancers who soon earned reputations as breakers or breakdancers. Although the popularization of certain dance movements, such as the robotic popping and locking moves, is credited to West Coast crews first seen on the syndicated television dance show *Soul Train* and on the early hip-hop films *Breakin'* (1984) and *Breakin' 2* (1984), when hip-hop arts caught the attention of mainstream media in the early 1980s, many thought that breakdancing was exclusively a New York City phenomenon. While partially true, New York City breakers advanced the popping and locking moves and mainly danced on concrete surfaces in parks, subways, and club jams as vividly seen in the hip-hop documentaries *Style Wars* and *The Freshest Kids* (2002). Characteristic of the New York breakers are additional moves from uprocking, toprocking, headspins, backspins, acrobatic movements, extensive use of footwork, and angular and freeze poses. Popular breakdance crews of New York City who dominated during the formative years of hip-hop were the Rock Steady Crew, the Rockwell Association (of the Bronx), the Dynamic Rockers (of Queens), and Rubberband Man and Apache of Brooklyn. The latter two incorporated salsa and the hustle dance moves to create uprock, a stylized move from Brooklyn.[48] It was common to see breakers perform impromptu at hip-hop jam parties, accompanying their favorite DJs.

By the mid-1970s, DJing had become extremely competitive, to the point that DJs soaked the labels off of their vinyl LPs to prevent would-be contenders from knowing the source of their break beats. Also, the invention of certain turntable techniques such as mixing, cutting, punch-phrasing, and scratching—all once done manually—required MCs. Certain DJs who were once solo acts, such as Kool "DJ" Herc, now comprised several crew members. Herc's crew, the Herculords, consisted of MCs Clark Kent and Jay Cee and the first lady of the crew, Pebblee-Poo. Afrika Bambaataa's crew consisted of MCs Cowboy (not to be confused with Cowboy of the Furious Five), Mr. Biggs, and Queen Kenya. Several DJ-MC crews proliferated, among them the Cheeba Crew, Fantastic 5 MCs, the Mercedes Ladies, and the Malachi Crew, but the one DJ-MCs crew that set the model for rhymin' to the beat of the music, trading rhyming couplets and ensemble shouts, was Grandmaster Flash and his MCs. Flash's MCs started as a trio but later added two more members to become known as Grandmaster Flash and the Furious Five. The Furious Five MCs included Melle Mel, Cowboy, Raheim, Mr. Ness, and Kid Creole.

Some DJs, however, did foray into MCing themselves, in particular Kurtis Blow and DJ Hollywood, the latter known for his consummate rhymin' skills, signature lines (appropriated by several MCs), and freestyle ability (to create rhymes "right-off-the-top-of-the-dome [head]"). Although the vernacular term for the MC was *rhymin' MC*, *rapper* soon gained mainstream currency and eventually replaced the term *rhymin' MC*.

Hip-hop flourished throughout New York City, earning a profit for its artists and awing listeners by its ingenuity, but it also steadily made its way throughout the eastern part of the United States, at first by way of underground mix tapes. Before it was first commercially recorded, rap music was recorded on cassette or eight-track tapes and sold to fans or friends at local performance venues. DJ Hollywood explained that, during his early career, after learning that he could use two turntables to make a tape, he would sell eight-track tapes for twelve dollars apiece.[49] As hip-hop became more and more popular throughout New York City, several clubs hosted hip-hop arts: Dixie Club, Club 371 of the Bronx, and Harlem's World of Manhattan Club. But the club that featured hip-hop on a nightly basis was Disco Fever, established by Sal Abbietello. Soon, the Fever would become a magnet for music entrepreneurs seeking to sign rap music talents. Others, such as Kool Lady Blue, an English-punk-clothing-entrepreneur-turned-hip-hop-promoter, promoted hip-hop at the famed Roxy (a former skating rink) and Negril, in lower Manhattan during the early 1980s.

Music industry entrepreneurs recognized the commercial potential of hip-hop music. Early independent record company owners included Bobby Robinson of Enjoy Records, Paul Winley of Winley Records, and Sylvia and Joseph Robinson of Sugarhill Records. The most successful of these labels was Sugarhill Records, which produced hip-hop's first successful commercial recording, "Rapper's Delight" (1979), featuring a trio of MCs from New Jersey called the Sugar Hill Gang. However, New York MCs challenged the originality of the Gang's rhymes; for it is commonly known that rhymes written by Grandmaster Caz of the Cold Crush Brothers were used by members of the Gang in "Rapper's Delight." New York MCs often credit "King Tim III" (1979), performed by the Fatback Band of Harlem, which featured a rhymin' MC, as the first rap song, circulating a few months before "Rapper's Delight."

As rap music moved farther into the mainstream, it eventually eclipsed the popularity and commercial potential of the other hip-hop arts. Nonetheless, music entrepreneurs from the generation of rap music artists, unlike the aforementioned record producers, started artist management companies for acts and formed rap music labels specializing in street production concepts: that is, underground promotion (i.e., pitching mix tapes of artists before their album officially "drops", or releases). These new school music entrepreneurs included Russell Simmons of Rush Productions Management, Simmons and Rick Rubin, cofounders of the legendary Def Jam Records, and Tom Silverman of Tommy Boy Records. Silverman's first successful rap music act was Afrika Bambaataa and his group Soul Sonic Force. Bambaataa's music introduced a synthesizer-, funk-, and electronic-driven sound called techno funk, as heard in his hit "Planet Rock" (1982). Other successful yet unique rap music acts during this period included the Fat Boys, a trio from Brooklyn known for popularizing the human beat boxvocal rhythmic simulation of drum beats,[50] Kurtis Blow, the first rap act to sign with a major label (Mercury Records), and female MCs Lady B and the trio Sequence, both signed to the Sugarhill Record label.

Between 1980 and 1985, other rap music acts surfaced throughout New York City. Among these artists were Big Daddy Kane, Biz Markie, Boogie Down Productions (started by KRS-One and Scott La Rock), Dana Dane, De La Soul, Doug E. Fresh & MC Ricky D (also known as Slick Rick), Eric B. & Rakim, Kool Moe Dee, Stetsasonic, the Juice Crew (featuring MC Shan and Roxanne Shanté), Jungle Brothers, the Real Roxanne, Ultramagnetic MCs, UTFO, and Whodini, as well as acts from neighboring cities such as Lady B, DJ Jazzy Jeff and the Fresh Prince, and Schoolly D of Philadelphia. During this period, rap music artists even collaborated with other popular music, including the punk group Blondie's recording "Rapture" (1980, featuring Deborah Harry)—leading some music critics to erroneously identify this as the first rap—and British punk-stylist-entrepreneur Malcolm McClaren's recording "Buffalo Gals" (1982).

Rap music also took the airwaves by storm with its first rap music radio show host personality, Mr Magic. Magic's radio show was launched on WHBI of Newark, New Jersey, in 1979 and later found its permanent home on New York City's WBLS. Magic's show was followed by New York's KISS FM and the hiring of its first hip-hop music host, DJ Red Alert. These shows inspired a legion of radio station programming, including KDAY of Los Angeles, the first radio station to play an all-rap format. KDAY's program director, Greg Mack, is credited for introducing established East Coast acts to West Coast audiences.

Contributing to the crossover success of rap music is Run-D.M.C., a trio from Queens, New York. Consisting of two MCs, Joseph "Run" Simmons and Darryl "D.M.C." McDaniels, with DJ Jam Master Jay, Run-D.M.C. established a rap music sound that combined rappin' over a rock guitar sound. Their single "Rock Box" from their debut LP *Run-D.M.C.*(1983) broke ground as the first rap song programmed for the syndicated rock-oriented video station MTV. After this achievement, Run-D.M.C. released their sophomore LP, *King of Rock* (1985), succeeded by their multiplatinum LP *Raising Hell* (1986) with its innovative rendition of "Walk this Way" by the hard-rock group Aerosmith, who appeared on the recording and in the video with Run-D.M.C.

Simmons's teaming up with Rick Rubin to create Def Jam Records led to other important innovations in rap music history. Their first solo artist was LL Cool J and the trio the Beastie Boys, a punk-style rappin' trio who proved the commercial viability of white rap music acts.[51] Ushering in the prototype of national consciousness was Def Jam's Public Enemy (PE), from Long Island. Dubbed the Prophets of Rage, PE's main lyricist Chuck D and his sidekick Flavor Flav, along with the Public Enemy's security

Run-D.M.C. Shown from left: Darryl McDaniels (D.M.C.), Jason Mizell (Jam Master Jay), Joseph Simmons (Run), as seen in *Krush Groove*, 1985.

Warner Bros./Photofest

constituent (known as Security of the First World and wearing attire reminiscent of the Black Panther Party) and its production team, the Bomb Squad, introduced listeners to black nationalist rhetoric via sampled speech material of Minister Louis Farrakhan and Malcolm X, revolutionizing the art of mixing or creating a recording. PE's production team, masterminded by Hank Shocklee, produced the music for the recording "Fight the Power" (1989). Their extensive use of breaks or beats via digital sampling and the coveted Roland TR-808 drum machine with its sonic boom or kick, producing an array of sound timbres and textures, was considered unprecedented for its time.

Public Enemy. Shown: Professor Griff (back left), Flavor Flav (front left), Terminator X (white cap), and Chuck D (front right).

Photofest

The success of these groups earned rap further popularity in the mainstream, aided by the creation of MTV's all-rap music programming *Yo! MTV Raps*, in 1988. The vee-jay, or video television host, was graffiti artist Fred Brathwaite, known in the hip-hop world as Fab Five Freddy. Following suit in the rap music–oriented television video programs were Black Entertainment Television's *Rap City* (now known as *Tha Bassment*) and *Video Music Box*. Rap music also ventured farther into the mainstream via television commercials that featured hip-hop music acts as spokespersons for name-brand clothing, sneakers, and soft drinks.

As hip-hop music expanded its roster to include female MCs during the mid-1980s, they, unlike previous MCs, introduced feminist-inspired themes to go with a rappin' style comparable to that of their male counterparts. Most noted in initiating this trend are MC Lyte and Queen Latifah. Another development that opened the doors for female MCs was the "answer-back" raps, or male/female sequels. These songs include "A Fly Girl," by the Boogie Boys, followed by "A Fly Guy," by Pebblee-Poo; "Girls Ain't Nothing But Trouble," by DJ Jazzy Jeff and the Fresh Prince, followed by "Guys Ain't Nothing But Trouble," by Ice Cream Tee; "The Show." by Doug E. Fresh and Slick Rick, followed by "The Show Stoppa," by Salt-N-Pepa; and a bevy of answer-back rap battles among female MCs such as Antoinette, The Real Roxanne, Roxanne Shanté, Sparky Dee, and MC Lyte. Although some of these female MCs, such as MC Lyte and Queen Latifah, sustained long careers in the hip-hop world, female MCs of the 1980s proved the viability and respectability of other female hip-hop artists. By the 1990s, these artists had inspired a legion of female MCs who revolutionized and diversified the images of women in hip-hop music: Bahamadia, Boss, Bytches With Problems (BWP), Da Brat, Eve, Foxy Brown, Harmony, Lady of Rage, Lil' Kim, Mia X, Missy Elliott, Monie Love, Queen Pen, Rah Digga, Remy Ma, T-Love, Trina, and Yo-Yo, just to name a few.

Although it is no surprise how graffiti and b-boy culture circulated on the national circuit, rap music slowly penetrated various regions, tailored to the musical taste and cultural milieu in respective areas. Forerunners of hip-hop music in Los Angeles comprised a techno-funk-quasi-rap style whose representative included Arabian Prince, the Dream Team, Egyptian Lover, Uncle Jam's Army, and World Class Wreckin' Cru, among a host of others. Primary contexts of early hip-hop culture in Los Angeles were skating rinks such as Skateland USA and World on Wheels and clubs such as the Radio (renamed Radiotron in the film *Breakin'*) and the Radio Lounge. This early sound would be replaced by a more funk-driven sound—in which lyrics about gang violence, police repression, and drug lore (such as crack cocaine) abounded—called G-funk or reality rap, and commercially known as gangsta rap.

The rise of gangsta rap styles can be traced to solo acts Toddy Tee with his mix-tape underground hit "Batterram" (1985), and rapper Ice T (dubbed the Original Gangsta) with his recording "Six in the Morning" (1985).[52] Incorporated in the presentation of gangsta rap is *cholo* culture, affiliated with Chicano gang culture. Cholo is characterized by "a distinctive street style of dress, speech [caló/Spanglish], gestures, tattoos, and graffiti that is a direct outgrowth of a 1930s–1940s second-generation Mexican subculture called *pachuco*."[53] Other images affiliated with cholo culture popularized in music videos depicting Los Angeles gang culture were lowriders, bandanas, oversized shirts, and baggy pants.

Augmenting the roster of gangsta rap was former drug dealer Eric "Eazy-E" Wright. In 1987, Wright founded Ruthless Records. During this same year, Eazy-E formed the group Niggas with Attitude or N.W.A, whose lyrics targeted issues regarding police brutality upon black and brown men and the ghetto life of Compton (gangbanging, drug dealing, and so on). Group members included MC Ren and DJ Yella, their main lyricist, Ice Cube, and soon-to-be-renowed-hip-hop-producer Dr. Dre. One of their most controversial songs, "Fuck tha Police," from their debut LP *Straight Out of Compton* (1988), generated much controversy and suspicion in the Federal Bureau Investigation (FBI) concerning what were believed to be cryptic messages propagating hate against the government.[54]

N.W.A.'s candid observations about gangs and ghetto culture of Los Angeles spurred a wave of artists who identified with the gangsta rap subgenre—Above the Law, Ice Cube and his affiliate groups, Da Lench Mob, and West Side Connection (featuring WC and Mac 10, and artists on the Death Row & Interscope labels (such as Snoop Dogg [formerly known as Snoop Doggy Dogg] and Tupac Shakur)—as well as Latino acts from Los Angeles: Kid Frost, Mellow Man Ace, and the collective Cypress Hill.

Alternative to the gangsta rap substyle was the gravelly voice of Tone-Löc with his party-oriented best-selling single hit "Wild Thing" (1988) and the Young MC, the songwriter for "Wild Thing," who followed up with "Bust A Move" (1989).

West Coast acts surfaced in other areas as well, including Oakland's Too $hort and MC Hammer and other acts from the Bay area: Blackalicious, The Coup, E-40, Hieroglyphics, The Luniz, Paris, Planet Asia, Spice 1, and Digital Underground.

Southern rap made its way into hip-hop music market, most notably in with the Geto Boys of Houston, who followed in the gangsta style, and the trio 2 Live Crew, masterminded by Luke Campbell of Miami, Florida. During the early 1990s, 2 Live Crew's LP *Nasty as They Wanna Be* (1989) featured sexually explicit content that spurred a wave of censorship debates involving right-wing organizations and the Parents' Music Resource Center (PMRC) that ultimately led to congressional hearings in 1994. Although the First Amendment protected the Crew as well as the other artists singled out (artists on the Death Row label), rap music artists responded by recording two versions of LPs deemed sexually explicit—a radio, clean version and an explicit version indicated by "explicit content" warning labels. Creating musical tracks via digital sampling and releasing recordings without seeking permission or clearing copyright also became a growing concern, prompting an amendment to U.S. copyright statutes to include the reproduction of any music via digital means.

By the 1990s, DJing had advanced into a complex system of turntable techniques, launching the turntable into a musical instrument category of its own. Those accomplished on the turntable at creating and making beats on the "wheels of steel" are referred to as "turntablists"—a term coined by DJ Babu of Dilated Peoples. Noted turntable artists, recognized for their unique art form, include the Beat Junkies, X-ecutioners (led by Rob Swift), Invisibl Skratch Piklz (featuring DJ Q-Bert, Mis Master Mike, and so on), Cut Chemist and Nu-Mark of the rap music collective Jurassic 5, and solo acts DJ Honda, DJ Shadow, DJ Symphony, and an array of others. Turntablism is a growing art form of its own, so much so that international competitions are sponsored by the popular turntable brand Technics as the Technics DMC World DJ Championship and the International Turntablist Federation Championship.

As rap music moved farther into the mainstream, business entrepreneurs and marketing strategists began adopting the term *hip-hop* as a cultural signifier for products with a street sensibility as expressed as a style of dress, language, dance, and an attitude. But some artists, such as KRS-One, expressed growing concerns about the commercialization of hip-hop, fearing that it threatened hip-hop culture.[55] But with the rise of hip-hop in the underground, as well as hip-hop community centers (such as Project Blowed in the Leimert Park area of the Los Angeles Crenshaw district and Representing Education Activism and Community through Hip-Hop [R.E.A.C. Hip-Hop, formerly known as the Hip-Hop Coalition]) that do not privilege one art form over the other, KRS-One's Temple of Hip-Hop, and political incentives such as Bikari Kitwana's National Hip-Hop Political Convention and Russell Simmon's Hip-Hop Summit Action Network (HSAN) conventions, such platforms could "serve as important renewal sites for remapping these interconnections."[56]

As hip-hop approached the end of the millennium, its presentation undoubtedly diversified beyond scope as nation-conscious rap, with such acts as Arrested Development, Black Star (with the duo Mos Def and Talib Kweli), Common, dead prez, the Roots, and X-Clan alongside Five Percenter rap (such as Brand Nubian, Lakim Shabazz, and Poor Righteous Teachers).[57] Verbally dexterous MCs include Busta Rhymes, DMX, Eminem, Jay-Z, Nas, the Notorious B.I.G., Pharoahe Monch, and collectives like Freestyle Fellowship and Wu-Tang Clan; the Latino hip-hop of Fat Joe and his Terror Squad; the Dirty South bounce substyle[58] popularized by Master P and his collective; and artists on the Cash Money label, including Juvenile, Lil Wayne, and B.G of the Hot Boys of New Orleans; Goodie MOb, OutKast, Ludacris, and T.I. of Atlanta; Chamillionaire of Houston; David Banner of Mississippi; Three 6 Mafia of Memphis; and the sing-songy style of Nelly of St. Louis. Another regional substyle of rap is crunk, "a fusion of Miami bass and Memphis buck—roughneck chants with [Roland TR-]808 beats and humming bass."[59] The crunk style originated in Memphis but was exploited by Atlanta-based artists; producer Lil Jon, self-proclaimed "King of Crunk"; and acts produced by him, including the East Side Boyz, Rasheeda, YingYang Twins, and YoungBloodz. Hyphy is another substyle that evolved in the 2000s. The term was coined by Keak Da Sneak and is associated with dance and music culture distinct to the California Bay Area. Among a select few hyphy artists are E-40, Messy Marv, and San Quinn.

The malleable quality of hip-hop music has lent itself comfortably to other musical styles, thereby creating the musical hybrids evidenced in jazz-rap hybrid acts A Tribe Called Quest, Digable Planets, and Gang Starr; the hip-hop–live-band concept advanced by the Roots and conceived by MC Black Thought (Tariq Trotter) and drummer ?uestlove (Ahmir Khalib Thompson); the rap-gospel or holy hip-hop acts Chris Cooper and S.F.C., Preachas in Disguise, and Soldiers for Christ, the hip-hop–reggae dance-hall hybrid *reggaetón* artists Alexis Y Fido, Calle 13, Daddy Yankee, and Ivy Queen; and the new jack swing introduced by Teddy Riley and his group Guy as a hip-hop–rhythm 'n' blues hybrid. Advancing this concept are Mary J. Blige, the Queen of Hip-Hop Soul, Akon, Erykah Badu, Beyoncé and Destiny Child, Chris Brown, Ciara, the Fugees (featuring Lauryn Hill), John Legend, Omarion, Ne-Yo, R. Kelly, Musiq Soulchild, and T-Pain, as well as those involved in the return of soul in the mid-1990s (neosoul) but with a hip-hop sensibility: India.Arie, Erykah Badu, D'Angelo, Alicia Keys, Jill Scott, and Angie Stone (a former member of Sequence), among others.

Popular culture has also witnessed the burgeoning hip-hop film genre, aptly called "new jack cinema." Often didactic in scope, these films present the grim reality of ghettos and street life, and the tough choices black youths face in order to cope—whether accepting reality or giving in to death. In an effort to bring about a sense of realism, rap music artists were cast to play serious character roles alongside renowned actors. It is worth mentioning a select few of these films and the hip-hop artists who starred in each: *Juice* (1991) with Tupac Shakur, *New Jack City* (1991) with Ice T, *Boyz 'N the Hood* (1991) with Ice Cube, *Menace II Society* (1993) with MC Eiht, *Above the Rim* (1994) with Tupac Shakur, and *Set It Off* (1996) with Queen Latifah. Of course, not all films with a hip-hop sensibility are dark in scope; satires and comedies have also been filmed, including *House Party* (1990), featuring Kid'N'Play, *Men in Black*, with Will Smith (also known as the Fresh Prince), *Living Out Loud*, featuring Queen Latifah (1998), *I Got the Hook Up* (1998), featuring Master P, and *8 Mile* (2002), a semiautobiographical film featuring Eminem. Eminem's performance of his song "Lose Yourself," from the film's soundtrack, received an Oscar for Best Song in a Film, making him the first rap artist to receive an Academy Award, followed by Three 6 Mafia, the second rap act to garner an Oscar for their song "It's Hard Out Here for a Pimp" from the film *Hustle and Flow* (2005). Additionally, rap artists Queen Latifah and Will Smith, received Oscar nominations for their roles in *Chicago* (2002) and *Ali* (2001), respectively.

Other hip-hop film genres consist of docudramas showcasing specific artistic elements: *The Show* (1994), *Rhyme and Reason* (1997), and *Freestyle: The Art of Rhyme* (2000), concepts about rhyming (e.g., freestyle and ciphers); *Nobody Knows My Name* (1999), a look at the struggles and challenges of female MCs; *Scratch* (2001) and *Keepin' Time* (2001), a sociohistory about turntablism; *The Freshest Kids* (2002), about the origins of b-boy/b-girl culture; *Style Wars* (1983, rereleased 2003), dealing with graffiti art/writer culture and followed by *Infamy* (2005), a profile of graffiti art/writer culture; and *Rize* (2004), which examines a hip-hop–dance subgenre identified with South Los Angeles, called krumping. The art of shooting or making music videos with a street edge sensibility (context, language, dress) opened doors for some music video directors into film directing, including Antoine Fuqua, F. Gary Gray, Brett Ratner, Jessy Terrero, and Hype Williams.[60]

Finally, hip-hop sensibility has influenced the entire scope of music production pioneered by small-scale neighborhood DJs or street-rap music producers, sending it to meteoric heights and launching independent rap music record label owners to mogul status.[61] Moreover, hip-hop continues to penetrate popular culture on its own aesthetic terms through the fashion-industry world with distinct name brands such as Echō and Enyce and clothing lines created by hip-hop artists—Rocawear (Jay-Z), Phat Farm (Russell Simmons), and Sean John ("Sean P. Diddy")—including footwear, such as Lugz and Timberland.

The existence of hip-hop in the twenty-first century proves its efficacy as a cultural expression embraced by youth around the globe.[62] An aesthetic base predicated on self-expression and originality has helped non–U.S.-based artists find their unique voices and linguistic spaces through a hip-hop prism. Contributing to its global success is the explosion of MTV, the circulation of hip-hop film classics, the formation and distribution of international record label subsidiaries by conglomerate music groups (such as Universal, BMG/Sony, and Warner Music Group), the proliferation of the Universal Zulu Nation international chapters, and the accessibility of the Internet. But, regardless of international magnitude, hip-hop remains a cultural practice deeply informed by African-based performance practices that define its aesthetic qualities.

NOTES

1. Some hip-hop critics argue that the human beat-box, a vocal rhythmic simulation of a drum and sometimes musical instrument, is an element. However, in the context of my research, I categorize beat-box or beat-boxing as a subcategory of MCing, because it is a vocal technique commonly exploited by MCs.

2. Paul Gilroy, *The Black Atlantic: Modernity and Double Consciousness* (Cambridge, MA: Harvard University Press, 1993), 103.

3. Afrika Bambaataa, interview with author, June 10, 1986, Manhattan, NY. Please note that all personal interviews with the author are deposited at the Ethnomusicology Archive, University of California, as part of the "Cheryl Keyes Collection, 1975–2001." Refer to the following Web site for further information: http://www.oac.cdlib.org/institutions/ark:/13030/kt2g501822.

4. Cheryl L. Keyes, *Rap Music and Street Consciousness* (Urbana: University of Illinois Press, 2002), 21.

5. Jacqui Malone, *Steppin' on the Blues: The Visible Rhythms of African American Dance* (Urbana: University of Illinois Press, 1996), 33; see also Kyra D. Gaunt, *The Games Black Girls Play: Learning the Ropes from Double Dutch to Hip-Hop* (New York: New York University Press, 2006), 47, with discussion about kinesthetic memory and kinetic orality, and Todd Boyd, *Young, Black, Rich, and Famous: The Rise of the NBA, The Hip-Hop Invasion, and the Transformation of American Culture* (New York: Doubleday, 2003), which comments about the cooperative influence of hip-hop and basketball.

6. Martha Cooper and Henry Chalfant, *Subway Art* (New York: Henry Hold and Company, 1984), 66; see also Robert Farris Thompson, *Flash of the Spirit: African and Afro-American Art and Philosophy* (New York: Vintage, 1983) and Robert Farris Thompson, "Kongo Influences on African-American Artistic Culture," in *Africanisms in American Culture*, ed. Joseph E. Holloway (Bloomington, IN: Indiana University Press, 1990), 148–184.

7. Keyes, *Rap Music and Street Consciousness*, 21.

8. Ibid., 23.

9. From Son House/J. D. Short, *Blues from the Mississippi Delta* (Smithsonian Folkways, 1963), FWO 2467.

10. Joyce M. Jackson, "The Black American Folk Preacher and the Chanted Sermon: Parallels with a West African Tradition," in *Discourse in Ethnomusicology II: A Tribute to Alan P. Merriam*, eds. Caroline Card et al. (Bloomington, IN: Indiana University Press, 1981).

11. Daryl Cumber Dance, *Shuckin' and Jivin': Folklore from Contemporary Black Americans* (Bloomington, IN: Indiana University Press, 1978), 198. A similar example of this toast can be found on the comedian Rudy Ray Moore's *This Pussy Belongs to Me* (Kent Records/Comedy Series, 1972), KST-002.

12. For further information, see Gaunt, *The Games Black Girls Play*.

13. Malone, *Steppin' on the Blues*, 70–110.

14. Keyes, *Rap Music and Street Consciousness*, 30.

15. Gilbert A.Williams, "The Black Disc Jockey as a Cultural Hero," *Popular Music and Society* 10, no. 3 (1986): 81.

16. Jack Olsen, *Black Is Best: The Riddle of Cassius Clay* (New York: Dell, 1967), 10.

17. Walter J. Ong, *Orality and Literacy: The Technologizing of the Word* (London & New York: Routledge, 2002 [1982]), 11.

18. Lumumba Carson, interview with author (June 16, 1986), Brooklyn, NY.

19. Afrika Bambaataa, interview with the author, ibid.

20. Ibid.

21. Melle Mel, interview with the author (June 7, 1986), New York, NY.

22. Norman C. Stolzoff, *Wake the Town and Tell the People: Dancehall Culture in Jamaica* (Durham, NC: Duke University Press, 2000), 41.

23. Dick Hebdige, *Cut 'N' Mix* (London: Comedia 1987), 72. The rude-boy image also graduated into an attitude called slackness. Eventually, rude boy was adopted by such reggae dancehall "gun lyrics" artists as Bounty Killer, Buja Banton, Ninja Man, Shabba Ranks (the first dancehall reggae artist to garner a Grammy), and "rude girl" Lady Saw. For further readings on the concept of slackness, refer to Carolyn Cooper, *Noises in the Blood: Orality, Gender, and the "Vulgar" Body of Jamaican Popular Culture* (London; New York: Macmillan, 1993) and Carolyn Cooper, *Sound Clash: Jamaican Dancehall Culture at Large* (New York: Palgrave Macmillan, 2004).

24. Norman C. Stolzoff, *Wake the Town*, 84.

25. An example of diasporic bonding via collaboration in hip-hop is Yellowman toasting on Run-D.M.C.'s recording of "Roots, Rap, Reggae" from the *King of Rock* (1986) LP.

26. Ransford W. Palmer, *Pilgrims from the Sun: West Indiana Migration to America* (New York: Twayne Publishers, 1995), 20.

27. H. Rap Brown, "Street Smarts," in *Mother Wit from the Laughing Barrel: Readings in the Interpretation of Afro-American Folklore*, ed. Alan Dundes, (New York: Garland, 1981), 336–353. Brown comments that some of the best dozen players were girls.

28. Ibid.

29. Keyes, *Rap Music and Street Consciousness*, 32.

30. Bambaataa, interview with author, June 10, 1986, Manhattan, NY.

31. Quoted in Steven Hager, *Hip Hop: The Illustrated History of Break Dancing, Rap Music, and Graffiti* (New York: St. Martin's Press, 1984), 49.

32. Portia K. Maultsby, "A Health Diversity Evolves from Create Freedom," *Billboard* (Black Music Spotlight Issue), June 9, 1979, BM10.

33. Nelson George, *The Death of Rhythm and Blues* (New York: Plume, 1988), 154.

34. Quoted in Vernon Reid, "The Vibe Q: Geroge Clinton," *Vibe*, November 6, 1993, 45.

35. Joseph G. Schloss indicates that the "Rap Sample FAQ, an online compendium of sample sources, list as almost two hundred songs that sampled from James Brown's "Funky Drummer," virtually all from the middle to late eighties—and the actual number is probably closer to several thousand . . ." For more information, see Schloss's *Making Beats: The Art of Sample-Based Hip-Hop* (Middletown, CT: Wesleyan University Press, 2004).

36. Quoted in R. J. Smith, "Lock, Pop, and Quarrel," *Vibe*, September 1998, 268.

37. Ibid.

38. Bill Adler, interview with author (May 23, 1986), Manhattan, NY.

39. Jim Rooney, *Organizing the South Bronx* (Albany: State University of New York Press, 1995), 46; see also the discussion in Keyes, *Rap Music and Street Consciousness*, 44–46; and Tricia Rose, *Black Noise: Rap Music and Black Culture in Contemporary America* (Hanover, NH: Wesleyan University Press, 1994), 27–34.

40. Nelson George, *Buppiess, B-Boys, Baps and Bobos: Notes on the Post-Soul Black Culture* (New York: HarperCollins, 1992), 11.

41. The Real Roxanne, telephone interview with author (July 30, 1986), Brooklyn, NY.

42. Hebdige, *Cut 'N' Mix*, 83.

43. Quoted in Andrew Emery, "Cutting Edge: Who is the Greatest Deejay Ever?" *Hip-Hop Connection* (May 1988): 26.

44. Bambaataa, interview with author, June 10, 1986, Manhattan, NY.

45. Ibid.

46. See Cooper and Chalfant, *Subway Art*, 27.

47. See "'Taki 183' Spawns Pen Pals," *New York Times*, July 21, 1971.

48. Joseph G. Schloss states that uprocking was a move first introduced around 1968 by Puerto Rican youth of Brooklyn. This discussion has led some critics to suggest that hip-hop may have first started in Brooklyn rather than the Bronx. I argue that *hip-hop* was a term initially used by a DJ from the Bronx, Lovebug Starski, and adopted by Afrika Bambaataa as a catchall term to embrace a collective of artistic forms rendered as graffiti, breakdancing (or b-boying), DJing, and, eventually, MCing. The geopolitical circumstances and faltering infrastructure germane to the Bronx during the 1960s and 1970s fostered an environment in which hip-hop arts coalesced as the interrelated expressions envisioned by Afrika Bambaataa rather than as separate or isolated forms. However, what is interesting is that uprock grew as an alternative art to gang violence initiated by Rubberband Man and Apache, of Brooklyn. Because there were offshoots of gangs from the Bronx in other boroughs, such as Brooklyn, uprocking was incorporated as a b-boy move in much the way that popping and locking were but was further reshaped and adapted as a move by b-boys in the Bronx. For further information on b-boy/b-girl dance culture, see Joseph G. Schloss, "'Like Old Folk Sound Handed Down from Generation to Generation': History, Canon, and Community in B-boy Culture," *Ethnomusicology* 50, no. 3 (2006): 411–432.

49. DJ Hollywood, interview with the author (August 18, 1986), Harlem, NY.

50. Although Fat Boys member Darren "The Human Beat Box" Robinson popularized the use of the human beat-box concept via recording, the origination of the human beat-box is credited to rapper MC Doug E. Fresh.

51. Def Jam also produced the white duo 3rd Bass. By the 1990s, Vanilla Ice (né Robert Van Winkle) was well on his way to becoming rap's first solo superstar. His career was shortlived after the controversy surrounding the unauthorized use of a chant from Alpha Phi Alpha, a black fraternity, as the basis of his song "Ice Ice Baby," from the album *To the Extreme* (1990). Many hip-hop-heads (hip-hop fans) questioned Vanilla Ice's originality.

52. Although Toddy Tee's underground mix-tape version "Batterram" (1985) is considered the first rap in gangsta style, Ice-T's "Six in the Morning" is considered the first West Coast commercial gangsta rap recording. The first gangsta rap

commercial recording, however, is thought to be Philadelphia MC Schoolly D's with "Gangster Boogie" (1984), followed by "PSK What Does It Mean?"

53. James Diego Vigil, *Barrio Gangs: Street Life and Identity in Southern California* (Austin, TX: University of Texas Press, 1994 [1988]), 3.

54. For an excellent source specifically dealing with gangsta rap in Los Angeles, see Robin D. G. Kelley, "Kickin' Reality, Kickin' Ballistics: Gangsta Rap and Postindustrial Los Angeles," in *Droppin' Science: Critical Essays on Rap Music and Hip Hop Culture,* ed. William Eric Perkins (Philadelphia: Temple University Press, 1996), 117–158.

55. See Margena A. Christian, "Has Hip Hop Taken a Beatdown or Is It Just Growing Up?" *Jet,* April 9, 2007: 54–56, 58–59; Michael Eric Dyson and Kevin Powell, "Two Sides: Is Hip Hop Dead?" *Ebony,* June 2007: 60–61; Tracy Sharpley-Whiting, *Pimps Up, Ho's Down: Young Black Women, Hip-Hop and the New Gender Politics* (New York: New York University Press, 2006).

56. Keyes, *Rap Music and Street Consciousness,* 228; see also Yvonne Bynoe, *Stand & Deliver: Political Activism, Leadership, and Hip-Hop Culture* (Brooklyn, NY: Soft Skull Press, 2004); Imani Perry, *Prophets of the Hood: Politics and Poetics in Hip-Hop* (Durham, NC: Duke University Press, 2004).

57. See Felicia Miyakawa, *Five Percenter Rap: God Hop's Music, Message, and Black Muslim Mission* (Bloomington, IN: Indiana University Press, 2005).

58. DJ Jubilee of New Orleans, who did a remake of Juvenile's "Back that Azz Up" (1998) is credited with ushering in the bounce style. The bounce style can be described as a sparse musical track with emphasis placed on a pulsing snare drum with booming kick drum (re)produced on a drum machine. The bounce style was exemplified by Jay-Z in his hit "Can I Get A" (1998) and further reshaped by other ATL (an abbreviation for Atlanta) artists to create crunk, a stylized funk affiliated with Lil Jon.

59. Roni Sarig, *Third Coast: Outkast, Timbaland, and How Hip-Hop Became a Southern Thing* (Cambridge, MA: Da Capo Press, 2007), 286.

60. Other noted music directors who have steadily worked in the hip-hop music video industry are Philip Atwell, Paul Hunter, Little X, Diane Martel, Dave Meyers, Chris Robinson, and Millicent Shelton, among many others.

61. Among some of the most successful DJs-turned-producers are DJ Premier, Dr. Dre, Lil Jon, Prince Paul, and Timbaland. Examples of independent rap music record labels that have become million-dollar enterprises are Dr. Dre's Aftermath Entertainment, Eminem's Slim Shady, Sean "P. Diddy" Comb's Bad Boy Entertainment, Jermaine Dupri's So-So Def, Queen Latifah's Flavor Unit Records, Jay-Z's Roc-A-Fella, and Russell Simmons's Def Jam.

62. A growing number of global specific studies on hip-hop are being written in various languages and published abroad. Within this paper, however, I will provide a partial list of English-language book-length works that address global hip-hop: Ian Condry, *Hip-Hop Japan: Rap and the Path of Cultural Globalization* (Durham, NC: Duke University Press, 2006); James G. Spady, H. Samy Alim, and Samir Meghelli, eds., *Tha Global Cipha: Hip Hop Culture and Consciousness* (Philadelphia, PA; Black History Museum Press, 2006); Ian Maxwell, *Phat Beats: Dope Rhymes: Hip Hop Down Under Comin' Upper* (Hanover, NH: Wesleyan University Press, 2003); Tony Mitchell, ed., *Global Noise: Rap and Hip-Hop Outside the USA* (Hanover, NH: Wesleyan University Press, 2001); and Adam Krims, *Rap Music and the Poetics of Identity* (New York: Cambridge, 2000).

6

The Blues

Don Cusic

Blues was the music of the black working class in the United States during the first half of the twentieth century. During the earliest part of the twentieth century there were essentially two types of blues. Vaudeville blues was descended from minstrel shows and featured performers with a band in a show staged to attract a paying audience, but Delta blues came from Southern cotton fields and was personified by a single man with a guitar.

Musically, the blues is a combination of British and European melodies and harmonies with African rhythms and work song call-and-response formats. The blues has been called an attitude, the self-expression of downtrodden blacks in a repressive white society, and a means of conveying heartfelt emotions to a hostile world. The blues as music certainly represented all of those factors—as well as a means of enjoying life, providing entertainment, and socializing on Saturday night.

Vaudeville blues and Delta blues evolved into rhythm and blues after World War II, the music of blacks who moved to Northern cities during the Great Migration. During the 1950s and early 1960s, rhythm and blues was a major component of rock 'n' roll; during the mid-1960s "Soul" music emerged from inner city blacks and studios in Memphis and Muscle Shoals, Alabama. During the 1970s R&B and soul music were key components of disco and dance music; from the 1980s forward rap and hip-hop have been the music identified with blacks (particularly urban blacks), the traditional blues relegated to a niche genre that sees musicians play before small but appreciative audiences in a subculture supported by a handful of clubs, record labels, magazines, and Web sites dedicated to blues and blues performers.

ROOTS OF THE BLUES

The roots of the blues in America go back to work songs African Americans sang in southern fields during the period of slavery in the United States. It includes field hollers, cries, calls, arhoolies, and spirituals, as well as washboard, jug, and string bands. As the blues developed in urban areas—when some blacks moved out of the rural South after the Civil War—this music became more rhythmic and included songs from marching bands, ragtime, gospel, pop, vaudeville, and minstrel shows.

Slavery in America began in 1619 when a Dutch ship with Africans arrived in Jamestown, Virginia. After 1808, the importation of slaves from Africa into the United States was illegal, but government officials tended to look the other way, and in 1859 more slaves were imported into the United States than had been in any year when the slave trade was legal. Thus, throughout the pre–Civil War South were slaves who had just arrived from Africa as well as slaves whose ancestors had been in America for several generations. Because of this, the African influence varied a great deal throughout the slave population.

In work songs done with a group, a leader generally set the tempo of the labor by singing while his fellow workers sang an answer in unison. This form of singing—called leader-and-chorus or call-and-response—has direct links to African traditions.[1] Drums and horns were banned by slave owners in the South because these instruments were used to send messages that could potentially lead to slave revolts, a constant fear among Southern whites before the Civil War.

The only instrument imported directly from Africa during the pre–Civil War years was the banjo, or "banjer" as it was called.[2] The instrument developed from lute-like instruments that had migrated from Middle Europe to West Africa, and then to the United States during the slave trade. In addition to the banjo, blacks learned to play fiddle; these two instruments became the nucleus for string bands on plantations. The songs played were most likely jigs and reels from Scottish and Irish traditions.

The major crops for plantations in the pre–Civil War South were tobacco and cotton, and these crops needed a large slave work force to make them economically profitable. Because cotton fields were large, the types of singing there included both individuals singing to themselves, generally in what were called "moans," and call-and-response, in which a leader sang out a line and others answered. "Hollers," or "hoolies," also developed, in which one singer sang or perhaps shouted while a long, loud melody rose and fell and perhaps broke into falsetto. This melody was picked up by another worker and reverberated like an echo around the field—or several might join in a chorus. This "holler," or "hoolie," replaced the group work song, for there was no need for cotton field workers to work together in unison.[3] If this hoolie was done in a cornfield, it was called an "arhoolie."[4] In both cases, notes were bent or struck slightly off-key or slurred. This "blues slur" comes when the third is flatted to a seventh or emotion is communicated by singing around a note.[5]

The work song and field hollers were of African origin and became an extension of the African tradition. However, it was not until blacks came to the United States that they had a common culture. It was here they had one language—English—rather than a number of tribal languages; and here they were influenced by the British folk songs and their harmonic patterns. Thus the blues arose from the blending of African influences with European folk songs, melodies, and harmonic structures in the American culture. In general, slaves took melody and harmony (only minimally a part of African music) and fused them with rhythm, a central part of African music not deeply embedded in European music.

Although slavery was abolished after the Civil War and the plantations broken up into small farms, the South kept gang labor through penitentiaries. Here, large gangs of men sang work songs as they split rocks, built roads and other public works, and rebuilt the South, which had been devastated by the Civil War. In work songs, the value of singing came from its comfort and solace as well as its efficacy in combining strength for more effective working in rhythm and unison.

In addition to work songs the blues had another source as well, rooted in the leisure activities of Saturday night.[6] The work songs and field songs served a function: they helped men and women get through their work days. But at night, particularly Saturday night, the ballads with the eight- and twelve-bar forms and conventional harmonic progression created another aspect of the blues. This was not the blues of people working; this was the blues of people at leisure.

BLUES ON RECORD

The first commercially successful blues recording was "Crazy Blues," by Mamie Smith, recorded in New York and released in August, 1920. The song was written by Perry "Mule" Bradford, an African American composer, manager, and entrepreneur. Bradford was born in Montgomery, Alabama, in 1895 but moved with his family to Atlanta in 1902, where he grew up in a home next to the Fulton Street Jail, where young Bradford first heard inmates singing the blues.[7]

Bradford entered vaudeville as a singer, dancer, and piano player in Atlanta then went on the road with Allen's New Orleans Minstrels in 1907 and came to New York, where he was involved in staging the musical revue *Made in Harlem*, which featured one of his compositions, "Harlem Blues." The song came from a number he learned in 1912, "Nervous Blues," and he revised the original. The song's melody had been used before; stride pianist James P. Johnson used it in his "Mama and Papa Blues" and part of the melody probably came from "Baby Get That Towel Wet," an old bawdy song played in sporting houses. Mamie Smith had been singing "Harlem Blues" regularly in *Made in Harlem*.

The first blues recording occurred during the early period of the Harlem Renaissance when the New York entertainment industry embraced black entertainers in Harlem, primarily because of Prohibition and the fact that so many "speakeasies" featuring black entertainment were located in Harlem. Bradford approached both Columbia and Victor about recording "Crazy Blues" with a black singer but was turned down.

Fred Hager, manager of OKeh, a small label belonging to the General Phonograph Company, financed by the German firm Carl Lindstrom, agreed to record "Harlem Blues" but insisted the song be sung by Sophie Tucker, a heavy-set Russian immigrant with a powerful voice who broke into show business in the early 1900s in New York.[8] Tucker's voice can be described as "soulful" and "bluesy"; early in her career she had performed "coon songs" in blackface and fit a "Mammy" stereotype. Later, she did away with the blackface but continued to record and popularize African American songs, including "St. Louis Blues" by W. C. Handy, which became the first million-selling blues song through sheet music sales in 1917.

Sophie Tucker could not do the session because of contractual commitments so Mamie Smith, Bradford's original choice, recorded the song. In recording the song, Bradford changed the name from "Harlem Blues" to "Crazy Blues" to avoid any possible copyright litigation by the musical revue backers.

"Crazy Blues" by Mamie Smith reportedly sold 75,000 copies during the first month of its release and during the first year of its release sold over one million copies. Perry Bradford supposedly received almost $20,000 in royalty fees, less than half what he was legally entitled to receive. However, at this time it was extremely difficult to get record labels to pay correct royalty fees, for record companies were the only ones who documented how many records were manufactured and sold.

"Crazy Blues" proved to be an astounding commercial success and led recording companies to look to African American musicians and consumers for future releases. This recording, by an African American singer released nationally, led white music industry executives to become aware of a large market for "race" music, realizing that the Negro population could and would buy recordings of blues singers and blues songs. It was a giant revelation to these white executives, who generally did not understand black music or the black culture—but merely sought to capitalize on it because there was money to be made.

FIRST RECORDINGS BY BLACKS

Although "Crazy Blues" marks the beginning of African American performers successfully recording blues numbers and record companies successfully marketing them to the African American population, this was not the first time the American public had heard blues or the first time that black performers had been recorded.

Thomas Edison's company recorded George W. Johnson, the only African American to record on cylinder; Johnson recorded his "Whistling Coon" minstrel number for the company. The Victor Talking Machine Company recorded comic Bert Williams, believing he would be popular with white audiences and hoping for sales in the African American community as well. Williams recorded fifteen titles for Victor, most of them show tunes or comedy routines from his stage repertoire; "Elder Eatmore's Sermon" sold over half a million units.[9]

The Dinwiddie Colored Quartet, who played authentic African American folk music, was recorded by Victor in 1902. The six songs recorded by the group were all slow spirituals sung a capella. The Fisk Jubilee Singers recorded in 1908, but the next major breakthrough for black recording artists did not occur until 1914 when James Reese Europe's Society Orchestra recorded for Victor as part of the series endorsed by the white dance team the Castles.

Although the major white-owned recording companies did not record many African American artists, they did record songs that were blues-influenced. (Columbia Record Company excluded black performers from recording until 1920; they turned down Bert Williams before the great Black performer recorded for Victor.) These songs were all done by white performers and were advertised as "negro novelty," "Up to date comic songs in negro dialect," "plantation airs," "Ethiopian airs," and, most often, "coon songs."

W. C. Handy

Tin Pan Alley songwriters wrote a number of songs derived from blues and African American folk songs, particularly after W. C. Handy moved from Memphis to New York in 1915. Handy and his partner, Harry Pace, established their own music publishing firms. Other African Americans who came to New York and opened publishing companies included Sheldon Brooks of Mobile, Alabama, Clarence Williams of New Orleans, Perry Bradford of Atlanta, and Bert Williams.

Before 1920, Handy had published his most famous blues compositions, including "Memphis Blues" in 1912, "Jogo Blues" in 1915, "Saint Louis Blues" in 1914, "Yellow Dog Blues" in 1914, "Joe Turner Blues" in 1916, and "Beale Street Blues" in 1917. Handy's success showed Tin Pan Alley the commercial potential for blues songs, and a number of derivative tunes came off the assembly line to satisfy the demand in vaudeville theaters, dance halls, and cabarets. By 1920, a form of the blues had entered mainstream popular music. This form was generally referred to as "vaudeville

Bessie Smith in the 1920s.

Photofest

blues" and was based on commercial, rather than folk, tradition. These used clichéd song formulas in the standardized twelve-bar, AAB stanza format. However, they became popular standards when performed by authentic African American vocalists or transformed by African American composers. Among the vocalists who popularized vaudeville blues were Ma Rainey, Ida Cox, Sara Martin, Alberta Hunter, Sippie Wallace, Mamie Smith, Victoria Spivey, and Bessie Smith. Composers included W. C. Handy, Perry Bradford, James and Rosmond Johnson, Spencer Williams, Porter Grainger, Clarence Williams, and Thomas Dorsey. Most of these composers and performers were connected to the South and traditional black folk music.

BLUES RECORD LABELS

The success of "Crazy Blues" led a number of small labels to record and release blues recordings. "The Jazz Me Blues" and "Everybody's Blues" by Lucille Hegamin were released on the Arto label, Lillian Brown released blues songs on Emerson, and Daisy Martin released sides on Gennett, all in 1921. Additionally, recording companies Perfect, Pathe, Ajax, Vocalion, and Paramount recorded and released blues recordings.

African Americans formed record labels in the 1920s, but success was difficult to achieve. Black Swan was begun by W. C. Handy and Harry Pace in January 1921.[10] They recorded Ethel Waters and Alberta Hunter and had an excellent year in 1921, but in 1924 they were deeply in debt and had to sell their assets to Paramount. The Sunshine label was begun in Los Angeles by two African American record store owners in 1922 and released songs by Roberta Dudley and Ruth Less and a jazz instrumental by Kid Ory's jazz band. This label also folded.

Meritt Records, formed by Winston Holmes in 1925 in Kansas City, lasted three years. Black Patti, begun by "Ink" Williams, the premier black talent scout in Chicago in the 1920s, was formed in 1927 but lasted less than a year. The major problem with Williams's label was that although he had access to the best African American singers and musicians in the business, he could not get his product distributed effectively outside Chicago.

It was difficult for any new label to get a foothold in the industry—and even more so for a black-owned label. However, the small labels did show the majors there was a market for blues recordings to African American consumers, and the major labels began recording traditional blues in earnest around 1926.[11]

FIELD RECORDINGS OF THE BLUES

After the initial recordings by the vaudeville blues singers—a field dominated by women—in New York, recording companies hit the road. During this early period, Paramount recorded more blues than any other label; other labels recording blues in the mid-1920s included OKeh, Columbia, and Victor. In 1926 Vocalion, owned by the Brunswick-Balke-Collender Company of Chicago, emerged as another major "race" label with Jack Kapp as head of the "race" division.

This began the heyday for traditional blues recording, the years 1926–1929, when the major labels did their first extensive field recordings. These labels generally recorded in Dallas, Memphis, Atlanta, and Chicago.

The first major blues artist to emerge from these recordings was Blind Lemon Jefferson, who recorded seventy-five songs for Paramount from 1926 to 1930. He was the best-selling rural bluesman of the 1920s. The songs recorded usually listed him as a writer (thirty-one listed him as composer), and the remainder listed no composer.[12] In reality, a number of these songs came from the folk and oral tradition, and the singer's contribution was one of interpretation, altering existing songs and adding verses.

The success of Blind Lemon Jefferson and other rural blues artists encouraged major labels to head south to conduct field recordings of African American artists. Perhaps the most successful of these field recorders was Ralph Peer, who visited Atlanta in the early twenties for the Okeh label and recorded blues singer Lucille Bogan. Peer then joined Victor and continued his field recordings.

Ralph Peer gave both "hillbilly" and "race" recordings their labels.[13] He named the music "race" because that was the term the influential black-owned newspaper, The *Chicago Defender* used, after a debate about whether the terms "Negroes," "colored," "African," "blacks" or something else should be used. African Americans who referred to themselves as "the race" during this time did so proudly.[14] Ralph Peer eventually recorded a number of well-known blues musicians, including Tommy Johnson, Blind Willie McTell, Furry Lewis, Gus Cannon and His Jug Stompers, and the Memphis Jug Band.

INFLUENTIAL BLUES ARTISTS IN THE 1920S

In 1928 Leroy Carr became famous with his "How Long, How Long Blues." Carr, born in Nashville in 1905 and raised in Indianapolis, became one of the most influential blues singers with his piano–guitar backing (Carr was a pianist and his guitar accompanist was Scrapper Blackwell) and his smooth, pop sounding vocals, a step away from the raw vocal sound of most early blues singers in the South. Carr was so popular and influential that when he died in 1935 there were two songs about his death. Bumble Bee Slim (real name Amos Easton) recorded "The Death of Leroy Carr" for Decca, and Bill Gaither recorded "The Life of Leroy Carr" on Okeh.[15]

Another early influential artist was Tampa Red (real name Hudson Woodbridge), who, with Georgia Tom, recorded "It's Tight Like That" in 1929. Georgia Tom was Thomas Dorsey, who later became the father of black gospel. "Tight Like That" was definitely not a gospel song; it was double-entendre blues. However, the song reportedly sold 750,000 copies and provided Dorsey with his first professional success.[16]

Tampa Red continued to record after Georgia Tom split and had hits with "Somebody's Been Using That Thing" and "It's All Worn Out." Another important blues act before the Depression was Memphis Minnie (Minnie Douglas), who had a hit in 1931 with "Bumble Bee" on Columbia.

After 1930 as the Great Depression grew and spread, the recording labels virtually abandoned blues recordings. The major reason was that the market dried up—blacks could hardly afford the basics of food, clothing, and shelter, much less records.

BLUES DURING THE GREAT DEPRESSION

Radio blossomed during the 1930s, and listeners heard big band and country music as well as comedy, drama, and soap operas; but the blues were not part of the early years of radio's golden age. First, blacks—with few exceptions—were generally barred from radio broadcasts, and even when there wasn't an "official" policy against African Americans on radio, business practices of the day excluded the exposure of music by blacks on radio.

The rate of unemployment for black males has been estimated to be about seventy-five percent during the Great Depression.[17] Because money was difficult to come by, especially for blacks, the record labels, although they continued to record some blues during the Depression, cut back significantly on their recordings and releases. In 1931 Paramount closed down, and Columbia and Brunswick discontinued their "race" series. In 1932 Vocalion discontinued its race series; in 1934 Gennett went bankrupt and OKeh discontinued its race series. Small labels, unable to survive the Depression, were absorbed by large labels until only two major recording labels existed during the early 1930s (Victor and the American Record Company) until they were joined by Decca, which began a race series in 1934 under J. Mayo Williams, who formerly worked for Paramount and Vocalion. For the most part, the major labels concentrated on big band and pop music, both of which were getting regular exposure on the radio and had a proven audience.

BLUES DURING THE 1930S

Although a few blues artists continued to record, the recording labels shifted their emphasis to the big bands, who were heard on radio, and to a limited number of country acts. The entertainment industry as a whole shifted toward movies made in Hollywood and toward radio, which was dominated by the networks.

Chicago emerged as a major source of blues talent during the 1930s, primarily through Lester Melrose, who owned a record store and was a major talent scout for labels who came to Chicago to record blues artists. Melrose generally published the songs these artists recorded and often kept the royalties, but he was an important source of talent as Chicago emerged as a center for blues musicians.

One of the most prolific blues recording artists found by Melrose was Big Bill Broonzy.[18] During the years from 1930 to 1934, Broonzy recorded for a number of labels under a variety of names. Broonzy was born in 1893 in Scott, Mississippi in a family with twenty-one children, sixteen of whom survived. His earliest musical influences included string band music. In 1920 Broonzy moved to Chicago as a manual laborer, where he found a thriving jazz scene. In 1926 Broonzy recorded his first sides for Paramount.

Important blues artists who recorded during the 1930s included Cryin' Sam Collins on Gennett; jazz guitarist Lonnie Johnson, who recorded with Duke Ellington; Louis Armstrong's Hot Five; the Harlem Footwarmers, whose hits included "I Got the Best Jelly Roll in Town" and "Don't Wear It Out"; Robert Brown, known as Washboard Sam, whose hits included "C.C.C. Blues," "Levee Camp Blues," "Diggin' My Potatoes," and "Back Door"; Robert Johnson, called the "Shelley, Keats, and Rimbaud of the blues" who only recorded twenty-nine sides before he was poisoned by a jealous husband when he was only twenty-seven years old and whose songs include "Me and the Devil Blues," "Hellhound on My Trail," "Dust My Broom," "Crossroad Blues," and "Love in Vain"; Roosevelt Sykes, who recorded under a variety of names until 1936 when he became known as "The Honey Dripper" for Decca ("honeydripper" is a blues colloquialism for a virile male); Sonny Boy Williamson, a harmonica bluesman who was murdered at the age of thirty-two; and Speckled Red (Rufus Perryman), a partially blind albino who played boogie woogie piano.

During the 1930s, many blues musicians cut their musical teeth in the lumber, levee, turpentine, and sawmill camps of the South. These camps were set up to harvest the South's rich crop of timber, and lumber companies set up a small "city" where workers were housed until the forests were cleared.

In these encampments, entertainment was provided by traveling musicians, who usually played in a shack set up as a bar. The bar itself was rudimentary—generally two barrels with a board across it: hence the term "barrel house." The music the lumber workers liked was loud, raw and raucous, or "barrel house" piano, which had a driving boogie woogie beat.

The songs often had blatant references to sex that were toned down when the musicians played before mixed audiences or when the songs were recorded. But these lumber camps and barrel houses were proving grounds for a number of black musicians. One musician who worked these lumber and levee camps was Arthur "Big Boy" Crudup. In 1940 Crudup came to Chicago with a gospel group, the Harmonizing Four, and made his first recordings for Bluebird. In 1954 the first record released by Elvis Presley was "That's All Right, Mama," a song Crudup wrote and recorded in 1948.[19]

THE ROOTS OF RHYTHM AND BLUES

In 1942 *Billboard* magazine instituted a chart for black artists, "The Harlem Hit Parade." The first charts were dominated by Decca, who had eight of the top ten records with acts such as the Ink Spots, Lionel Hampton, Lucky

Millinder, Bea Booze, Ella Fitzgerald, and Charlie Barnet. The only "indie" on the charts was Savoy with "Don't Stop Now" by the Bunny Banks Trio.

The most successful black artists on major labels during the World War II years were the Ink Spots, the Mills Brothers, Ella Fitzgerald, Louis Jordan, and Nat King Cole, who all appealed to white audiences with a smooth sound that sounded much like the sound of white groups. The major black artist to emerge during this period was Louis Jordan, whose biggest hits, "G.I. Jive" and "Is You Is, or Is You Ain't (Ma' Baby?)," which reached the pop charts. "Is You Is" was featured in four Hollywood movies.

Louis Jordan, known as "the Father of Rhythm and Blues," was the pivotal figure in the development of rhythm and blues because of his success with record sales, on the radio, and in personal appearances. Jordan demonstrated that a large market existed for black-styled music for both white and black audiences. Jordan began recording for Decca in 1938 and had his first chart hits in 1942: "I'm Gonna Move to the Outskirts of Town" and "What's the Use of Getting Sober?" In 1943 Jordan had hits with "Five Guys Named Moe" and "Radio Blues" and in 1945 had a huge hit with "Caldonia." Also in 1945 Jordan had his biggest hit, "Choo Choo Ch' Boogie," written by Vaughn Horton and country songwriter Denver Darling. Jordan played a happy, fun-loving music with a "jump" band, a pared down big band with horns, bass, and drums.[20]

THE GREAT MIGRATION

During the Great Migration, a period covering roughly from World War I until 1970, more than six-and-a-half million blacks left the rural South and moved to Northern cities. The major migration occurred during the 1940s; in 1940, seventy-seven percent of African Americans lived in the South and forty percent in the rural South; in 1970, about half of all African Americans lived in the South, and less than twenty-five percent lived in rural areas. After 1940 five million blacks moved north, a huge exodus with ramifications that were felt in music and popular culture. Before World War II, most black Americans were strongly tied to agriculture; after World War II, black Americans inhabited cities to such an extent that "urban music" became a euphemism for "black music."[21]

Musically, there was a shift in taste from the rural-based blues to rhythm and blues, a music characterized by the electric guitar in a band that played loud and long in clubs. This music was a product of segregation. Both a black section of town and a white section of town existed, and in the black section were businesses, banks, and clubs owned and operated by blacks. Blacks wanted to hear a music created by and for a black audience playing on their jukeboxes in the numerous establishments. Blacks in the cities were more "worldly" and dismissive of rural blacks who seemed backward;

Blues musician Muddy Waters performs at New York's Palladium Theater in a benefit performance for the New York Public Library in 1977.

AP Photo

young urban blacks dismissed early blues as "field nigger music" and concentrated on rhythm and blues.

The older blues almost died out, except for a few singers and musicians, until the urban folk revival of the late 1950s and early 1960s, when young, white music fans searched for and discovered early "roots" music—folk, hillbilly, and blues. This led to the rediscovery of older blues performers who were then booked on folk and blues festivals. The rediscovery of early blues by British teenagers led to a second blues revival during the British Invasion of the mid-1960s, when some of those

British teenagers became rock stars and popularized many old blues songs and performers.

Another blues revival occurred in 1990 when Columbia issued *The Complete Recordings* of Robert Johnson, the legendary blues artist who died in 1938. During the CD era, when consumers shifted from vinyl and tape to CDs, the major labels issued a string of releases from legendary blues performers such as Bessie Smith and Muddy Waters that sold well to consumers and inspired them to look for more blues releases and to seek out blues performers at festivals and in clubs.

In the twenty-first century the blues is a thriving, though relatively small, genre of the contemporary music industry. Blues "stars" such as Keb'Mo, Robert Cray, Kenny Wayne Shepherd, Joe Bonamass, Buddy Guy, and the granddaddy of current blues performers, B. B. King—as well as white acts such as the late Stevie Ray Vaughn and John Hammond—continue to sell blues recordings.

Twenty-first century blues is rooted in the sounds of the black blues from pre–World War II up to the rock 'n' roll era of the mid-1950s. The music is integrated with both white and black performers, but the essence of the blues, a heavy, sweaty music that wears a smile through hard, tough times, remains intact.

NOTES

1. Paul Oliver, *The Story of the Blues* (Boston: Northeastern University Press, 1998), 7.

2. Samuel Charters, "Workin' on the Building: Roots and Influences," in *Nothing But the Blues: The Music and the Musicians*, ed. Lawrence Cohn (New York: Abbeville Press, 1993), 14; Francis Davis, *The History of The Blues: The Roots, The Music, The People From Charley Patton to Robert Cray* (New York: Hyperion, 1995), 35–36.

3. Oliver, *Story of the Blues*, 7.

4. Ibid., 18.

5. Ibid., 26; Charters, *Workin' on the Building*, 27.

6. Oliver, *Story of the Blues*, 26.

7. William Barlow, "'Fattening Frogs for Snakes': Blues and the Music Industry," *Popular Music and Society* 14, no. 2 (Summer 1990): 18–19; Perry Bradford, *Born With The Blues: Perry Bradford's Own Story* (New York: Oak, 1965).

8. Barlow, *Fattening Frogs for Snakes*, 19.

9. Ibid., 15.

10. Ibid., 21.

11. Ibid., 21–22.

12. Alan Govenar, "Blind Lemon Jefferson: That Black Snake Moan: The Music and Mystery of Blind Lemon Jefferson," in *Bluesland: Portraits of Twelve Major American Blues Masters*, eds. Pete Welding and Toby Byron (New York: Dutton, 1991), 35.

13. Russell Sanjek, *American Popular Music and Its Business: The First Four Hundred Years, Volume III: From 1900 to 1984* (New York: Oxford University Press), 31; Nolan

Porterfield, *Jimmie Rodgers: The Life and Times of America's Blue Yodeler* (Urbana: University of Illinois Press, 1979), 92.

14. Taylor Branch, *Parting The Waters: America in the King Years* (New York: Simon and Schuster, 1988), 45; Barlow, *Fattening Frogs for Snakes*, 11.

15. Mark A. Humphrey, "Holy Blues: The Gospel Tradition," in Cohn, *Nothing But the Blues*, 159–163.

16. Ibid., 163–165.

17. Robert S. McElvaine, *The Great Depression: America 1929–1941* (New York: Times Books, 1984), 187.

18. Davis, *History of the Blues*, 178.

19. David Evans, "Goin' Up The Country: Blues in Texas and the Deep South," in Cohn, *Nothing But the Blues*, 80.

20. Arnold Shaw, *Honkers and Shouters: The Golden Years of Rhythm & Blues* (New York: Macmillan, 1978), 61–65.

21. Nicholas Lemann, *The Promised Land: The Great Black Migration and How It Changed America* (New York: Vintage, 1992), 6.

BLUES RESOURCES

Museums

Beale Street Blues Museum, Memphis, Tennessee
Chicago Blues Museum, Chicago, Illinois
Delta Blues Museum, Clarksdale, Mississippi
Experience Music Museum, Seattle, Washington
Highway 61 Blues Museum, Leland, Mississippi
R&B Museum, Memphis, Tennessee
Rock and Roll Hall of Fame, Cleveland, Ohio
Stax Museum, Memphis, Tennessee
Texas Music Museum, Austin, Texas

Web Sites

http://www.alabamablues.org
http://www.bluesdatabase.com
http://www.bluesland.net
http://www.blues101.org
http://www.bluesrevue.com
http://www.kingsbiscuittime.com/magazine
http://www.livingblues.com
http://musicmoz.org
http://www.nothinbutdablues.com
http://www.realbluesmagazine.com
http://www.texasmusicmuseum.org

Magazines

Big Road Blues
BlueSpeak
Blues Revue
King Biscuit Time
Living Blues
Real Blues
Texas Blues

FURTHER READING

Brooks, Tim. *Lost Sounds: Blacks and the Birth of the Recording Industry 1890–1919.* Urbana: University of Illinois Press, 2004.

Charters, Samuel. *The Roots of the Blues: An African Search.* Boston and London: Marion Boyars, 1981.

Cohn, Lawrence, ed. *Nothing But the Blues: The Music and the Musicians.* New York: Abbeville Press, 1993.

Davis, Francis. *The History of the Blues: The Roots, The Music, The People From Charley Patton to Robert Cray.* New York: Hyperion, 1995.

Dixon, Robert M. W., John Godrich, and Howard Rye. *Blues & Gospel Records 1890–1943.* New York: Oxford University Press, 1997.

Gordon, Robert. *Can't Be Satisfied: The Life and Times of Muddy Waters.* Boston: Little, Brown, 2002.

Lomax, Alan. *The Land Where the Blues Began.* New York: Pantheon, 1993.

Oliver, Paul. *Blues Off the Record: Thirty Years of Blues Commentary.* New York: Hippocrene Books, 1984.

Oliver, Paul. *The Story of the Blues.* Boston: Northeastern University Press, 1998.

Shaw, Arnold. *Honkers and Shouters: The Golden Years of Rhythm & Blues.* New York: Macmillan, 1978.

Welding, Pete and Toby Byron, eds. *Bluesland: Portraits of Twelve Major American Blues Masters.* New York: Dutton/Penguin, 1991.

7

Jazz: An American Art Form

Ronald C. McCurdy

Jazz music, a uniquely American art form, evolved in specific cultural, social, and historical circumstances. Although African Americans were the primary architects of this music, people of all walks of life and various ethnicities have added to the body of work we call jazz. Jazz music directly evolved from the blues, especially in the area of instrumental performances, which are derived from the vocal practices found in the blues. Some of these practices include scooping, sliding, whining, growling, and playing in the upper register. In jazz performance, the artist is just as important as the composer. The intent is for the artist to place a personal "stamp" on each performance. Jazz music is an amalgamation of both European and African performance practices.[1] The harmonic and formal structures of jazz are closely related to that of European styles. For example, the 12-bar blues or the AABA 32-bar structure are symmetrical forms similar to Western art traditions. This kind of formal symmetry does not exist in African genres of music. Many of the harmonic principles found in Western art traditions are also part of the harmonic structures prominent in jazz compositions.

The tonal system in Western art traditions (i.e., intervals of half-steps and whole-steps and major and minor tonalities) are also part of the systems found in jazz composition and performance. The primary difference is that jazz has its own vocabulary, language, nuances, and syntax. It relies heavily on the oral tradition.[2] Even though there is sometimes a written score, the artist is expected to understand and interpret the notation in such a manner as will allow a higher degree of jazz authenticity to exist during the performance. Jazz relies on "call and response" as a means of creating tension and release within the ensemble. One of the most important elements of jazz is improvisation. This is the opportunity for the artist to spontaneously compose melodies while engaged in performance. The artist is expected to improvise in tandem with other musicians. In effect, the artist is engaging in a sort of musical conversation. In many examples, the melodies in jazz serve as a launching pad for the improvisations. Improvisation was the opportunity for musicians to personalize music by making individual statements. A skilled improviser, like a skilled writer, painter, or dancer, is able to create art that resonates with an audience.

It is important to note that jazz did not miraculously appear. Like other genres of music, it evolved from earlier forms of music. As mentioned earlier, jazz is a direct descendent of the blues. As time has passed, the genre of jazz has evolved to become world music. It is not uncommon to travel almost anywhere in the world and hear jazz music or jazz-influenced music. In order to fully understand the evolution of jazz, we must examine the genesis of this music and the circumstances that allowed jazz to be born in America.

AFRICAN TRADITIONS

In order to have a clearer understanding of the origin of jazz, we need to revisit Africa. In examining the functions of music in African society, we will be able to see some of the parallels of how jazz evolved once the slave trade started in the Americas—particularly in North America. Most African slaves were transported to America beginning in 1619 and came primarily from the West Coast of Africa. This region was known as the Ivory Coast, the Gold Coast, and the Slave Coast. Some of the tribes included the Fanti, Ashanti, Ewe, Yoruba, Ibo, and many others.[3] In West Africa, music was a part of everyday life. Music, dance, and poetry were inextricably connected. Everyone sang, danced, and was engaged in poetry. The idea of a separation between audience and performer did not exist. Songs were designed for all segments of society and for various occasions, including hunting, fighting, and harvesting crops. There were songs sung by men, by women, and by children. Songs existed for religious purposes, to celebrate the birth of children, and for marriages and funerals. Music was used for litigation.[4] Professional musicians known as griots recounted the deeds of royalty within each tribe through song and poetry. Because African society depended upon oral tradition, nothing was written down. The griots performed extemporaneously. Usually, these skills were passed from one generation to the next.

If we compare the performance practices of Western art traditions, we see value placed on the idea of authorship or composition, and an emphasis on a finished product rather than on a continuously evolving tradition. The artist is expected to interpret what is written on the musical score without any deviation. There are opportunities for subtle interpretations, but the Western tradition expects the original composition to remain intact. In African traditions, one of the most important aspects of performance practice is the improvisational nature of the performance. This is where we are able to view some of the initial parallels between African and jazz perform-ance practices. As in jazz performance (in both forms), the African musi-cian always personalizes the performance. Regardless of the composer, the performer's task is to tell his or her story, thus making each performance unique.

Another very important aspect of African music is the strong correlation with language. Because most African languages are tonal, whatever can be verbalized can also be played on the drums. A slight alteration in pitch can alter the meaning of certain words. This became one of the major reasons that American slaves were denied access to drums during the colonial period, prompted by fears of their ability to communicate through drum-ming. Slave masters feared insurrections and felt that the less communica-tion among slaves, the better.

As we further examine the instruments employed in Africa, we can once again draw parallels between African instruments and how some evolved into equipment used by modern jazz musicians. Four primary categories of African instruments existed: membranophones (drums made of animal skin), idiophones (bells, shakers, rattles), aerophones (wind instruments, elephant tusks), and chordophones (string instruments).[5] All these instru-ments helped Africans to communicate musically. Perhaps the most impor-tant ingredient of this music is its rhythmic complexity, known as polyrhythms, or the layering of two or more rhythms to create what is known as syncopation (the deliberate interruption of the rhythmic pulse). A per-fect modern-day example is rap or hip-hop music. Without syncopation, the music of Kanye West, P-Diddy, or 50 Cent could not exist. Again, we are able to observe some musical parallels as we move toward the beginnings of jazz.

AFRICANS AND THE PRE–CIVIL WAR PERIOD

The pre–Civil War period was a critical time for the development of African music in America. We know that slavery was nothing new to the Americas—slaves were brought to the West Indies and South America. The transportation of slaves from West Africa to the Americas begs the question why jazz developed in the United States instead of in other regions of the world? What unique feature of the experiences in the United States allowed jazz to develop?

For years scholars have attempted to answer this question. Perhaps the most compelling explanation came from author Ernest Borneman, who explains a dichotomy in the transformation process of African music in the new world. Borneman states that during the fifteenth century, Britain had no slavery and no understanding of the Greek or Roman concepts of slav-ery. During the sixteenth century, the Mediterranean people had a place in their society for slavery, but the British had none. Spanish and

Portuguese slave owners assumed that slavery only affected the body of the slave—not the mind. The British, on the other hand, found slavery morally indefensible and thus decided that slaves must be inferior and subhuman. Borneman contends that the dynamics of slavery under Spanish control demanded less drastic changes, thus allowing slaves to continue many of their tribal customs, including music. British control, which dehumanized the African slave, made change and the need for code languages necessary, creating an opportunity for jazz music to manifest itself.[6]

One of the early manifestations of this code language was the spiritual. Several religious groups took a special interest in saving the souls of the African slaves and Native Americans. Such groups as the Catholics, Moravians, Quakers, and Methodists attempted to convert slaves to Christianity. Slaves embraced the notion of Christianity largely because they could relate to many of the stories from the Old Testament of the Bible, particularly those that spoke of Moses fleeing Pharaoh's army. They saw themselves in a similar oppressed predicament. As part of this religious conversion came the Spiritual, which had a dual function: (1) praising God and (2) planning for escapes from the harsh brutality of the plantation.

Spirituals were part of a larger genre known as Slave songs. These songs are considered folk music, indicating their lack of designated composers. These Slave songs were at times religious and at others secular. One of the most important performance practices in spirituals was the element of improvisation, which made each performance different.

A very charismatic preacher named Rev. Richard Allen (founder of the African Methodist Episcopal Church) was able to improvise and create spirituals extemporaneously. Rev. Allen also created what were called wandering refrains, allowing members of his congregation to improvise certain aspects of the performance.[7] In many ways, these techniques were precursors to jazz performance.

On the secular side, slaves spent part of their leisure time dancing. This is important because jazz's most popular period saw a strong connection between music and dance. Because drumming was outlawed, particularly in southern states, the slaves compensated by creating rhythms through hand clapping and foot stomping. However, one location in New Orleans, called Place Congo Square, allowed slaves to drum and dance, assembling and practicing their traditional dances, singing and playing their percussion instruments. This practice continued until the Civil War.[8]

RAGTIME AND BLUES: PRECURSORS OF JAZZ

Toward the end of the nineteenth century a new piano style began to emerge: ragtime. It evolved from songs, dances, and marches brought to America by European immigrants.[9] In 1897, Thomas Turpin published

Harlem Rag, the first rag published by an African American. This was a major event, one of the first times an African American composer actually notated his compositions, originally intended for dancing and entertainment, allowing them to later evolve into occasions for listening.[10] Although Scott Joplin is credited as the father of ragtime, others played this music before Joplin published "Maple Leaf Rag" in 1899. Joplin's compositions were known as "classic ragtime."

This is one of the first examples of the fusing of African American elements and European forms and techniques. Piano rag is a multisectional form usually consisting of sixteen measures in each section, called "strains" or "themes." Some of the most common forms were ABAC, ABACB, and ABCD (each letter denotes a section or theme).[11] The score was to be performed as written but did, however, employ the syncopated rhythms that would later be associated with jazz.

One of the most prominent ragtime pianists of the early twentieth century was the self-proclaimed inventor of jazz, Ferdinand Morton (better known as Jelly Roll Morton). Morton and his band, the Red Hot Peppers, helped to shift the ragtime style closer to a contemporary jazz style by making improvisation a major part of their performance practice. Unlike the rigid and exactingly composed rags of Joplin, Morton often improvised sections of his rags.

ADDITIONAL PIANO STYLES/STRIDE PIANO

One of the piano styles that was a continuation of ragtime was known as stride piano. This style was played primarily by a group of New York (Harlem)–based pianists. Some of the most notable pianists, or "ticklers," were James P. Johnson, Willie "The Lion" Smith, Eubie Blake, and, later, Fats Waller, Art Tatum, Duke Ellington, and Count Basie. Stride piano evolved effortlessly from a group of East Coast ragtime piano players.[12]

The main characteristic of stride piano is its "oom-pah" sound. The left hand plays a single note in the lower register of the piano on the first and third beats (the "oom"). The chords are played in the middle register on beats two and four, also by the left hand. The left hand functions much as it does in ragtime, but from the right hand greater virtuosity is expected, playing looser melodic figures. The stride pianists were able to play long variations on popular tunes of the day, as well as original compositions.

RENT PARTIES

One early practice in Harlem that provided performance venues for stride pianists, in addition to bars and sporting houses (brothels), was an event called a rent party. These were gatherings at the apartments of individuals having challenges paying their monthly rent. The tenant invited a pianist and charged admission, earning enough money to pay the rent for the month. Often, two or more pianists would attend and engage in a "cutting" contest, a friendly competition to judge the best player in the group.

James P. Johnson seldom, if ever, lost a cutting contest. Johnson recorded "Carolina Shout" in 1921, one of the most influential recordings for the next generation of young piano players, most notably Duke Ellington, who first learned to play "Carolina Shout" note for note from the first version recorded on a piano roll by Johnson in 1918. Similarly, Thomas "Fats" Waller also learned "Carolina Shout" and even had the courage to perform this composition for Johnson upon their first meeting. Waller would become one of Johnson's most prized protégés. Beyond his clowning and showmanship, he was a flawless technician and prolific composer, author of such hits as "Ain't Misbehavin'," "Honeysuckle Rose," and "Jitterbug Waltz."

Johnson too, had his share of well-known classics. His most popular composition was "The Charleston," which helped create a dance craze that swept the country. Johnson devoted much of his time to composing works in the classical genre as well (his composition "Yamekraw" premiered at Carnegie Hall in 1928). Despite his versatility as a composer and pianist, Johnson continues to be known as the Father of Stride.[13]

BOOGIE-WOOGIE

The next piano style to emerge had elements of both ragtime and stride piano. This style was known as boogie-woogie and was characterized by an ostinato (repeated) pattern in the left hand accompanied by melodic figures played in the right. Clarence "Pine Top" Smith is credited as the innovator of this style. Boogie-woogie was usually part of the arsenal of gifted piano players, but was seldom the only style played by any pianist. Smith recorded only twice, but his version of "Pine Top's Boogie Woogie" became part of the standard jazz repertoire.[14] Many well-known jazz pianists employed this style at one time or another. Count Basie, Fats Waller, and Mary Lou Williams are a few who made this part of their performance. Other boogie-woogie piano players included Jimmy Yancey, Meade Lux Lewis, Cripple Clarence Loften, and Albert Ammons. This style continued during the rock 'n' roll period, played such artists as Fats Domino and Little Richard.

BEBOP PIANO

Piano playing changed dramatically during the bebop era (*c.* 1945–1955). Few of the elements of ragtime, stride, and boogie-woogie existed in this new style. Basie and Earl "Fatha" Hines had begun to initiate the transition of the formerly rigid left hand into a new role known as "comping" (accompanying).

It is important to note that the previous styles had seen the piano functioning as a solo instrument filling the role of an entire orchestra. This new style, however, usually saw the piano played within the context of a rhythm section (combining piano, bass, and drums). The role once executed by the left hand in ragtime, stride, and boogie-woogie was now played by the bass. The driving rhythms were now provided by the drums. Tad Dameron, Thelonious Monk, and Bud Powell were the three innovators of the bebop style—Powell developed a style allowing the right hand to engage in long scale-like improvisations as the left hand continued to comp.[15]

THE BLUES

While ragtime was in vogue, blues was also developing in America. Blues emerged from spirituals, work songs, and field hollers, which were sung as solos, sometimes accompanied and sometimes not. Although this blues style was being performed by bluesmen all throughout the South, W. C. Handy is credited as the father of the blues, because he was among the first to notate his compositions.

Handy's "Memphis Blues," published in September 23, 1912, created a large market for this style of music as well as awareness that the traditions of the blues were well intact.[16] This was the first time that the music had had a commercial aspect. The early bluesmen performed in the same manner as those who had been enslaved fifty years earlier, singing for the personal gratification. No monetary compensation was attached to their performance prior to the publishing of the compositions of Handy and others of the era.

One such artist was Huddie Ledbetter (1885?–1949), known as "Leadbelly." Leadbelly spent most of his life in and out of prison. In 1918, he served a thirty-five-year sentence in Texas's Sugar Land Penitentiary, for murder. He was able to forge a kind of friendship with the warden and later the governor. While in prison, Leadbelly constantly sang songs that resonated with his fellow inmates and prison guards. He was often given the opportunity to provide music (work songs) as the other prisoners engaged in physical labor. His music was so well received that the governor shortened his sentence, releasing him from prison in 1925. He found himself back in prison in 1932, this time in Louisiana's Angola State Penitentiary, for attempted murder. Leadbelly was introduced to the folklorists John and Alan Lomax, who visited prisons looking for folk songs. Lomax was able to intercede on Leadbelly's behalf and in 1934 was once again released from prison. Lomax served as a kind of manager for Leadbelly, arranging concerts for him. Leadbelly toured with Woody Guthrie, Josh White, and Big Bill Broonzy and served as a musical influence to a series of younger bluesman, including Blind Lemon Jefferson.

Leadbelly, who seemed to always find trouble, returned to prison on at least two more occasions. Once released, he resumed his concert schedule.

Huddie William Ledbetter, aka Leadbelly, circa 1930s.

Photofest

Although a series of serendipitous circumstances allowed Leadbelly to parlay his musical talents into commerce, the important point is that Leadbelly initially performed for himself, for personal gratification. Potential for income was not the original reason he initially sang.[17]

COUNTRY/RURAL BLUES SINGERS

One of the most creative blues artists of the early twentieth century was Robert Johnson. The contributions of Robert Johnson were extremely important because of the influences he would have on the development of what would become jazz. The first country blues singers were men who were itinerant musicians from the South and Southwest.[18] Johnson and many of his contemporaries were similar to the African griots: storytellers. They sang about the challenges of their era: relationships, chain gangs, oppression. Not all their songs were negative; some told of good times and the lighter moments of life. Many of the songs were composed spontaneously.

Distinct differences emanated from various locations of the country. Texas Blues, Blues of the Mississippi Delta, and Blues of the Carolina Piedmont all had different qualities, but their common denominator is that they all reflected black culture from the late nineteenth and early twentieth centuries.[19]

The 12-bar blues form was established during this period, later becoming a very important formula practiced by all subsequent jazz bands. The same 12-bar blues performed by Johnson can be heard by such musicians as Duke Ellington, Count Basie, Chick Webb, and Jimmy Lunceford even up to modern times (such as by Wynton Marsalis and the Lincoln Center Jazz Orchestra). The 12-bar blues was not limited to only jazz bands. This formula also found its way into the Rhythm and Blues styles of the 1950s. The music of Little Richard, Fats Domino, and many others relied heavily on the blues progression that Robert Johnson helped to create.

One of the most well known compositions by Robert Johnson is "Hellhound on my Trail." This composition, and others by Johnson, helped to transform the blues into an art form. The vocal lyrics help us better understand the form of the blues. The melodic and textural structure uses AAB.[20] Notice how the lyric is repeated by both A sections, with the "punch-line" representing B:

"Hellhound on my Trail"
I got to keep movin', Blues fallin' down like hail.
I got to keep movin', Blues fallin' down like hail.
I can't keep no money, with a hellhound on my trail

URBAN/CLASSIC BLUES SINGERS

This style of blues was dominated by women. The earliest documented recording was made by Mamie Smith in 1920. Smith recorded "Crazy Blues" and "It's Right Here for You." This landmark recording set the stage for additional recordings when the financial potential of catering to a black demographic became apparent.

In 1921, the OKeh Record label was formed, beginning a phenomenon known as race records. Clarence Williams, a music director, was dispatched to seek and record the best black talent available. Later that year, Louis

their short time together. Chick passed away by 1939, and his band was renamed Ella Fitzgerald and her Famous Band. Ella's range, flexibility, and clarity have been the standard by which all other jazz vocalists have been measured. In this area, she has no peers. Ella's improvisations were as fluent and inventive as any instrumentalist's. She had tremendous instincts for melody, phrasing, and harmony and recorded for the Decca label for 22 years.[25]

In 1938, Ella recorded "A Tisket, A Tasket," which proved to be a huge hit for her. In the mid-1940s, she met Norman Grantz, who created the Jazz at the Philharmonic concerts. These concerts led to a series of recordings that paid homage to American songwriters who included George Gershwin, Cole Porter, Jerome Kern, Hoagy Carmichael, and Duke Ellington.

In 1986, Ella underwent quadruple bypass heart surgery. During the surgery, it was discovered that she was diabetic, something that led to Ella's poor eyesight. Because of her poor circulation, both her legs had to be amputated below the knees. On June 15, 1996, Ella passed away. She had made over 200 recordings and had appeared in Carnegie Hall more than twenty-five times, leaving behind her a body of work that will probably never be surpassed.

EARLY NEW ORLEANS JAZZ

New Orleans was one of the most culturally diverse and complex cities in North America during the colonial period. It was a major port of entry for goods and materials, fueling the economy at that time. The city was founded in 1718 as part of the French colony. In 1763, Spain took control, and by 1803, France was owner of the territory once more. Later that year, France sold the colony to the United States in what was called the Louisiana Purchase.

The dynamic in New Orleans was quite different from the rest of the country. Central to New Orleans was the Creole culture, which was Catholic and French-speaking. The entire region was much more liberal when it came to accepting a variety of cultures blended together. In addition, European influences were joined by a strong West African presence.

By the eighteenth century, people of African descent (both free and enslaved), made up half of the city's population. There were individuals from the West Indies and the Caribbean Islands. As the numbers of black Americans increased in New Orleans, so did the variety of music. Blacks brought with them their blues, religious music, and dances to add to the mix of an already vibrant musical culture in New Orleans. One very important part of the culture was the emergence of a segment of the population known as Creoles of color, people of mixed African and European blood. Most were educated and very astute in business and many were formally

Louis "Satchmo" Armstrong.

Photofest

trained musically, performing in some of the best professional orchestras in New Orleans.

An example of New Orleans's influence on jazz and ragtime is evidenced by the use of syncopation in early New Orleans brass bands. Marching bands became a big part of the culture as a result of the military bands. Blacks begin to form their own brass bands, which participated in a variety of community activities, including funerals and Mardi Gras celebrations.[26] The "front line" in the brass band consisted of the trumpet, trombone, and clarinet. The trumpet usually played the melody and the trombone and clarinet the countermelody. The "back line" consisted of the banjo, drums, basses, and guitar, functioning as the rhythm section.[27] Collective improvisation became a main characteristic of the performance and created a polyrhythmic effect in which all the "front line" instruments played simultaneously, a practice that disappeared over time in trends toward more modern jazz styles.

Early in the twentieth century, New Orleans had become a major sea and river port and was active in the entertainment area as well. All kinds of theaters and vaudeville acts made the city their home, and the music publishing business was also thriving. Illegitimate businesses were found in the red-light district near Canal and Rampart Street. The shores of Lake Ponchartrain were a site where bands competed for audiences at amusement parks and resorts; there were always opportunities for dancing.

A more "earthy" style of dancing became popular in New Orleans in dances done mostly by blacks. Toward the end of the nineteenth century, musicians who could not read music begin playing more improvisational music for dances and other occasions. One of the best-known cornet players who began to incorporate improvisation into his music was Charles "Buddy" Bolden. Bolden proved to be a transitional figure as jazz grew in popularity and other musicians began imitating some of his techniques.[28]

Segregation laws were passed to retaliate against Reconstruction in the 1890s, increasing the amount of discrimination against anyone of African ancestry in New Orleans. That discrimination was extended to Creoles of color as well. Any previous accommodations they had enjoyed were no longer an option.

In many ways, this collective discrimination against anyone with black blood ultimately strengthened the musical bond between the Creoles of color and blacks. Because of this bond, blacks were now privy to the kind of formal training that many of the Creoles of Color had enjoyed for years. This proved a means for improving the overall musicality of blacks. Several major artists developed their skills while growing up in New Orleans. During the first decade of the twentieth century, trumpeter Freddie Keppard was the featured soloist with the Original Creole Orchestra.

An all-white group of musicians who called themselves the Original Dixieland Jazz Band recorded the first commercially successful jazz recording in 1917.[29] The "Livery Stable Blues," which Nick La Rocca claimed to have composed, was more a novelty composition than an actual jazz composition. The trumpet and clarinet imitated barnyard animal sounds, which generated tremendous enthusiasm from the public. Very soon, the Original Dixieland Jazz Band was touring the world playing their brand of jazz.[30]

The popularity jazz was now receiving provided opportunities for several black artists to leave New Orleans to tour nationally and internationally. The list of very innovative artists who hailed from New Orleans included clarinetists Sidney Bechet and Johnny Dodds, drummer Baby Dodds, trombonist Edward "Kid" Ory, and cornetist Joe "King" Oliver.

Perhaps the most innovative jazz figure of the first two decades of the twentieth century was Louis Armstrong. Armstrong grew up poor in New Orleans. His mother was a part-time prostitute, and he never had much of a relationship with his father. As a young boy, Armstrong was sent to the Waifs Home for Boys for allegedly shooting a gun in public. While in reform school, he was given his first music lessons. After a year, he was released and began doing odd jobs around New Orleans. King Oliver befriended Armstrong and helped develop his skills as a trumpeter.

Armstrong later joined King Oliver and his Creole Band. The band included Honore Dutrey on trombone, Lil Harding on piano, Bill Johnson on banjo, Baby Dodds on drums, Johnny Dodds on clarinet, and King Oliver on cornet. Upon the closing of Storyville in 1917, many jazz artists began to tour nationally and internationally. Oliver moved to Chicago and summoned Louis Armstrong in 1922. This stint with Oliver's band lasted until 1924. Armstrong teamed with Lil Harding (whom Armstrong married in 1925) to form two major bands that would establish Armstrong's legacy as a jazz artist. The bands were known as the Hot Five and Hot Seven (1925–1928) and were commercially successful and popular. These bands were the best example of New Orleans–style performance. Johnny Dodds, on clarinet, was in a class by himself, and Kid Ory was a superb technician as well.

Armstrong was able to transform the way jazz was performed and extended the range of the trumpet. Armstrong was innovative with a technique known as "scat singing," an improvisation technique that used nonsense syllables. This would be a technique that jazz vocalists such as Ella Fitzgerald, Sarah Vaughan, Joe Williams, Mel Torme, and many others would embrace.[31] "West End Blues" is an example of Armstrong's brilliance as a trumpet player. The introduction, by Armstrong, one of the classic trumpet solos in jazz history, demonstrates Armstrong's extensive range and flexibility. The brass bands suggested the beginnings of an ensemble sound that would begin in the 1920s with the big bands. Bandleaders such as Fletcher Henderson, Duke Ellington, Jimmy Lunceford, Chick Webb, and many others furthered the concept of ensemble playing in an era known as the Swing Era.

THE SWING ERA (ca. 1930–1945)

The collapse of the stock market in 1929 did not have an immediate affect on jazz in America. Eventually, bands that had worked regularly found themselves out of work; but America was moving toward another style of music that involved dancing. The Roseland Ballroom and Savoy Ballroom were two major venues where literally thousands of young people could be found on any given night dancing to the big band sounds of the period. The Swing Era was the most popular period in jazz's history. In short, jazz was the pop music of its era. There were more people dancing and listening to jazz on the radio than ever before—or since.

The ensembles grew from quintets and septets to what were called "big bands," consisting of fifteen to twenty pieces in some instances. These ensembles generally consisted of three to five saxophones, three or four trumpets, and three or four trombones, as well as a rhythm section composed of a piano, a string bass, drums, and a guitar. The clarinet and tuba, once part of New Orleans ensembles, were replaced by the saxophone and acoustic bass, respectively. Because of the number of musicians who were now receiving formal education in music, the level of technical proficiency improved exponentially. The tempos became much faster, and the tone quality and pitch accuracy also improved. Instead of improvising freely through many of the New Orleans compositions, the Swing Era presented full elaborate arrangements as the standard.

One very important figure who helped to establish the configuration of what would be known as the big bands was Fletcher Henderson. He and his co-arranger Don Redman organized the big band, establishing the independence of each section within the band (i.e., saxophone, trumpet, trombone, and rhythm sections). This set the standard that big bands would emulate throughout jazz history in a configuration that continues even today.[32] White bandleaders such as Guy Lombardo and Paul Whiteman presented a combination of popular songs and quasi-classical works before the public.[33]

The most popular white leader of a big band was Benny Goodman, who was known as the "King of Swing." Goodman was part of the Austin High Gang, a group of young high school students who took a special interest in jazz. That group included Gene Krupa, Jimmy McPartland, Frank Teschmacher, Bud Freeman, Dave Tough, and Muggsy Spanier.[34] Goodman had a long and successful career as a jazz clarinetist. (In addition to being an exceptional jazzist, he also played classical music.)

In 1938, Goodman took his integrated band to perform in Carnegie Hall. This was a historic event, for America was still very much a segregated society. The band members were Lionel Hampton on vibraphone, Teddy Wilson on piano, and Gene Krupa on drums. In 1935, Goodman was leading his own band, playing several arrangements by Fletcher Henderson that helped propel his commercial success. He also was able to infuse black musical sensibilities into a white big band. The jazz impresario John Hammond was now backing Goodman's band, which led to appearances on NBC's three-hour program, "Let's Dance." That same year, Goodman enjoyed success performing at the Palomar Ballroom in Los Angeles.

As mentioned, the Swing Era was the most popular time in history for jazz music. Jazz was the pop music of the day in the 1930s. Black bands also benefited from dance music's surge in popularity, and several black bands enjoyed success. Fletcher Henderson, Don Redman, Chick Webb, Benny Moten, and Jimmy Lunceford were among some of the more successful black bandleaders of the day. Sy Oliver served as the principle arranger for Lunceford's band; he, like Henderson and Redman, possessed a formally trained approach for arrangement and composition that made his arrangements very sophisticated and well received by audiences all over the country. The driving four-beat rhythm, the fast, danceable tempos, and the strong ensemble shout choruses were the hallmark of what made the swing era big bands so exciting.

Two of the most popular and most successful swing bands were the Count Basie and Duke Ellington Orchestras. Both bandleaders lived long, fruitful lives and made significant contributions to the body of literature in the band genre. They both had careers that lasted more than fifty years. Each band had its own distinctive sound and style—both resonated with the jazz listeners and dancers.

William Basie (1904–1984) was born in Redbank, NJ. He studied piano from his mother and from a German lady named Holloway. Basie initially wanted to be a drummer but early on found the piano and organ his instruments of choice. When Basie finally got to Harlem, he heard pianist Fats Waller. They became fast friends, and Waller showed Basie the stride piano style and how to "swing." A stint at the Roseland Ballroom, arranged by John Hammond, helped launch Basie's popularity. It was around this time that his band was known as the Big Swing Machine. In 1937, Basie assembled for his first recording some of the top jazzmen of the day. Among the many vocalists who sang with Basie's band, vocalist Jimmy Rushing, also known as "Mr. Five by Five" because of his girth, was one of the most distinctive voices ever to perform with the Basie Orchestra.[35]

Count Basie and his band, circa 1940s.

Photofest

The Basie band evolved over the years and employed some of the most noted musicians in the country. Basie developed and launched the careers of many future jazz stars. Coleman Hawkins, Lester Young, Marshall Royal, Ernie Wilkins, Ben Webster, Chu Berry, Don Byas, Buddy Tate, Frank Foster, and Frank Wess were among some of the noted saxophone players. Some of the brass players included Buck Clayton, Oran "Hot Lips" Page, Harry "Sweets" Edison, Clark Terry, Thad Jones, Dickey Wells, J. J. Johnson, and Benny Morton. The rhythm sections included such names as Jo Jones, Walter Page, and Freddie Green. Even though Basie passed away in 1984, the Basie band continues even today, and the same musical concepts still exist.

One of the stylistic characteristics of the Basie band was known as a riff style, in which a two-measure musical motive becomes the melodic material for a composition. Many of the compositions were steeped in the 12-bar blues progression. One of the most well-known compositions to employ the riff style is "One O'Clock Jump." Other compositions that exemplify Basie's driving style include "'Doggin' Around," "Taxi War Dance," and "Lester Leaps In," three recordings featuring Lester Young.[36]

Count Basie led his band for more than forty years. Around 1950, Basie discovered that he was the victim of poor management. His managers were profiting from Basie's talents but thrusting him into more debt and into troubles with the IRS. From that moment on, Basie made attempts to take control of his financial destiny. He began to make better choices in his hires for his band, and he gave up alcohol and cigarettes in 1960. He suffered a heart attack in 1977 and was diagnosed with spinal arthritis and confined to a wheelchair. Basie continued to perform and travel with his band until he was hospitalized in 1984, soon after passing away, on April 26, 1984.

The other major big bandleader of the swing era was Edward Kennedy "Duke" Ellington (1899–1974). Ellington was born into a middle-class family in Washington, D.C., on April 19, 1899. Ellington grew up in a household maintained by his mother while his father was a butler for a wealthy Washington family. The family in which Edward and his younger sister grew up was a religious one.

Even as a child, Ellington carried himself with a certain degree of confidence that caused one family member to call him Duke. The name stuck, and he kept it throughout his life. Ellington's first love as a child was baseball, but his mother decided that piano lessons would be a good idea. Like many kids, Ellington resisted and was less than studious when it came to preparing for his lessons. As Ellington entered his teens, he heard a pianist named Harvey Brooks who introduced Ellington to the music of James P. Johnson. Ellington learned to play Johnson's "Carolina Shout."[37] When Ellington also realized that the piano was somewhat of a magnet for girls, he became even more serious about honing his craft. He began playing for school dances and other occasions around Washington, D.C. Even at a young age, Ellington demonstrated a keen eye for business. Another one of Ellington's talents was painting and drawing: instead of paying a manager to book his gigs, he began booking himself and painting signs advertising his own performances and availability.

After a few failed attempts to relocate to New York beginning in 1922, Ellington finally returned to New York in 1926 with a four-year performance stint at the Kentucky Club. Some of Ellington's early sidemen included Sonny Greer on drums, Otto Hardwick on saxophone, Arthur Whetsol on trumpet, and Elmer Snowden on guitar. It was during the Kentucky Club engagement that Ellington met a young impresario named Irvin Mills.

Mills became Ellington's manager. Mills (who was white) was able to book Ellington's band into venues to which most other black bands were denied access. Ellington's band was listed on various record labels as Duke Ellington (Victor), The Jungle Band (Brunswick), and the Washingtonians (Harmony).[38] In 1927, Mills was able to broker a deal to have the Ellington Band perform at the Cotton Club. On December 24, 1927, Ellington opened for what would be a nearly five-year engagement at the Cotton Club.

Duke Ellington (seated) and members of his famous Ellington Orchestra.

Photofest

This arrangement was to last from 1927–1932. During the Cotton Club engagement, Ellington and his musicians served as the house band for the club. The band's duties included backing up singers, tap dancers, and chorus girls. The Cotton Club was a venue operated by gangster Owney Madden during Prohibition. All the musicians and other entertainers were black. The dancing girls, although black, were required to pass the "brown paper bag test": if their hue was darker than a brown paper bag, they were not allowed to dance at the Cotton Club, all of whose patrons were white.

One of the trademark sounds of the band was the growling trumpet. Bubba Miley was one of the first to fill that role, adding to one of the billings that advertised Duke Ellington and His Jungle Band. Later, the growling trombone sound was added by "Tricky" Sam Nanton. When Miley left the band, he was replaced by Cootie Williams. Other notable artists who were part of Ellington's band included Johnny Hodges, Harry Carney, and Barney Bigard on saxophone; Juan Tizol and Lawrence Brown on trombone; Arthur Whetsol, Freddie Jenkins, and Cootie Williams on trumpets; Freddie Guy on guitar; Wellman Braud on bass; and Sonny Greer on drums. Ellington was no ordinary band leader. This nearly five-year stint in the Cotton Club proved a valuable time in Ellington's musical growth. The shows at the Cotton Club were broadcast nightly over radio in homes all across America. He also recorded several records, and the band had obtained national and international acclaim.

When Ellington's tenure at the Cotton Club ended in 1931, he was ready to move forward with more recordings and embark upon an international tour. Throughout Ellington's long career, he would be the recipient of many awards and honors. In 1969, toward the end of his life, he would be invited to perform at the White House for President Nixon. During the time spent at the Cotton Club, Ellington amassed a repertoire that allowed him to play for a variety of engagements. One composition in his repertoire became the mantra of many of the big bands. The song featured Ivie Anderson on "It Don't Mean a Thing, If It Ain't Got That Swing." One of the most distinctive aspects of Ellington's band is that he composed music to fit the abilities of his personnel.

One of Ellington's long-time collaborators was a diminutive man by the name of Billy Strayhorn. Strayhorn, hired in 1939, also played piano and once aspired to become a concert pianist. But the social climate of the time made being a concert pianist simply not an option for Strayhorn. A man of seemingly small ego, Strayhorn was content to remain in the shadows of Ellington. "Sweet Pea," as he was called by Ellington, composed many of the band's hits, including what would become one of Ellington's theme songs, "Take the A Train." Strayhorn was someone of impeccable talents. He composed the haunting ballad "Lush Life" when he was sixteen years old. Other compositions include "Chelsea Bridge" and "Upper Manhattan

Medical Group (UMMG)". Strayhorn remained with Ellington for the remainder of his life, up to his death in 1967.[39]

Ellington maintained a working band for nearly fifty years. At a time when America's musical tastes were shifting and all kinds of social change abounded, he managed to reinvent himself and keep his band on its feet. Over that half-century, some of the most celebrated jazz musicians were part of his band. Members included Clark Terry and Ray Nance on trumpet, Louie Bellson and Sam Wooodyard on drums, Ben Webster and Paul Gonsalves on tenor saxophones, Oscar Pettiford on bass, and Jimmy Hamilton on clarinet and saxophone. Ellington composed over three thousand compositions that ranged from dance pieces, suites, and sacred music to music for television, as well as a host of other self-commissioned works.

Ellington was a tireless composer who viewed all of his compositions as works in progress. No composer since Ellington has been able to escape the influence he exerted on the development of the big band. Even while Ellington was hospitalized, only weeks before he passed away, he requested that a piano and manuscript paper be brought to his room so that he could continue to work. He worked until his death on May 24, 1974.

BEBOP AND BEYOND

The bombing of Pearl Harbor on December 7, 1941, changed life in America drastically, summoning America into the World War II. It became difficult for musicians to travel, and younger musicians were becoming tired of playing the same arrangements in the big bands each night. The second generation of jazz musicians wanted to push the creative envelope. The style they created was called bebop. Charlie Parker, John Birks, Dizzy Gillespie, Thelonious Monk, and Bud Powell were among the young lions who were pushing music forward. It was common for the musicians to meet after work at jam sessions that served as laboratories in which to incubate this new music.

Bebop-style music was quite different from big-band. Ensembles shrank from eighteen pieces to quartets and quintets, and the tempos of the compositions sped up. Harmonies became more complex and melodies more difficult to sing. The young musicians who had played in big bands for audiences who expected to hear the same arrangements (in some cases the same solos) each night were now playing for themselves. In short, jazz was becoming a connoisseur's art—which meant that jazz audiences suddenly decreased in size and appreciation. Dancing, which had been a huge part of the swing era, was prohibited by many jazz clubs. This virtuoso music in many ways was a social commentary on the disdain the musicians had for having to play music for dancing. The intent of the bebop era was to raise the artistic standards of jazz musicians.[40] Minton's Playhouse (an after-hours joint in Harlem) became one of the favorite spots for the emerging music. Such tunes as "Thriving on a Riff," "Groovin' High," and "Hot House" became standard tunes associated with the bebop era. The musicians enjoyed playing the popular tunes of the day, written by some of American's most gifted composers, including Jerome Kern, Cole Porter, and George Gershwin. In almost all examples, the musicians phrased the songs differently from the originals, even composing alternate melodies over the chord progression, as when, for example, Kern's "All the Things You Are" became "Prince Albert." This technique is called a contrafact.[41] Gershwin's music was some of the more popular embraced by jazz musicians. The chord progression for "I Got Rhythm" became a standard for jazz musicians; hundreds of compositions were written that embraced its chord progression, "Moose the Mooch," "Shaw Nuff," and "Thriving on a Riff" among them.

COOL JAZZ

Early in the 1950s yet another style emerged, called cool jazz. Miles Davis, Lennie Tristano, and Stan Getz are three musicians credited with creating this new sound in jazz, considered less abrasive and more accessible to the general public.[42] Although dancing was not associated with this style, it seemed more inclusive to a lay audience than bebop with its slower tempos, simpler harmonies, and less fiery improvisations (though just as virtuosic).

Third Stream

A byproduct of cool jazz was a style called third stream. The term was coined by composer and conductor Gunther Schuller. The style represented the fusion of classical music and jazz elements; ensembles were enlarged to include woodwinds (such as flutes and clarinets) and French horns. Charles Mingus and Teo Marcero were two of the most successful jazzists to incorporate this new style.[43]

WEST COAST JAZZ

In the 1950s, a style known as west coast jazz became popular. It resembled the Capital recording sessions of Miles Davis, which included smaller ensembles—a complete trumpet or trombone section was trimmed to one trumpet and one trombone.[44] Some of the more successful west coast jazz musicians included Gerry Mulligan and Chet Baker. Dave Brubeck also had tremendous success, especially on college campuses, with such hits as "Take Five" and "Blue Rondo Ala Turk."

HARD BOP

A reaction seemed to take place as each innovative style developed. The east coast musicians, mostly black, resenting what they perceived as the unemotional aspect of the mostly white west coast jazz, developed a style called hard bop. This style was more "earthy" in quality and employed melodies more accessible to listeners. Many of the tunes had a gospel-like flavor, and their harmonies were less complicated. Clifford Brown, Horace Silver, Bobby Timmons, and bandleader Art Blakey were the primary innovators of this style; "Moanin'" and "Dat Dere" were compositions that represented the hard bop style.

SOCIAL CHANGE

During the 1950s and into the 1960s America was undergoing a radical transformation. Many of the perennial jazz icons, such as Ellington, Basie, and Dizzy (Parker died in 1955 and Clifford Brown died in 1956), were still active, though playing to much smaller audiences. Many had to reinvent themselves in an effort to remain on the scene. The civil rights movement was in full motion by the end of the 1950s and into the 1960s. Boycotts, sit-ins, and race riots had become the norm by the mid-1960s within the African American community. America was engaged in a very unpopular war, and this, coupled with civil unrest, made for an extremely turbulent time in the country. Among young kids, drugs such as LSD and marijuana accompanied the new style called rock 'n' roll. America's musical taste had begun to shift. The Beatles and the Rolling Stones were two groups from England who enjoyed tremendous success in America, as did Bill Haley and His Comets and a young man from Memphis named Elvis, who would become known as the King. All of these changes in society helped create a generation gap.[45]

FREE JAZZ

The turbulent times in society and within the black community were reflected in the music of the time. Free jazz, the next innovation, reflected African American discontent. Ornette Coleman is the father of free jazz. In many ways this new style rejected the traditional ways of playing jazz. Tonal centers were obscured or did not exist at all, which meant improvising on chord changes was no longer an option. Traditional forms such as the 12-bar blues and the AABA form were also obscured. One such example is a composition by Ornette Coleman called "Bird Food," a blues-based composition that forces the 12-bar blues into an AABA format. Each of the A sections uses a symmetrical approach to the blues. The first A uses nine-and-a-half

Miles Davis on trumpet and John Coltrane on tenor saxaphone in St. Louis in 1956.

Photofest

measures of a blues chorus, the second A is eleven measures, and the last A uses eleven measures.[46] This is hardly a conventional approach to composition or performance such as was embraced by artists prior to the free jazz movement. This style ventured into the realm of intellectual art music, leaving even further behind any notion of pop music that might include dancing.

Other, more traditional jazz artists begin to follow in the avant-garde style of Coleman. John Coltrane, who had played in a more conventional style with Miles Davis's Quintet of 1955 was now experimenting with free jazz. Coltrane's inclusion of Middle Eastern scales and departure from conventional formal structures and running chord changes was now the order of the day.

Coltrane's 1965 recording (two years before his death) of "A Love Supreme"[47] is a classic example of his artistic evolution. Other artists who embraced the free jazz movement included Don Cherry, Eric Dolphy, Charles Mingus, Cecil Taylor, and groups such as the Art Ensemble of Chicago. Even these were but a few of those who were striking out in new directions with jazz.

JAZZ FUSION

The emergence of rock 'n' roll, which featured such artists as Jimi Hendrix, Three Dog Night, and many others, moved jazz into yet another direction. Miles Davis, who was never opposed to change, began experimenting in the late 1960s with a style known as jazz fusion. This style was characterized by elements of both jazz and rock. One of Miles's best-known examples was his 1969 recording of "Bitches Brew."[48]

Other groups, such as Weather Report, led by Joe Zawinul and Wayne Shorter, and the Mahavishnu Orchestra, led by John McLaughlin, represented additional examples of how jazz responded to the proliferation of other popular styles. Horn bands such as Blood, Sweat and Tears, Chicago, and Tower of Power continued to include both jazz and rock elements in their playing.

CODA

Jazz has endured now for more than one hundred years. It has undergone a series of transformations and has been a reflection of society in all its tragedies and triumphs. It has been a snapshot of American society and has taught Americans how to feel, and to realize that anything is possible when the human spirit is challenged. Americans have witnessed the genius of icons such as Louis Armstrong, Duke Ellington, Miles, and Ella Fitzgerald and seen the emergence of younger talents who continue to carry the torch, moving the music forward.

Individuals such as multi-Grammy-winning trumpeter Wynton Marsalis and his older brother Brandford have been consistent contributors to the furthering of jazz. Terence Blanchard, Roy Hargrove, Brad Meldau, Joshua Redman, and Christian McBride are among some of the younger artists who are continually making significant contributions. Since the moment that dancing was no longer a part of jazz, it has struggled to maintain the kind of audiences it once enjoyed during the swing era of the 1930s—yet the music has endured. More individuals are playing this music in schools and youth groups all over the world than ever before. Jazz has truly become world music. It can be heard in practically every country on the globe.

Yet, despite the national and international acceptance jazz has enjoyed, it is a genre that continues to struggle financially. Jazz artists find it difficult to earn a living, and they play to relatively small audiences. But the music continues to move. Who knows what genius will emerge next? Thousands of young artists flock to New York every year to pursue their dreams.

It is likely that jazz will continue to evolve by incorporating styles from other cultures, much as Dizzy Gillespie did with the Afro Cuban movement. Continuous collaborations, much like that of Herbie Hancock and Bobby McFerrin, will continue to work with artists and genres outside the realm of jazz. Regardless of what happens, jazz will continue to move forward.

NOTES

1. Frank Tirro, *Jazz: A History* (New York: W. W. Norton & Company, 1977), 368.
2. Ibid., 369.
3. Ibid., 31.
4. Eileen Southern, *Music of Black Americans: A History* (New York: W. W. Norton & Company, 1997), 5–8.
5. Ibid., 9–12.
6. Tirro, *Jazz*, 42.
7. Southern, *Music*, 79.
8. Tirro, *Jazz*, 47.
9. Donald D. Megill and Richard S. Demory, *Introduction to Jazz History* (Englewood Cliffs, NJ: Prentice Hall, 1996), 45.
10. Southern, *Music*, 320.
11. Ibid., 321.
12. Lewis Porter and Michael Ullman, *Jazz: From Its Origins to the Present* (Englewood Cliffs, NJ: Prentice Hall, 1993) 87.
13. Ibid., 91.
14. Frank Tirro, *Jazz*, 327.
15. Ibid., 279.
16. Ibid., 52.
17. Megill and Demory, *Introduction*, 9.
18. Ibid., 14.
19. Southern, *Music*, 376.
20. Tirro, *Jazz*, 126.
21. Southern, *Music*, 371–374.
22. Megill and Demory, *Introduction*, 117.
23. Porter and Ullman, *Jazz*, 181.
24. Megill and Demory, *Introduction*, 112–115.

25. Porter and Ullman, *Jazz*, 425.

26. Megill and Demory, *Introduction*, 54.

27. Southern, *Music*, 368.

28. Tirro, *Jazz*, 149–151.

29. Ibid., 86–87.

30. Ibid., 176.

31. Ibid., 185–186.

32. David W. Megill and Paul O. W. Tanner, *Jazz Issues: A Critical History* (Dubuque, IA: Brown and Benchmark, 1995), 57.

33. Tirro, *Jazz*, 176.

34. Ibid., 233.

35. Ibid., 249.

36. Megill and Demory, *Introduction*, 109.

37. Porter and Ullman, *Jazz*, 98.

38. Megill and Demory, *Introduction*, 100.

39. Porter and Ullman, *Jazz*, 107–108.

40. Tirro, *Jazz*, 293.

41. David Baker, *How to Play Bebop* (Van Nuys, CA: Alfred Music Company, 1985), 45.

42. Tirro, *Jazz*, 293.

43. Ibid., 300.

44. Ibid., 301.

45. Ibid., 335.

46. Ibid., 345.

47. *A Love Supreme*, John Coltrane, Atlantic Records 5003.

48. Porter and Ullman, *Jazz*, 297.

8

Superheroes and Comics

M. Keith Booker and Terrence Tucker

In one episode of the animated television series *The Boondocks*, young Huey Freeman, a radical African American ten-year-old, is asked what a superhero based on him would be like. They'd never base a superhero on him, he replies, because he wouldn't be commercial enough. "Besides," he goes on, "all the black superheroes are corny. They'd probably give me a metal headband and a yellow disco shirt or something stupid." The reference here is obviously to the original Luke Cage, one of the first black superheroes in the comics and one of several black superheroes to debut in the 1970s under the clear influence of the Blaxploitation movement in film. Indeed, black superheroes began to appear in any significant number only as late as the 1970s, largely the result of an effort (inspired, as was Blaxploitation film itself, by the emerging Civil Rights movement) to correct a long and baleful legacy (effectively detailed by Erik Strömberg)[1] in which African Americans had either been absent from the comics or depicted in largely demeaning and stereotypical ways.

Cage, who first appeared in the self-titled serial comic *Luke Cage, Hero for Hire* in June 1972, is in many ways the prototypical African American superhero. Born Carl Lucas and growing up in the streets of Harlem, Lucas is wrongly convicted of murder and sent to prison, thus becoming an emblem of at least one strain in the experience of young black men in America. In prison, he undergoes still more emblematic experiences when he is abused by vicious (white) prison guards, then ultimately pressured into participating in medical experiments in the hope of receiving better treatment. When the experiment goes wrong (sabotaged by one of the prison guards), Lucas is unexpectedly given superhuman strength and toughness (the emphasis on his "skin of steel"—or "titanium" in some modes—echoes the emphasis on his skin color as an African American), which he uses to escape from prison. He then returns to Harlem determined to clear his name by tracking down his former best friend, Willis Stryker, who had framed him for murder in a dispute over a woman they both loved. When he finds that Stryker has been killed in a dispute with rival mobsters, Lucas finds that his task is more difficult than he first expected. Noting the publicity received by other (Marvel) superheroes in the New York area, he decides to become Lucas Cage, Hero for Hire, hoping to use his powers to help him earn a living.

He is successful, though only barely: his difficult battles with a variety of supercriminals never quite earn him the fortune he had originally envisioned. Instead, he occupies a seedy office in a rundown Times Square movie theater, struggling to attract clients and eking out a living while in the meantime avoiding identification as an escaped convict. This situation places him somewhat in the situation of the hardboiled private detective, but even more in the tradition of outsider Blaxploitation heroes, such as the protagonists of the 1971 films *Shaft* and *Sweet Sweetback's Baadasssss Song*—except with superpowers. He is, however, somewhat more successful than the typical Blaxploitation hero in eventually joining the mainstream; he is eventually cleared of the original murder charge, and his exploits ultimately place him in contact with a number of other Marvel superheroes, whose circle he joins, if uneasily and marginally, now bearing the more conventional superhero name of Power Man.

Cage/Power Man was not Marvel's first African American superhero. That honor would go to The Falcon, who first began appearing in *Captain America* comics in 1969. Eventually sharing top billing in the *Captain America and The Falcon* series, The Falcon joined Captain America somewhat in the tradition of the popular interracial pairing of Bill Cosby and Robert Culp in the television show *I Spy* (1965–1968). By pairing with Captain America, the embodiment of American patriotism and nationalism, The Falcon becomes a nonthreatening figure who seeks to embrace the democratic spirit of America. He sits in the tradition of race men—Ralph Ellison, Cosby himself—who often project a racelessness that implicitly critiques the presence of Jim Crow segregation. The portrait of the Falcon finds a figure whose belief in America is so complete that it rivals Captain America's and alleviates fears of blacks as violent threats or retaliatory agents, much in the spirit of Martin Luther King's philosophy of nonviolence. Indeed, when Captain America quits out of frustration with the Watergate Scandal—the preeminent twentieth-century challenge to American idealism—Falcon not only dons the Captain America persona but eventually convinces Captain America to return. Just as Captain America's popularity is based on the promotion of American nationalism against international threat (World War II, the Cold War), the presence of the Falcon addresses anxieties about racial integration. The Falcon and his alter ego Sam "Snap" Wilson eventually come to resemble the middle-class integrationist image presented in the early years of the Civil Rights movement. This image contrasts with the working-class and underclass world of Luke Cage, the first African American superhero with his own series, who appeared in the midst of the Black Power movement. But the initial appearance of the Falcon found him in stark contrast to the royal blood of African super-heroes the Black Panther and Storm of the X-Men. As "Snap," Sam Wilson is a thug and hustler who accidentally crashes on Exile Island and is manip-ulated by Captain America's enemy, Red Skull, to become Captain America's ideal partner and eventual destroyer. However, as Wilson takes on the Falcon identity and trains under Captain America, he eventually joins his mentor to defeat Red Skull. Ultimately, Wilson becomes a social worker in Harlem, helping its black residents locally while presenting a united racial front nationally and internationally in his partnership with Captain America. What becomes obvious in the initial and subsequent appearances of the Falcon is that Wilson does not possess the ideal charac-teristics that would make him a natural hero in the vein of Superman's Clark Kent or the Black Panther's T'Challa. Instead it is only by becoming the Falcon, erasing his past, that Wilson becomes acceptable in the Captain America universe. Thus, although the Falcon might seem to "represent the ultimate fantasy—to be endowed with incredible powers that fall literally, from the sky," as Christopher Knowles points out,[2] Wilson's former status as a hoodlum—and the stereotypical linkage of blackness to criminality—seems to make him unworthy of being a solo hero: he needs Captain America to legitimize his heroic role. Even the Black Panther's willingness to provide the Falcon with a harness to mount his wings—a nod to the hopeful Americanization and integration of black Americans—does not result in an extended consideration of race. Despite the appearance of Luke Cage, Marvel's *Black Goliath* (1975) was only minimally successful, as was DC Comics' *Black Lightning* (1977), although Black Lightning demonstrates the shift in representations of African Americans that coincided with the shifting ideas of black political ideology and African Americans' self-identification.

The politics at work in previous black superhero comics became more explicit with Black Lightning, DC's first black superhero. Born Jefferson Pierce, Black Lightning avoids the criminal justice problems of the Falcon and Luke Cage by turning to his Olympic training to get out of the ghetto. Like those characters, however, Pierce returns to the ghetto as a teacher as an attempt to help inner-city youth. In true Blaxploitation form, Pierce becomes Black Lightning as a way to battle drug dealers, the 100 Mob. The Black Lightning series failed to last even two years, perhaps because the character moved beyond mere images of "authentic" blackness to contend with issues of race and class in ways that moved away from the Blaxploita-tion mode and more toward black nationalism. Black Lightning declines to join a superhero team (in this case the Justice League), because he believes they only want a token black hero. His eventual membership in the Batman-supported group the Outsiders is then in part because of their willingness to move beyond the status quo. Moreover, Black Lightning highlights the eventual problem with the Blaxploitation era on which it sought to capitalize. Specifically, white conceptions of blackness frequently missed the original intent of black-authored texts such as *Sweet Sweetback's Baadasssss Song* or the original *Shaft*. Tony Isabella, whom Braford W. Wright calls "one of the few black writers working in the field," argued that "even open-minded white writers found it difficult to portray minority characters in a way that was not offensive or patronizing."[3] In contrast with the liberal writers who sought to construct black superheroes in a way that made color secondary to heroism, comics featuring black superheroes in the 1970s played toward what many considered "authentic" images of African American life. Neither strategy seemed to fully capture the complexity of the characters' heroic standing—and the hope it engendered—and the reality of their lives as African Americans living in America. Perhaps the epitome of this paralysis comes in a well-known episode of the explicitly political Green Lantern comics of the 1970s (*Green Lantern* #85, 1972). After saving a slum lord from angry tenants, Green Lantern is confronted by an older African American man who demands to know why Green Lantern has failed to help African Americans in the fight against racism. Green Lantern hangs his head in shame, unable to respond. The scene reflects the paralysis of the comic book industry in attempting to balance popular/critical acclaim with nonstereotypical representations of African Americans.

Ironically, Green Lantern's negotiation of race encompasses the comic book industry's attempt to provide characters that accurately reflect multicultural American while responding to the expectations of comic book fans. Like the X-Men, the Green Lantern Corps provides an opportunity for a variety of characters to be featured, whether human, meta-human, or alien. Readers are thus allowed their choice of characters instead of being restricted to a single character, who may be loved by some readers but disliked by others. The result is the expansion of the number and face of the fan base. In the case of the X-Men, for example, the African princess Storm was complemented by anti-heroes such as Wolverine and traditional heroes such as Cyclops. Similarly, the intergalactic makeup of the Lantern Corps minimizes concerns about race through a classic science fiction technique, namely the privileging of the lives and commonalities of humanity—regardless of race—in the face of unknown aliens, galaxies, and realities. Thus, the emergence of African American architect John Stewart in January 1972 (*Green Lantern* #87) as Hal Jordan's backup does not seem to be a move that seeks to explicitly add an African American character, even though Stewart's appearance was consistent with the arrival of the Falcon and Luke Cage. Jordan, who followed the original human Green Lantern Alan Scott, was considered the most popular Green Lantern, and Stewart's connection to Jordan legitimized him in much the same way that the Falcon

Justice League, 2001. Shown: Green Lantern, The Flash.

Cartoon Network/Photofest

became accepted through his association with Captain America. Stewart appears as a working-class black very different from both Sam Wilson and Luke Cage. Although out of work from time to time, Stewart does not have a criminal background or negative experiences with the police. Stewart's devotion to his assignment as a Green Lantern—he continues to serve despite opportunities to resign—mirrors the Protestant work ethic that sits at the center of American ideals.

Unlike the Falcon, Stewart's elevation to hero status does not include an erasure of an "unworthy" past. Nor does he achieve his powers because of royal blood. Stewart appears as a man whose history, though filled with the "fantastic," is one familiar to the African American experience: the grandson of African Americans who migrated North to Detroit from Mississippi, son to a father who worked on the assembly line because of the industrial jobs African Americans were able to work, and helped as a child by an extended family that stepped in when his mother died of cancer. His refusal to wear a mask, unlike other Green Lanterns and, in fact, many superheroes, echoes a tendency within Blaxploitation films, such as *Shaft, Gordon's War* (1973), and *Three the Hard Way* (1974): the defiance of its heroes. Like those characters, Stewart feels that his efforts are nothing to hide behind and thus, when his identity is revealed on television soon after he becomes Green Lantern, he continues. His dedication, goodness, and effort make him an ideal candidate for a superhero. In particular, Stewart's characteristics make him important because he was one of the first African American characters to take a superhero identity traditionally reserved for whites and was soon followed by Steel, Captain Marvel, and the Punisher. However, in having to live up to a largely white historical terrain—in both his lives (as his secret identity and as the superhero)—Stewart forged his own distinct identity. Aside from his refusal to wear a mask (a standard superhero trope), he joined the Darkstars, which rivaled the Lantern Corps as a galaxy police force, and became a regular Green Lantern to serve with the Justice League of America, even though Hal Jordan was a founding member. Indeed, when the Cartoon Network revived the animated series of the Justice League of America (JLA) in 2001, featuring Superman, Batman, the Martian Manhunter, Wonder Woman, Flash, and Hawkgirl, John Stewart was chosen as the Green Lantern. Many purists objected to the decision, and some suggested that Stewart was chosen because he was African American, despite the presence of heroes who were not originally members of the JLA. Stewart is thus representative of the possibility of African American superheroes and the challenge of incorporating them into the superhero.

As Jeffrey A. Brown notes, the limited success achieved by the various black superheroes produced by mainstream comics publishers Marvel and DC Comics in the 1970s may have come about because these heroes were too closely based on and identified with the heroes of the Blaxploitation phenomenon in film.[4] One hero of the era who escaped this identification was the Black Panther. Often regarded as the first modern black superhero (though he is African, not African American), the Black Panther has also been one of the most enduring. Although several different characters in the history of the Marvel universe have used the Black Panther name, the modern-day Black Panther was created for Marvel Comics by Stan Lee and Jack Kirby, first appearing in *Fantastic Four* Vol. 1, #54, in July 1966. The character thus predated the founding of the Black Panther Party by three months, though his status as a strong representative of black identity has sometimes caused readers to assume that his name refers to the party. (Indeed, his name was briefly changed to the Black Leopard in the late 1960s to avoid this confusion, but the change didn't stick.) The Black Panther is the superhero identity of one T'Challa, king of the African nation of Wakanda, though many of his adventures are set in the U.S. His first extended role in the Marvel universe, for example, occurred when he traveled to New York to join the Avengers superhero team as a supporting character. His first starring role came in *Jungle Action* Vol. 2, #6–24 (Sept. 1973–Nov. 1976); written by Don McGregor, this sequence involved one of the first self-contained, multi-issue story arcs in comics history, though that device would later become quite common. The Black Panther was then featured in his own self-titled series, mostly written and drawn by Kirby, that ran from January 1977 to March 1979. A four-issue miniseries, also titled *Black Panther*, appeared in 1988, written by Peter B. Gillis and drawn by Denys Cowan, who later became a founder of Milestone Comics, the first mainstream comics publisher to focus on multicultural (and especially African American) superheroes.

A stylish new *Black Panther* series, which received considerable critical acclaim, was introduced in 1998, written by Christopher Priest and illustrated by Mark Texeira. This updated series includes a quick reiteration of the Black Panther's background story and the history of Wakanda (which is one of the world's most technologically advanced nations, thanks to its unusually rich mineral resources and T'Challa's wise governance). The series also includes some clever narrative innovations, such as initially telling the story largely from the point of view of the rather ordinary (white) State Department functionary Everett K. Ross, who is assigned to look after T'Challa and his considerable entourage when the African king comes to America, seeking to solve the murder of a young black girl and to investigate the corrupting of the Tomorrow Fund, a U.S. charity funded mostly by the Wakandan government. The Black Panther received still another makeover with the appearance of a new ongoing series beginning in 2005, written by Hudlin and drawn by John Romita Jr. (among others).

Sporting a costume noticeably similar to that of Batman, the Black Panther is a superhero very much in the vein of Batman, depending on athleticism, special training, and high-tech gimmicks in the absence of actual superhuman abilities. However, the Black Panther does have somewhat enhanced abilities, thanks to the effects of a magical African herb that he alone, as chief of the Panther tribe, is entitled to ingest. Many of his adventures have little to do with his race, although his status as an African king foregrounds his cultural and ethnic background. This status also introduces a number of political elements into the Black Panther comics, as when the initial plot arc of the Priest–Texeira reboot deals centrally with T'Challa's efforts to fight off a coup attempt in Wakanda. The royal status of T'Challa is also reflected in his unerring nobility that at times borders on the stereotypical; similarly, the representation of the royal and tribal politics of Wakanda sometimes spills well over into the stereotypical in its vision of Africa as a pre-modern locale. Nevertheless, as opposed to the individualism of many superheroes (especially black heroes such as Luke Cage and Sabre), T'Challa does display considerable political skills and leadership abilities, as when he becomes the leader of a black superhero team including Luke Cage, Blade, and Brother Voodoo in the Hudlin Black Panther series. The Black Panther's various interactions with other superheroes (including his membership in the Avengers) also indicate his status as an important part of the mainstream Marvel universe while also reflecting the general intertextuality that helps to give that universe coherence.

If African American superheroes stand out for their rarity in the world of the comics, African American superheroines are marginal to their world because of both their race and their gender. In a mostly white world dominated by male readers and male characters, African American women tend to be absent, present but invisible, or simply represented as the object of masculine desire. The most widely known black heroine is Storm from Marvel's *X-Men*. Storm does not appear in the original version of the X-Men, published in 1964, but in *Giant Size X-Men* #1 in 1975. Although retaining Cyclops and Professor Xavier from its original incarnation, the newer version presents an international team that includes the Russian Colossus, the German Nightcrawler, and the Canadian Wolverine. Although the latter became a runaway favorite of the comic, Storm was also popular and, perhaps more importantly, became perhaps the most indispensable character. Although introduced as an African princess (and eventual queen of Wakanda), Storm (Ororo Munroe) is the child of an African mother and an African American father. Her long white hair and blue eyes clearly contrast with the more Afro-centric look in the tradition of Angela Davis or even Grace Jones and might initially raise questions about Storm's construction in comparison to her black male counterparts. Her "distinct" look is merely the most immediate example of a character who "reconciles a whole gamut of conflicting myths and ideologies. An elemental force of nature, she is the least spontaneous and most withdrawn of the X-Men. Asexual (even for a superheroine) she sports perhaps the most revealing and fetishistic black costume of any 1970s Marvel of DC character."[5] Also, her powers—which range from the ability to control the weather to the ability to perform magic and witchcraft—hint at a black nationalist ideology that situates Africa as the cradle of civilization. Much of her power, specifically her psychic resistance, emerges as much from her traditional heritage as from her status as a mutant. Moreover, as Richard Reynolds notes, Storm "is certainly an exciting and original creation—her powers have great visual appeal, and her long white hair and dark complexion provide the kind of contrasting visual image that gives credibility to the underlying pretext of the mutant theme."[6] Storm's role as one of the leaders of the X-Men—usually alongside the American Cyclops—embodies the emergence of African Americans as critical, equal partners in positioning America as a leader of the world. For example, she is above the consistent tension created by Wolverine's challenges to Cyclops's authority as well as the anxiety Colossus could produce in the midst of Cold War America. Indeed, when Cyclops leaves the team (*Uncanny X-Men* #138), Storm takes over as the team leader and maintains that leadership when Cyclops again vies for it in *Uncanny X-Men* #201.

Like the meeting between the Falcon and the Black Panther (whom Storm eventually marries), which symbolizes the significance of African American identity, Storm's heritage represents the complex presence of blacks in America—specifically the journey of blacks—literally and culturally—from Africa to America. So, while Storm is frequently identified and influenced by her African heritage, there is a clear narrative of Americanization. In the 1990s' animated TV adaptations of both the *X-Men* and *Spiderman* comics Storm's African heritage appears only minimally and she is frequently voiced without the African accent she is thought to have in the comic. In the three X-Men films—*X-Men* (2000), *X2: X-Men United* (2003), and *X-Men 3: The Last Stand* (2006)—Storm is played as an African American by African American actress Halle Berry. In the final film, which incorporates parts of the Phoenix Saga from the comic, Storm takes over as the leader of the mutant school and as the leader of the X-Men after the deaths of Professor Xavier and Cyclops.

Storm's place in the hierarchy of the X-Men command structure not only symbolizes the elevation of African Americans and women by the Civil Rights movement and the second wave of feminism but also acts as a way to demonstrate an ideal American collective that encompasses all genders and ethnic groups. Reynolds argues, for instance, that "Storm—despite her name—is on all occasions an advocate of calm and the healing of divisions within the X-Men team or outside it."[7] It is Storm who is able to stabilize Jean Grey when, as the Phoenix, she threatens the universe after she is corrupted and starts to come psychically unhinged. Yet Storm's stability, or more specifically her willingness to bring stability to the team, augments and complicates her presence as an African American female heroine. Jean Grey's sexuality is manifested through a traditional romantic relationship with Cyclops, but Storm seems to combine—though not necessarily reflect—elements of the black mammy in her privileging of the X-Men over her own desires as well as the "exotic," overly sexual black female. By combining these characteristics, however, her depiction avoids falling into stereotype, especially when she takes up a romantic relationship with the mutant Forge and eventually marries the Black Panther. Also, her seclusion from the rest of the team is based on her life as an orphan and her absence of friends but also highlights a similar seclusion of African Americans, who have been the sole black faces at schools or at work before and in the wake of the Civil Rights movement. Nevertheless, Storm became a successful character (both critically and commercially) because of the integral role she plays in the practical and imaginative structure of the X-Men. As a black woman, she succeeds as a character for a predominantly white male readership because she is the stabilizing force in a groundbreaking team even as she pushes the boundaries for traditional representations of superheroes. Thus, although Reynolds believes that "Storm reflects many of the traditional solutions to devising a female superhero in a team context,"[8] when considered against previous images of black women and black heroes of the era, Storm is one of the most innovative figures in the African American superhero canon.

Other black superheroes of the era remained more in isolation from the comics mainstream, largely because they were published by marginal presses. A key example is *Sabre*, a 38-page trade paperback written by Don McGregor and illustrated by Paul Gulacy. Appearing in 1978, *Sabre* became the first publication issued by Eclipse Enterprises, which would go on to become Eclipse Comics. It can also lay claim to being one of the first graphic novels, appearing in the same year as Will Eisner's *A Contract with God*, which is widely (though not quite accurately) cited as the first graphic novel. *Sabre* is also historically important because the original paperback was sold exclusively through comic-book stores, proving the viability of that method of distribution for longer and more expensive comics. The initial *Sabre* paperback, now again in print in a twentieth-anniversary edition published by Image Comics in 1998, was followed by a fourteen-issue comic-book series, the first two of which reprinted the original black-and-white graphic novel in color. All of the *Sabre* comics feature the same eponymous African American hero, given his name by his favorite weapon, though he also totes a fancy high-tech pistol.

Sabre and his beautiful-but-deadly (white) lover-sidekick, Melissa Siren, have no actual superpowers, but both are preternaturally tough, courageous, and skilled in combat. Sabre, in particular, has become a hero and has developed his own staunchly held code of beliefs, tempered in the fires of a difficult upbringing in a series of rehabilitation centers, none of which was able to quell his fierce individualism and resistance to oppressive authority. He continues in this vein in the comics, which take place in a postapocalyptic America in which the social system has collapsed beneath the pressures of greed and conformism. As Sabre explains to Melissa in one key (postcoital) sequence, his rebellion against society began when he realized that most in the general population were being "narcotized" by their "sensory video systems," a sort of futuristic form of television. As he puts it, "the materialistic carrot held under their noses" has caused most people to give up their individuality, while "I.Q. scores and salaries became more important than a sense of honor, or a measure of dignity in dealing with yourself or others."[9]

Melissa shares Sabre's romantic rejection of the coldly calculating world around her, though from a different point of view that arises from her status as the first "test tube fetus," a product of a project designed, in a mode somewhat reminiscent of Aldous Huxley's *Brave New World*, to do away with sexual reproduction altogether, freeing up humans for "more important things." Melissa, however, feels that something important has been lost in freeing conception from its "orgasm origins." That something, she concludes, is "magic," a quality that is entirely lacking in the thoroughly routinized world in which she grows up.

In the *Sabre* graphic novel, the total triumph of consumer capitalism has led to an almost total collapse of civil society, creating a post-apocalyptic atmosphere of chaos and despair in which a few unscrupulous individuals have seized power, creating a (rather dysfunctional) dystopian state the power of which is resisted by only a few determined rebels. The routinization theme is emphasized in the way Sabre and Melissa must make their way across a bizarre Disneyland-like amusement park in order to try to free a group of these rebels who have been taken captive. The implication is clear: any apparent magic in this world is a mere simulacrum of magic, contained and commodified, bottled for mass consumption in carefully controlled doses. This park is run by the Overseer, a mysterious and sinister figure, though much of the actual work is carried out by his henchman Blackstar Blood, a villain with a certain sense of honor that ultimately leads him to come to the aid of Sabre and Melissa at a crucial moment, helping them to defeat the Overseer, though even more powerful enemies remain on the horizon.

Sabre's romanticism now seems a bit quaint, while its portrayal of Melissa is a bit sexist: despite the fact that she is strong and courageous, she functions in the text largely as a sexual object who must be rescued from a sexual fate worse than death by the hyper-masculine Sabre. Sabre himself is a hero somewhat in the Blaxploitation vein, though his swashbuckling style is modeled more directly on Errol Flynn's Captain Blood. Indeed, Sabre's race is largely beside the point, serving mainly to help establish his status as an outsider to the society around him, though that is a status he shares with more mainstream heroes such as Luke Cage.

Meanwhile, the reference to Cage in *The Boondocks* suggests the problematic nature of black superhero comics, which have often either failed to address genuine issues of racial politics or have addressed these issues in limited and stereotypical ways. *The Boondocks* itself, based on the daily syndicated comic strip of the same title by Aaron McGruder, is largely an attempt to rectify this situation by aggressively addressing such issues through the medium of comics. And this attempt has been successful in that the syndicated strip of *The Boondocks* (which has also been collected in several bound volumes) has been one of the most prominent examples of African American comics in recent years. This strip (like the animated TV series based on it) satirizes a number of aspects of American politics and culture, largely from the point of view of Freeman, an inner-city Chicago kid who is transplanted, along with his younger brother, to the suburbs (the Boondocks of the title) so that they can grow up in safer surroundings. McGruder has forayed into the world of comic books and graphic novels as

The Boondocks, 2005. Shown from left: Huey Freeman (voice: Regina King), Riley Freeman (voice: Regina King), Robert "Grandad" Freeman (voice: John Witherspoon).

Cartoon Network/Photofest

well, as in the case of the graphic novel *Birth of a Nation* (2004), coauthored with filmmaker Reginald Hudlin. Based on the questionable circumstances surrounding the presidential election of George W. Bush in 2000, this novel focuses on the largely black (and poor) city of East St. Louis, Illinois, where numerous residents are fraudulently denied the right to vote in a presidential election, swinging Illinois (and the country) in favor of Governor Caldwell of Texas, a Bush-like presidential candidate. In protest, East St. Louis secedes from the Union (and, surprisingly, manages to maintain its independence), presenting numerous opportunities for outrageous satire that are made all the more effective by their uncomfortably close resemblance to real-world situations and events.

As with comic books in general, however, much of the action involving African Americans in comics has centered on superheroes. Although many of these comics have also dealt quite explicitly with questions related to race and racism, race itself is often not particularly an issue in such comics, except that the very fact that the heroes are black obviously has strong implications given the way in which comic-book superheroes often serve as fantasy role models for young male readers. Brown puts great emphasis on this aspect of superhero comics in his study of the black superheroes created by Milestone Comics in the 1990s, arguing that characters such as Icon, Hardware, and Static, the staples of the Milestone line, helped to "facilitate a progressive interpretation of black masculinity which incorporates intelligence with physicality," producing "models which stress holism rather than the one-dimensional hypermasculinity found in other contemporary comic books."[10]

The Milestone line of "multicultural" (which mostly meant African American) comic book heroes was an overt attempt to correct both the shortage of black superheroes in mainstream comics and the stereotypical representation of black superheroes when they did appear in such comics. However, Milestone (whose principals included established artists such as Dwayne McDuffie and Denys Cowan) took a moderate approach, both in the style and content of their comics and in their business practices, leading to considerable controversy. For example, their decision to contract with DC Comics to distribute their various comic books was seen by many (including rival, but more radical, African American comic book publishers such as Ania) as a sell-out to the white establishment. Meanwhile, heroes such as Icon (who has largely the same superpowers as Superman) were described by Milestone's critics as a sort of "Superman in blackface." Even attempts by Milestone to rectify the problematic representation of black superheroes in the past (as when Luke Cage was parodied in *Icon* #13 as Buck Wild, Mercenary Man) were sometimes seen as sellouts. Nevertheless, Milestone, while never a huge commercial success, did reach a larger audience than smaller rivals such as Ania. Still, even this effort was short-lived. Milestone debuted in 1993 with the titles *Hardware, Icon, Blood Syndicate*, and *Static*, which remained the mainstays of the company until 1997, when its comic book division was shut down. Today, the company's products are probably best known through the *Static Shock* animated series, which took the *Static* comic book to television from 2000 to 2004 on Kids' WB and has been rerun on the Cartoon Network.

The limited success of Milestone Comics in the 1990s indicates the marginal position of African American characters to the comics even today, though it is certainly the case that such characters did make some significant advances during that decade. For example, the Marvel cyborg superhero *Deathlok*, who had briefly appeared in the 1970s, was resurrected in the early 1990s (with McDuffie and Cowan as key creative forces) as the alter ego of African American pacifist intellectual Michael Collins. After discovering a secret weapons project, Collins is murdered and then resurrected in the body of an unstoppable cyborg killing machine. However, he manages to use his intellect (and expertise in cybernetics) to gain control of the machine and turn it into a force for good, installing among other things a "no-kill" order as a prime directive. Still, Collins experiences ongoing conflicts between his identity as a person and the identity that has been thrust upon him in the form of the cyborg body, a dilemma that has obvious ramifications in terms of African American masculine identities. Indeed, the parallel between cyborgs and African Americans is made quite overt in the very beginning of this resurrected series in a four-issue serial collectively entitled "The Souls of Cyber-Folk," in which Collins liberally quotes from W. E. B. Du Bois while himself becoming aware of the status of cyborgs such as himself as a sort of outcast minority whose half-human, half-machine status echoes the "double consciousness" of African Americans, per Du Bois.

Because of his intense pacifism (which often brings him into conflict with more violent Marvel superheroes, such as the urban vigilante the Punisher), Deathlok (who prefers to be called simply Michael Collins as he struggles to separate himself from the killing machine that houses his consciousness) is a special case among the superheroes of the 1990s. Still, even African American heroes who remained ultraviolent often became more sensitive and more humanized during the decade. One of the most successful African American superheroes of the 1990s, for example, was Todd McFarlane's Spawn, who began appearing in his own self-titled comic in 1992. Though ostensibly part of a trend toward generally darker, grittier, and more brutal superheroes that began with *The Dark Knight Returns* (1986) and *Watchmen* (1987), Spawn also represents a counter-current to this trend in that he is also presented as a sensitive and tormented soul who is not entirely comfortable with his own violence and his own superhuman status.

Spawn is also unusual (though not unprecedented) as a superhero in that his powers have supernatural origins. He begins as Al Simmons, an African American hit man for the CIA, gradually growing more and more concerned at the corruption and sinister shenanigans afoot in that organization, especially due to the machinations of his boss, Jason Wynn. As a result, Wynn has Simmons assassinated, after which the former hit man finds himself in hell. Due to his background and training, Simmons is identified as the perfect leader for the army that is being mounted in hell for an all-out assault on the forces of heaven. Desperate to see his beloved wife

Wanda Blake one more time, Simmons makes a deal with the demon Male-bolgia to be resurrected as a "hellspawn" so that he can return to earth for a visit with Wanda. Simmons, however, does not entirely understand the terms of his deal with Malebolgia. Moreover, he finds that he is returned to earth after an absence of five years, during which time Wanda has married Simmons's former best friend, with whom she has a fifteen-month-old child. Simmons also finds that most of his memories have been erased, so that he finds himself confused and disoriented, a situation made even worse by the fact that he does not understand the superhuman powers with which he has been gifted as part of his resurrection. These powers include preternatural strength and toughness, but many of them reside in his elaborate costume (a living thing in its own right), which gives him numerous additional abilities.

Much of the early storyline of *Spawn* has to do with Simmons's explorations of these considerable powers and his attempts to avoid domination by Malebolgia and his sinister henchman, the Violator, who often appears in the guise of a grotesque clown. He also begins to battle various villains (such as a virtually indestructible cyborg hit man who works for the mob), clearly placing him within the realm of the superhero, despite the unusual origins of his powers. As the series progresses, however, Spawn (perhaps not surprisingly, given the circumstances) becomes darker and darker, evolving into something of an anti-hero—who at one point seizes power in hell and becomes the King of Hell. Later, Spawn achieves godlike powers and is able to reconstruct the world after it is destroyed in the Armageddon that has been looming throughout the series. God and Satan, however, have no part in this new world, being excluded by Spawn because they refuse to cease their incessant bickering and battling.

Widely heralded for its innovative content and striking artwork, *Spawn* has now appeared continuously for more than fifteen years, making it perhaps the most successful comic book series of all time to feature an African American protagonist—no mean feat given that it has been published by Image Comics and thus lacks the distribution and marketing clout of the larger Marvel and DC. It has also inspired a number of spinoff comics, as well as action figures and video games. The *Spawn* comics have also provided the basis for a 1997 live-action film and for a widely acclaimed animated miniseries, *Todd McFarlane's Spawn*, which aired on HBO for three seasons from 1997 to 1999, winning two Emmys. The overall *Spawn* phenomenon thus indicates the possibility of success for African American superheroes in contemporary American culture, though it is also the case that race is not usually a particularly central issue in the *Spawn* stories. Race, in fact, becomes virtually irrelevant as the protagonist moves beyond the human, though this fact itself potentially defamiliarizes our view of race within the human world.

In contrast, the character Blade (another entry in the darker and grittier vein of superhero comics of the 1990s) is clearly African American, while his status as half-man, half-vampire gives him a duality similar to the one African Americans face daily. Born Eric Brooks to a mother who was murdered by the vampire Deacon Frost while she was pregnant, Blade first appeared in *Tomb of Dracula* #10 (July 1973) but did not become the solo focus of a comic until *Blade: The Vampire Hunter* #1–10 (July 1994–April 1995). Like Spawn, Blade is a vigilante who often conflicts with other superheroes, like Spiderman, because of his single-minded pursuit: hunting vampires. Also like Spawn, Blade has no secret identity, whose own story would have presented an opportunity to explore his life as a black man. Meanwhile, Blade (as played by Wesley Snipes) has gone on to become the central figure in a series of successful films that represent the only serious attempt to produce superhero films with a black superhero, thus standing in sharp contrast to superhero spoofs such as *Meteor Man* (1993) and *Blankman* (1994), starring Robert Townsend and Damon Wayans, respectively. In comparison with serious films featuring white superheroes (such as Tim Burton's two *Batman* films) such films appear as "bumbling spoofs. Although well-intentioned films, with ultimate true heroism from the comedic protagonists, they are overwritten by the image of the black-costumed hero as a failure, as a buffoon incapable of exercising real power."[11] Even the appearance of Steel, the African American member of the Superman family, was undercut by the casting of Shaquille O'Neal in the film version, along with a generally campy, low-budget presentation.

The treatment of Blade highlights a continual and fundamental tension in the superhero universe. As Reynolds points out, "A key ideological myth of the superhero comic is that the normal and everyday enshrines positive values that must be defended through heroic action," which leads to a situation in which "almost by definition the superhero is battling of behalf of the status quo."[12] As a result, direct challenges by the superheroes themselves to that status quo—with obvious exceptions such as a crime-ridden Gotham—would be anathema. The presence of African American superheroes may strike some as more an affirmative action effort than an opportunity to take comics into new directions. Even the Falcon, preceding Black Lightning's refusal to join the Justice League, was accused of being mere "quota representation" for the Avengers team (*Avengers* 181–194), despite the endorsement of Captain America. The tension of how to integrate African Americans into the comics becomes embodied in their presence on superhero teams. Their presence becomes more acceptable as the teams are less mainstream and more willing to take less traditional "heroic" action. Blade's own partnerships have been made possible by their tensions with heroes known for privileging the safety of humans over capturing villains. African American superheroes, then, become acceptable within the context of more famous or popular white superheroes or amongst a sub-genre that minimizes racial difference in favor of a comprehensive rejection of mainstream interpretations and ideologies of classic superhero mythology.

The success of series such as *Spawn* and *Blade* has also cleared the way for more nuanced treatment of race issues in the comics of the early twenty-first century. In contrast to Milestone's more moderate approach, black independent publishing company Stickman Graphics published the graphic novel *The Festering Season* (2002), written by Kevin Tinsley with artwork by Tim Smith 3. The novel follows Rene Duboise, a young black female who suspends her voodoo training in Haiti to return to New York City after the death of her mother, who has been killed at the hands of the police. Rene is forced to navigate a multi-gendered, multi-racial, multi-faith world with competing, complex interests at work. She remains confident in her knowledge and abilities yet displays a hesitancy that comes from incomplete training and the scope of the forces with which she must contend. While still mourning her mother's death, Rene contends with an arena filled with vengeance, sorcery, police brutality, political maneuvering, and racial divisiveness. The novel combines the genres of science fiction, horror, and crime fiction alongside an explicit sociopolitical commentary that moves beyond the rhetorical debates one might see in the Green Lantern/Green Arrow comics or even the Milestone family. Amid Rene's eventual discovery that the dark magic that seems to permeate her mother's death may be initiated by the drug lord/philanthropist Gangleos, she must contend with a city in the midst of two controversial trials and teaming with anxiety about racial tensions, police brutality, and disease scares. Gangleos uses anxieties that mirror those in America at the end of the twentieth century, including an explicit disregard for the poor and homeless, to execute a plan to turn the city into an army of zombies. Thus, the commentary on race and politics become dominant themes on par with the more traditional story of a superheroine coming of age and into her powers.

Rene stands as a black female protagonist whose own racial and gendered position becomes central to resolving the novel. She mixes thoughtfulness, common sense, toughness, and vulnerability but also recognizes the frustration of the African American community and the impact of Gangleos's plan, despite skepticism from those who dismiss magic and voodoo. Like Storm, Rene exists as black female protagonist in a pop cultural milieu dominated by (white) men. As a result, she finds herself navigating a world dominated by men within the comic as well. Yet the novel remains relatively female-centered, especially when Rene meets Isabella Delsento, who seeks to avenge the death of her brother Hernesto, whom she believes was murdered by Gangleos. The women, typically enough, frequently find themselves fighting off groups of men with their fists and with magic, remaining surrounded by men attempting to impose their will on the city and its communities. Whether it is Gangleos, Reverend Shefield, the African American minister and community leader who protests Rene's mother's death, or the male-dominated political structure under fire for its policies and police action, Rene and Isabella face numerous foes and find that they are compelled to find solace with each other in an attempt to discover the truth. An exception is Paul Whythe, who works as an anthropologist at NYU and NYPD. The novel positions Rene as a black female voodoo priestess who comments on race, gender, and faith. She sees not only racial tensions and gender dynamics, but Gangleos's manipulation of the city's ignorance of and hostility towards the Voodoo and Santeria communities, whom he attempts to eliminate because they are capable of discerning his larger plan. In Chapter Five, after her aunt encourages her to convert to Christianity, she informs her aunt that she rejects religious doctrine and dogma that she sees as divisive.

What becomes clear is that *The Festering Season* makes sociopolitical issues inseparable from the plot of the comic. The novel depicts a pre-9/11 New York filled with fear, apprehension, and resentment. Indeed, in the Afterword, author Kevin Tinsley reacts to the post-9/11 reimagining of New York as a national site of trauma and the casting of Rudy Giuliani as a national hero. The result is what Tinsley describes as a realization of "how oblivious the rest of the country is to the police state that was New York City throughout the 1990s."[13] Giuliani, according to Tinsley, had "a local reputation for being an extremely divisive mayor who never hesitated from trampling his constituents' constitutional and civil rights."[14] In particular, Gangleos uses the death of Rene's mother (based on the real-life shooting of Amadou Diallo in 1999) and the possible riot after the murder trial of his own brother to produce enough bloodshed to enact a spell that would transform the city into zombies. The riot at her funeral is based on a similar tension caused by an unwanted police presence at the funeral of Patrick Dorismond, who was also killed by police officers. The powder that triggers the spell is transported throughout the city by trucks spraying insecticide because of public fears about the West Nile virus. Thus, by explicitly situating sociopolitical issues at the center of *The Festering Season*, Tinsley and Smith make the distinct experience of its black female protagonist vital to understanding the narrative itself and less likely to be dismissed or considered blackface representations of classic (white) superhero tales.

Similarly focused on the political experience of African Americans is the revisionary Captain America tale, *Truth: Red, White, and Black* (2004), written by Robert Morales and drawn by Kyle Baker. The original (white) Captain America was a sickly man who was given an experimental serum in order to give him enhanced (though not, strictly speaking, superhuman) strength, agility, and endurance so that he could contribute to the U.S. war effort in World War II. In *Truth*, this background is explored further with the suggestion (based on historical realities such as the Nazi-like experiments conducted on black sharecroppers from 1932 to 1972 in the Tuskegee Study of Untreated Syphilis in the Negro Male) that such a potentially dangerous serum would have likely been tested largely on African American subjects. Here, the treatments lead to mostly disastrous results, though one subject, Isaiah Bradley, does manage to become a supersoldier in the Captain America vein. However, even Bradley experiences considerable negative long-term side effects from the treatments and of course is never allowed to become an American icon like Captain America, eventually finding himself imprisoned until he is pardoned during the Eisenhower administration. By focusing on a hero specifically created as an icon of Americanism, and by linking the story to the actual historical fact of medical experimentation on black men, Morales and Baker create a graphic novel with powerful social and political implications. As the black comics scholar William H. Foster III puts it in his tellingly titled collection of his own commentaries on African American superhero comics, *Looking for a Face Like Mine*, "in a world where most white people still doggedly deny the presence of discrimination, let alone racism, this was as bold a step as has ever been taken in the history of comics."[15]

Another recent superhero graphic novel that deals with race and racism in a particularly overt manner is *The American Way* (2007), written by John Ridley, penciled by Georges Jeanty, and inked by Karl Story and Ray Snyder. Set in the early 1960s, this comic features an alternative-history Cold War scenario in which a government-sponsored band of superheroes, known as the Civil Defense Corps (CDC), is a major part of the U.S. defense strategy. These heroes have legitimate superpowers, thanks to a high-tech gene therapy administered to them by the government. However, their role is otherwise a sham, and the various battles they fight (against alien monsters and various other villains) are secretly staged by the government as a sort of public relations gimmick designed to foster a sense of confidence in the American population and to serve as a warning against the Soviets. In this sense, the title of the novel is clearly ironic, suggesting that the oft-touted "American way" is shot through with deceit and deception, more image than substance. However, the principal irony in the title lies in the way the comic explores the deep-seated racism that runs through the supposedly egalitarian society of America.

The American Way is told largely from the point of view of Wesley Chatham, an advertising executive for an automobile company, who is hired by the Kennedy Administration to serve as the "Marketing Director" for the CDC. This very title suggests the element of manipulation of public opinion that is key to the government's strategies, though Chatham himself is shocked as he begins to learn the extent of the deception that underlies the operations of the CDC. However, despite the best efforts of the government to use the CDC to stir up feelings of patriotism and solidarity among Americans, American society seems to be falling apart, largely because of racial tensions. In an effort to bring African Americans into the fold, the government decides to create the first black superhero, recruiting Jason Fisher, a black soldier with a chip on his shoulder, for the role. Fisher is given Superman-like powers: he has great strength, can fly, and is essentially invulnerable, though his gene therapy is intentionally altered so that he can still feel pain, thus limiting his power to some extent. Further, his racial identity is kept a closely guarded secret, even from the other heroes in the CDC. Thus, in his superhero guise as the New American, he is given a costume that covers all of his skin, including a visored helmet that hides his face.

The New American's racial identity is revealed when he breaks his face-mask in a battle with another hero, who has gone insane. The public reacts largely to the revelation with racist outrage, and many Southern members of the CDC refuse to work with the black hero, eventually withdrawing from the CDC to form a separate Southern Defense Corps (SDC) that operates only in the South. Things come to a head when a vicious serial killer known as Hellbent (one of the CDC's periodic show enemies) is released from prison and assigned to kill a delegation of Cuban diplomats who have been sent to the United Nations. Instead, Hellbent (who is white) goes AWOL and attacks a busload of black freedom riders, killing all of them except Fisher's brother, whom he intentionally leaves crippled and maimed, but alive. In the process, he defeats a group of CDC heroes (who are unaccustomed to real battles and thus ineffectual), killing one of them. In response, Fisher tracks down and kills Hellbent, after which the ultra-racists decide to go after Fisher because he has killed a white man—something they cannot tolerate, even if the white man is a crazed murderer. The CDC comes to the aid of the SDC, and a fierce battle ensues. Meanwhile, the government, unscrupulous as always, launches a nuclear strike, hoping to destroy all the superheroes. Instead, as the result of a madman's plot, missiles are diverted toward several major U.S. cities, though the heroes manage to divert them at the last second. One of the heroes gives the full classified file on the CDC to reporter Tannis Darling, who has been investigating the CDC throughout the novel, which ends as Darling is apparently about to blow the lid off the government's nefarious operations, though the government has already launched a furious spin effort to blame it all on a Communist conspiracy.

The American Way is a biting piece of political satire, typical of its time in its cynical assumption that the U.S. government is involved in a variety of dishonest manipulations, intricate conspiracies, and blatant cover-ups, though it is perhaps unusual in the way it extends this vision of the government back to the Kennedy administration, still thought by some to be a shining beacon of virtue in the days before Watergate and before the Vietnam War became a major issue in American life. The novel is also unstinting in its presentation of the extent and ugliness of American racism, especially in the South. Indeed, virtually all white Southerners come off as overt racists in the novel; even Northerners, who tend to support Fisher and eschew blatant racism, still harbor subtle racist tendencies beneath the surface.

NOTES

1. Fredrik Strömberg, *Black Images in the Comics: A Visual History* (Seattle, WA: Fantagraphic Books, 2003).

2. Christopher Knowles, *Our Gods Wear Spandex: The Secret History of Comic Book Heroes* (San Francisco: WeiserBooks, 2007), 131.

3. Bradford W. Wright, *Comic Book Nation: The Transformation of Youth Culture in America* (Baltimore: Johns Hopkins University Press, 2001), 249.

4. Jeffrey A. Brown, *Black Superheroes, Milestone Comics, and Their Fans* (Jackson: University of Mississippi Press, 2001), 4.

5. Richard Reynolds, *Super Heroes: A Modern Mythology* (Jackson: University Press of Mississippi, 1992), 94.

6. Ibid.

7. Ibid.

8. Reynolds, *Modern Mythology*, 95.

9. Don McGregor, *Sabre* (Fullertin, CA: Image Comics, 1978).

10. Brown, *Black Superheroes*, 2.

11. Ibid., 178.

12. Reynolds, *Modern Mythology*, 77.

13. Kevin Tinsley, "Afterword," in *The Festering Season* (New York: Stickman Graphics, 2002), 228.

14. Ibid.

15. William H. Foster III, *Looking for a Face Like Mine: The History of African Americans in Comics* (Waterbury, CT: Fine Tooth Press, 2005), 37.

9

Standup Comedy

Leon Rappoport

What is standup comedy? Where did it come from? Why has it become an increasingly prominent and valuable part of contemporary African American culture? As each of these questions is considered, it should become apparent that hardly any aspect of mainstream American culture, whether language, music, or history in general, has not been directly or indirectly shaped by African Americans. Because of this, much of what follows is significant for virtually all racial and ethnic groups in our society.

DEFINING STANDUP COMEDY

We all think we know it when we see it, of course, but as an art form, contemporary standup comedy is still ambiguous enough that writers even disagree about whether to spell it with or without a hyphen. And there is no standard dictionary definition. A Google search only brings up a relatively formal Wikipedia entry describing it as a style of comedy performed by a single comedian who usually uses a microphone to speak directly to the audience. The performance itself, called a monologue, typically consists of a rapid series of jokes, satirical funny stories, ironic parodies, mimicry, and bits of slapstick, most of it aimed at ridiculing conventional values and attitudes. This seems quite accurate, yet for most practical purposes, it may serve just as well to stay with the more comprehensive one-liner description of standup provided by Ronald Smith. In his book about the lives of famous comedians, he simply asserts that standup is nothing more or less than ". . . the art of getting up in front of people and being funny—one of the easiest sounding, most difficult things in the world."[1] This is also accurate, but unlike the contemporary focus of the Wikipedia statement, it suggests that standup has a very long history. Both of these perspectives are outlined below, although in order to appreciate the unique features of African American standup, it will be necessary to consider the historical factors that have shaped its development.

THE CONTEMPORARY PERSPECTIVE

The relatively short and probably most widely accepted perspective on standup comedy follows from the style and content of comic monologues that began to gain popularity in nightclubs during the mid-1950s and early 1960s. Jewish and black performers such as Mort Sahl, Lenny Bruce, Dick Gregory, Godfrey Cambridge, and Bill Cosby (Richard Pryor arrived at the end, in 1962) initiated the style we can see today on HBO and other popular venues, in which the performer typically engages the audience in a type of one-way, meandering conversation that can range from intimate sexual matters to controversial social and political topics, often with a good deal of obscene language mixed in. By dealing with such previously taboo topics and language, these so-called "rebel comedians" were making a sharp break from the familiar, feel-good humor of the past, the bland routines of traditional white headliners such as Jack Benny, Bob Hope, Fred Allen, and others who made their reputations on radio after emerging from music halls and vaudeville theaters.[2] The remarkable recent history of standup, extending from the comedians of the 1950s and 1960s to such stars of the present as Chris Rock, Whoopi Goldberg, and the Wayans brothers, will be more fully examined in a later section dealing with the contemporary comedy scene. Meanwhile, it will be useful to consider material indicating that standup has a very long history dating back at least to the ancient Greeks and Romans, if not earlier. Centuries upon centuries ago, performers staked their livelihoods—and sometimes their lives—on their ability to get up in front of people and be funny.

THE MORE REMOTE ORIGINS

When introducing their recent book about the history of humor, Dutch historians Jan Bremmer and Herman Roodenburg noted that most scholars have only recently begun to recognize humor "as a key to the cultural codes and sensibilities of the past."[3] In other words, to understand the ways that most ordinary people were thinking and acting in any given historical era—the social norms, values, and attitudes governing their behavior—find out what made them laugh. More to the point of this chapter, find out *who* made them laugh. These ideas clearly apply equally well to the present; so far as we can tell, the comedians of the ancient world were surprisingly similar to those we know today.

Among the ancient Greeks, humor was provided by (1) actors who performed plays and improvised skits poking fun at women, politicians, and foreigners they considered to be barbarians, (2) politicians who became famous for speeches ridiculing their opponents, and (3) philosophers such as Socrates, who, according to Plato, couldn't resist amusing his students by showing up the stupidity and prejudices of the local "gentry."[4] Further-more, Bremmer mentions an account from the fourth century BC describing the performance of a professional entertainer called a *gelotopoios* (literally "laughter-producer" or buffoon) who was hired to liven up banquets or wedding parties by telling jokes, doing mimicry, and performing slapstick. Such entertainers could not have been very different from modern standup artists.

The Romans assimilated many of the Greek culture's traditions, and, having conquered most of the Western world, also developed a rich stock of insulting stereotypes to apply to everyone who was not a Roman . . . and even to some who were. Thus upper-class Romans, who prided themselves on being rational, disciplined, and in control of their emotions, apparently enjoyed ridiculing the primitive, impulsive behavior they attributed to plebians, women, barbarians, and slaves. In a famous case in point, Cicero attempted to ridicule and demean Mark Antony for his loss of self control caused by heavy drinking. Laughter at the expense of anyone who became disabled or was afflicted with a noticeable deformity was also a normal aspect of Greek and Roman culture.[5] The Romans were also easily amused by the sight of gladiators trying to kill each other or wild beasts attacking unarmed Christians—although that isn't quite what we're dealing with here.

Brief as they are, the foregoing summaries should be sufficient to show that the Greek and Roman founders of Western civilization enjoyed at least some of the same varieties of humor that we enjoy today, including a few that seem close to contemporary standup. It may be even more surprising—because much less knowledge is available about historically remote African societies—to find that what *is* known indicates traditions of humor similarly close to what we have today. Tribal groups did not leave many written records behind describing their cultural histories, let alone their forms of humor, but anthropologists have been able to learn a good deal by examining oral accounts handed down to storytellers and elders through the generations.

Mel Watkins provides a convenient review of this diverse material, pointing out that in African tribal groups there were typically one or more storytellers who would explain the world to young people by passing on origin myths, legends, and instructive parables. More specifically, it is believed that in West Africa there were exceptionally talented, quick-witted storytellers called griots. Part of their stock-in-trade was aggressive, satirical rhyming and joking that could easily intimidate onlookers.[6] They would be employed by tribal leaders as public entertainers and were often assigned to either praise or ridicule particular groups or individuals. During the early eighteenth century, an English traveler in Africa who observed griot performances considered them similar to traditional European court jesters.

Oversimplified as it may be, the image of medieval court jesters or fools presented in countless Hollywood films is not entirely false. During the Middle Ages, talented individuals who often combined the skills of a clown, the quick wit of a standup performer, and the agility of an acrobat or juggler could make their way in the world as entertainers to the rich and powerful. Some of them were fortunate enough to gain a permanent position in the court of a king or aristocrat. Once accepted as an official fool, they often had license to not only make fun of other aristocrats, but also, with some discretion, their own patron. Instead of undermining authority, however, it has been suggested that such humor served to reinforce it by demonstrating that only a fool would dare to criticize those in power.[7]

Most medieval performers had no permanent base. They traveled between towns and villages in small groups that usually included a mix of musicians, acrobats, actors, and storytellers who were collectively known as *jongleurs.* They put on shows on public feast days and special occasions, yet because they were frequently on the move and had no firm place in the organization of medieval society, church and community leaders perceived them as amoral and a potential danger to public order. They were, after all, childish people who engaged in make-believe and didn't stick around very long after their shows—and thus were not to be trusted. Accordingly, they were frequently treated as hardly different from thieves, con men, and prostitutes.[8] Some parallel exists here to the way itinerant minstrel show performers of the nineteenth century were perceived. It is noteworthy that the traditional idea of people in show business as being more or less disreputable, amoral, or just childish and untrustworthy has remained with us as a persistent stereotype.

SLAVERY AND THE RISE OF MINSTRELSY

Having sketched the distant origins of performance humor, including some of the surprising precursors of standup that existed among the Greeks and Romans, Africans, and medieval Europeans, it is necessary to skip forward several hundred years to reach the story of how, in the context of slavery, African Americans created the comedic style that has arguably become a dominant feature of contemporary popular culture. It began on seventeenth- and eighteenth-century Southern plantations where, during their off-hours, black slaves were permitted to fraternize and comfort themselves by chanting, singing, and dancing to drum beats as they had traditionally in Africa. These spontaneous gatherings were soon recognized by most plantation owners as a useful means of supporting the morale, and, therefore, productivity, of their enslaved workers. What the slave owners did not recognize was that as time went on, such gatherings fostered the growth of an increasingly sophisticated "underground" culture in which slaves developed their own language (a mixture of abbreviated, oddly pronounced English, local slang, and some African expressions) and used it to deceive or ridicule their masters.[9] Some of these slaves might well have been inspired by *griot* traditions they brought with them from Africa (although there is no clear evidence to support this intriguing supposition).

In any case, the satiric trend that became a part of slave gatherings was inadvertently facilitated by plantation owners and managers. Their castoff garments were the main source of clothing for slaves, who then sewed and patched, mixed and matched the items to dress up in ways allowing them to entertain themselves by acting out parodies of their masters. High-stepping dances such as the cakewalk are said to have originated as an exaggerated imitation of the strutting posture of plantation owners. As slave gatherings became more elaborate, some of the performers who stood out because of their exceptional abilities for songs, dances, and repartee received special privileges from their owners and were encouraged to put on shows for visiting white dignitaries. By the first half of the nineteenth century, African slaves had created a substantial repertoire of ironic performance humor based on their own folk culture of music, dance, and language. Many elements of this culture were carried across the country by the growing number of slaves who gained their freedom. In some instances, newly freed slaves even published accounts of how they had made fools of their former owners.[10] At the same time, during the 1820s and 1830s, white theater performers called "Ethiopian delineators" began to popularize the idea of blacks as comic objects by appearing in blackface makeup to do songs and dances supposedly demonstrating absurd forms of slave behavior.

The beginning of minstrelsy is said to have occurred when one of these "delineators," named Danny Rice, noticed a black stable hand in ragged clothing hopping about in odd dance steps while singing this catchy song to himself: "Wheel about, turn about and do jus so, and every time I wheel about I jump Jim Crow." Rice bought the man's clothes, learned the song and dance, and became a big hit when he took it on stage. (Following the Civil War, the phrase "Jim Crow" became a synonym for racial segregation laws, but the reason for this remains obscure.) Rice's act was quickly copied by other blackface actors who added new routines they copied from the plantation performers. "Widely imitated were the jigs and jubas of the black field hands and the cakewalks of the house servants."[11]

Calling themselves the "Virginia Minstrels," four of the blackface actors who found themselves out of work in New York in 1843 organized a group show that became an immediate success. Traveling minstrel shows proliferated, and by the 1850s they were the most popular form of entertainment in the country. A standard and especially popular part of all these shows was a comedy routine in which a serious looking character called Mr. Interlocutor fed straight lines to one or two raffish, childlike characters called Mr. Bones or Mr. Tambo, who then responded with silly punch lines while carrying on in any bizarre fashion likely to get laughs.[12] This routine, which probably originated as a way for slave performers to entertain their masters, if not themselves, clearly seems the model for all future comedy acts involving a straight man and a funny looking comic in baggy pants.

During the Civil War, a few groups of free blacks formed their own minstrel shows, but the one that became most successful, touring through much of the country and later in Europe as well, was called the "Georgia Minstrels." Initially organized and managed by a talented black performer named George Hicks in 1865, the troupe went through several incarnations over the next dozen or more years, with various managers and new performers. One thing that remained constant, however, was the use of blackface makeup, apparently because black performers did not appear black enough to meet the stereotyped expectations of white audiences that had grown accustomed to the exaggerated makeup of white actors in the original minstrel shows.[13] Several major black minstrel ensembles played successfully around the country for the next twenty years or more, steadily adding new talent and improving their music, dance, and comedy offerings. But their popularity began to wane in the 1890s as the novelty of seeing a group of imitation or genuine blacks acting out reified stereotypes wore out. A noteworthy attempt to reverse this trend that didn't last very long was the first openly mixed-race troupe formed in 1893 called "The Forty Whites and Thirty Blacks."[14] Furthermore, by this time, minstrelsy was being replaced by the somewhat more sophisticated popular entertainment known as vaudeville.

THE VAUDEVILLE ERA

The vaudeville era lasted for approximately fifty years, starting in the early 1880s in Boston, when B. F. Keith opened a family oriented variety show theater under the title "vaudeville" in Boston. It gradually ended in the 1930s as most popular entertainment shifted to movies and radio. During its heyday, however, there were two major networks of vaudeville theaters known as the Keith Circuit and the Orpheum Circuit.

The shows that played these circuits were largely stripped of the scatological and sexually suggestive material that had been a part of minstrelsy, lest such material offend middle-class sensibilities, but widely accepted racial and ethnic stereotypes were still prominent. In general, the well-attended vaudeville theaters presented variety shows not very different from the popular TV variety shows of the 1950s, which typically consisted of a series of separate music, dance, and comedy acts designed to appeal to respectable middle-class audiences that included women and children.

Although the careers of many talented black performers did not survive the decline of minstrelsy, some of the more exceptional stars reinvented themselves in vaudeville. For the most part, this was worked out in the segregated black vaudeville theater circuit run by an organization called the Theater Owners Booking Association (TOBA). It paid most performers so little that they referred to it as Tough On Black Actors and the "chitlin circuit."[15] The best-known and most successful black performer was Bert Williams, who according to Watkins, was considered by many to be "the best comedian of all time."[16] His comedy act included standup monologues as well as remarkable song-and-dance skills that were shown off in the context of comic dialogues with his partner George Walker. Williams was so talented that he soon moved beyond vaudeville to become one of the first African Americans to star in Broadway shows such as the Ziegfeld Follies.

Watkins provides what may well be the most thoughtful, detailed discussion of how African American performance comedy began evolving toward a new and much more sophisticated level at the end of the nineteenth century. He cites evidence showing that black comedians such as Bert Williams, George Walker, and Bob Cole were no longer depending on the old reliable funny faces and buffoonery to get laughs but were shifting the focus of their humor toward more subtle material. Accordingly, he notes that leading black comedians now began to take on the persona of traditional African tricksters—presumably the griots noted earlier.[17] Their acts involved less buffoonery and greater amounts of clever verbal material. Although Watkins does not mention it, further support for his thesis can be found in the more or less parallel development of the rhyming calypsonian comedians who were becoming an important cultural force in Trinidad.

The changing tone and content of performance comedy by African Americans in the early years of the twentieth century can best be understood as a reflection of the profound changes that were going on in the larger society. During what was called the "Progressive" Era, represented by the presidency of Teddy Roosevelt—who outraged mainstream racists by inviting the black scholar and educator Booker T. Washington to dinner at the White House in 1901—America was becoming an urban industrial country. As more African Americans migrated to the Northeast and Midwest to take advantage of minimal but slowly expanding economic and educational opportunities, the old stereotyped barnyard and slapstick humor leftover from the plantation days became an embarrassment to them, as well as to increasing numbers of whites. During this same period, waves of immigrants from Europe were also beginning to significantly influence American culture, including African American humor. The new Irish, Italians, Jewish, Germans, Swedish, and other arrivals all brought their own varieties of humor that eventually meshed with the African American tradition, but initially the new arrivals simply provided both black and white comedians with a rich new stock of ethnic stereotypes and greenhorn jokes. In the big city music halls and vaudeville theaters, Sambo material could now be replaced or supplemented with Goldberg, Murphy, or Giovanni jokes. The big city venues were also the places where a slight touch of integration could be experienced. Although segregation was the order of the day, and some white performers refused to perform on the same stage as blacks, the music was often ragtime (black composers Noble Sissle and Eubie Blake had their own popular stage act; Irving Berlin did not invent ragtime), there was usually at least one black comedy or song and dance act, and some whites, like Al Jolson and Eddie Cantor, portrayed sympathetic characters in blackface makeup. There is no clear evidence of the extent to which African American and white comedians may have influenced each other, but W. C. Fields and Eddie Cantor, who played on the same vaudeville bills as Bert Williams, both admired his work. Fields was quoted as calling him "the funniest man I ever saw," and Cantor claimed that he learned his sense of timing from Williams.[18] Furthermore, because vaudevillians were notorious for stealing jokes and copying material from each other, it is hard to imagine that some of this didn't go on between the black and white comedians.

Although black performers emerging from the minstrelsy period went on to work in all the venues open to them: vaudeville houses, nightclubs, music halls—even Broadway shows in a few instances, by the 1920s, a new generation of comedians born after the turn of the century began seeking the limelight. They included people such as Mantan Moreland (born 1902); Lincoln Perry, known as Stepin Fetchit (1902); Loretta Mary Aiken, known as Moms Mabely (1894); Dewey "Pigmeat" Markham (1904); and Eddie "Rochester" Anderson (1905). Whether deliberately planned or not, the laughable, self-demeaning stage names they adopted allowed them to present themselves as innocuous figures of fun not to be taken seriously, and thus not likely to upset white audiences. This was important at a time when white anxieties were excited by the aggressive assertiveness of Jack Johnson, who became the first black heavyweight champion of the world and had the temerity to consort with white women in public. Furthermore, films such as *The Birth of a Nation* were also spreading the Ku Klux Klan view of blacks as a threat to white women, if not to all of white civilization.

The African American performers who came of age in the 1920s would spend most of the next thirty years suffering all of the insults and injustices associated with racism. Their work was mainly done in segregated theaters and nightclubs, and the few who found work in white venues, including films, were generally hired to reproduce the Sambo or Mammy stereotypes. On Broadway, however, an important exception was the success of all-black musical comedy shows. One of the best known was *Shuffle Along*, written and performed by the young comedians Flournoy Miller and Aubrey Stiles in 1921. They followed this with another hit called *Runnin' Wild* in 1923. According to research by Darryl Littleton, Miller and Stiles also created the idea for the Amos 'n Andy radio show, which became an immediate success when it was performed by the white team of Freeman Gosden and Charles Correll in 1928. Flournoy Miller later wrote material for the show in the 1940s.[19] Also noteworthy in this context is that although some of the boundaries for what was considered by whites to be acceptable black humor were loosening, it was still true in the 1930s and 1940s that black comedians could only deviate from the established patterns of stereotypes at their own risk, or in all-black venues. When playing the role of Jack Benny's servant Rochester on radio and TV, however, Eddie Anderson became one of the first black comedians who consistently got laughs by making fun of a white man.[20] Like Eddie Anderson, a number of other black comedians in the 1930s and 1940s played the stereotyped role of wise-cracking servants on radio shows and in films. In some cases they had to be coached in order to deliver their lines using the black vernacular dialect that whites had come to expect. Mel Watkins refers to this as the verbal equivalent of the black comedians who had to wear blackface makeup in vaudeville.[21] Along with all Americans of their generation, however, the African American performers who spanned the years from minstrelsy and vaudeville to television would eventually witness a comedy revolution when legally enforced racist practices finally began to be outlawed during the 1950s and 1960s.

THE NEW AFRICAN AMERICAN COMEDY CULTURE

All authorities on popular culture and humor generally agree that our contemporary, "anything goes" form of standup comedy began with a handful of white and black performers who have been called "the rebel comedians of the 1950s and 1960s."[22] Their so-called "rebellion" involved a radical reversal in the style and focus of comedic material. Instead of relying on the familiar themes employed by mainstream stars such as Jack Benny and Bob Hope, who got laughs by appealing to social stereotypes, bits of slapstick, and mother-in-law jokes, the rebels began to get laughs by ridiculing the familiar social stereotypes and those foolish enough to believe they were true. They also would delight small avant-garde audiences by dwelling on previously unmentionable topics such as mixed race sex, masturbation, homosexuality, and the joys of smoking grass. As might be expected, this sort of critical, satiric humor, targeting established middle class social and political values, was not an immediate popular success. Respectable people were further dismayed by the casual conversational style in which performers like Lenny Bruce discussed outrageously obscene material. In the mid- to late 1950s, such humor was generally performed in small, racially integrated venues—clubs, coffee houses, and bars—in big cities such as San Francisco, Chicago, and New York, attracting audiences of idealistic college students, artists, and intellectuals, most of whom shared the critical attitudes expressed by the comedians.

The leading white rebels were Mort Sahl, who delivered ironic monologues typically related to political and philosophical issues in the style of a thoughtful college professor, and Lenny Bruce, who ridiculed religion and law enforcement while celebrating drugs and sex—the kinkier the better— in the style of a black jazz musician or street hustler. In fact, black musicians, comedians, and hustlers were among his closest associates. He was sometimes called a white Negro, and "conveyed a comic *attitude* reflecting prominent aspects of genuine black American humor. He adopted the swagger and assertive impiety of the black hipster."[23] About the same time (1957–1958) that Bruce was becoming a hit with large, integrated club audiences in San Francisco, black comics such as Nipsey Russell, George Kirby, and Slappy White were starting to do their acts for primarily white audiences. But, unlike Bruce, who forcefully ridiculed the prejudices of middle class whites, the black comedians had to be far more cautious about using material that might upset white audiences. Dick Gregory was the breakthrough black artist who would change all this.

After a record-breaking performance at Hugh Hefner's Playboy Club in 1961, Gregory was written up in news magazines, invited on TV talk shows, and given a recording contract. In his autobiography, he explained that his success sprang from his discovery of something like a formula for the performance of anti-racist humor by African American comedians. It was necessary, he reasoned, to make audiences feel relaxed and secure and to get them on his side at the beginning of his act. So he would spend the first few minutes making jokes about himself with little or no references to race. Having once gained their confidence in this fashion, Gregory then challenged audiences by presenting an increasingly hard-edged series of stories and observations poking fun at racist stereotypes in a way that encouraged his listeners to laugh with him at the absurdities of prejudice.[24] Like many brilliant insights, this one sounds quite simple, but Gregory did not come to it easily. Born during the depression and raised in an impoverished area of St. Louis, he attended Southern Illinois University on an athletic scholarship before starting his stage career in small black Chicago nightclubs during the late 1950s. His breakthrough insight seems to have followed from having grown up and come of age in urban environments straddling the divide between traditional black culture and the dominant white society. In effect, his athletic skills, attractive appearance, and university experience, combined with his diverse background performing in small clubs and his quick verbal intelligence, made him an ideal crossover entertainer.

Dick Gregory in 1961.

Photofest

Although he later used his celebrity status to advocate for a variety of sociopolitical causes growing out of the civil rights movement, his contribution to the development of African American standup was profoundly important as well. Lenny Bruce could rivet audiences with his aggressive outlaw stage presence, presenting an angry, often obscene series of fantasies and parodies directed against mainstream American institutions, but he was not someone most people would want to take to lunch. By contrast, by the time Dick Gregory had finished seducing and more or less gently introducing anti-racist humor to his audience, many of them would be ready to invite him home for Sunday dinner. It would be another decade or more before some young black comedians would come along and successfully adopt the hard-nosed, defiant style associated with Lenny Bruce. In the meantime, it was Gregory's outstanding success that cleared the way for an exciting new generation of black standup artists who would deliberately copy or spontaneously imitate his brilliant performance model.

The new wave included Godfrey Cambridge, Flip Wilson, Richard Pryor, and, most significantly during the early and mid-sixties, Bill Cosby. Cambridge and Wilson followed the trail blazed by Dick Gregory and became mainstream sensations for awhile, whereas Richard Pryor's astonishing success did not set in until the 1970s. But, by the late sixties, Cosby had become the best-known black comedian in America. As Gerald Nachman put it, "Dick Gregory cracked the color line, Godfrey Cambridge crossed it, and Bill Cosby whited it out."[25]

All accounts indicate that Gregory and Cosby had very similar backgrounds. Cosby's relatively impoverished childhood in Philadelphia was like Gregory's in St. Louis. Like Gregory, he gained an athletic scholarship to college (Temple University) and then left college to start performing in bars and third-rate clubs, where his tall good looks and smart self confidence contributed to his reassuring stage presence. Cosby even began his career using jokes and anti-racist material he copied from Gregory. The similarity broke down, however, when Cosby and his agent and friends realized that hard-edged racial humor did not suit his stage persona. Instead, what worked best for him were monologues about the universal human comedy and stories and observations with no particular bearing on race or ethnicity that could resonate with almost anyone's range of experience. Furthermore, his performance style conveyed both a sense of confident authority and good-natured, charming decency to audiences (he had decided early on to work without using obscene language). If Gregory could seduce an audience, Cosby could charm them right out of their seats. After working in Greenwich Village clubs in 1962, he became a great hit on the Tonight Show in 1963 and then took on an unprecedented costarring role with a white actor in a dramatic TV series (*I Spy*) in 1965. The rest, as they say, is history.[26]

All in all, his qualities as a standup performer led some commentators to describe him as an African American version of Mark Twain, more of a philosophical storyteller than a comic. Commentators over the years have suggested that the TV and film performances of Bill Cosby and Sidney Poitier, have probably done more to erode white prejudices than have any formal programs of education or integration. Cosby's career has had its ups and downs as he moved from standup to dramatic roles in films and TV. As will be noted later, he became a major critic of comedians' use of obscene language and the infamous n-word. Oddly enough, Richard Pryor, who became the polar opposite of Bill Cosby, achieving wide fame while using obscenities throughout his act and referring to all blacks as niggers, began his career by trying to emulate Cosby's style and material. In the mid-sixties, he was even being publicized as the new Bill Cosby.[27]

Richard Pryor Live on the Sunset Strip, 1982.

Columbia Pictures/Photofest

Richard Pryor eventually developed the creative voice and sensibility that revolutionized standup comedy in the 1970s, but no sign of this could be seen in either his background or his early nightclub act, patterned after Cosby. Born and primarily raised by his grandmother, who ran a brothel and boarding house in the black section of Peoria during the 1940s, he was a frail, sensitive child who grew up to be a quick-witted, smart-alecky teenager. A good part of his education was gained from listening to stories told by the itinerant characters who hung out in his grandmother's parlor. His formal education ended after he was expelled from high school for hitting a teacher. At eighteen, he joined the army, and after serving for two years, he began doing standup in small clubs in the Midwest. By 1963, his act was good enough to get him club dates in New York and then guest appearances on a TV variety show and on major talk shows. He later called the routines he was doing during this period "white bread humor," and his stage presence was a perfect fit. He would come on stage in a hesitant, rather timid fashion: a young, thin, short, black man looking a bit embarrassed to be the center of attention. It was the opposite of the confident Gregory and Cosby style, but it worked very well for him. Audiences were usually sympathetic and were all the more impressed after he strung them along to a clever punch line.

Even though the white bread humor brought him substantial success, he became increasingly disgusted with it, and with himself for doing it. The repressed anger and frustration he felt while going along with the expectations of white audiences and club managers began to show up in his act in the late sixties. An early example of his effort to find a more authentic comedic voice is the satiric routine called "Super Nigger" that appeared on his first record album in 1969. Once he found an authentic voice based on black ghetto street jargon and language rhythms—or at least what whites generally took to be the genuine elements of black ghetto culture—his career took off like a rocket. Much of his act was now based on his genius for acting out a wide range of character types, from redneck Southern sheriffs and teenage black drug addicts to the streetwise and philosophical old black man he called Mudbone. His parodies of middle-class whites, including their vocal tones and body language, never failed to break up white middle-class audiences as well as blacks.

Because of Pryor's subsequent success in other domains—he was a gifted comedy writer who wrote much of the script for the film *Blazing Saddles* with Mel Brooks, a popular starring actor in several Hollywood films, and the creator of brilliant one-man TV comedy concerts—his effect on the art of standup may not be appreciated. Fundamentally, and in many ways like Lenny Bruce, he violated most of the conventions that had previously restricted the style, subject matter, and language of standup, but he did this far more effectively than Bruce. His style rested on his exceptional ability to create and convincingly act out characters in sustained comic narratives, and his subject matter extended over a wider range of racial and ethnic topics. Although his language was just as obscene as Bruce's, he went much further in his use of the previously forbidden n-word. Thus, before Pryor, it is hard to imagine that anyone would have thought of bringing out a record album with "nigger" in the title, yet in 1974 and 1976, respectively, he received Grammy Awards for albums titled *That Nigger's Crazy* and *Bicentennial Nigger*.[28]

All in all, it is almost impossible to exaggerate Pryor's effect on both black and white standup comedians. The field of standup comedy was never the same after him; to this day, every working comedian acknowledges a debt to his groundbreaking work. Apart from the notorious excesses and eccentricities of his personal life, however, the one cloud hanging over his legacy concerns "That Word." Pryor himself clearly had no particular qualms about referring to himself and other blacks as niggers; he had grown up with it, and when he began infusing his act with authentic racial humor, it became a potent means of enhancing comedic effects. Furthermore, its usage in the street between people of color was not always insulting. When soul singer James Brown was sometimes called "a straight up real nigger," it was said as a gesture of respect for his authentic personal style and assertion of racial pride. In his book devoted to "the strange career of a troublesome word," the African American scholar Randall Kennedy noted that nigger could also be used by African Americans as a token of affection, of comradeship, or as a defiant gesture against white prejudice.[29]

Nevertheless, use of the word remains a hot point of contention among black comedians as well as African Americans in general. In the wake of Pryor's immense success, many black performers, and a few whites too, attempted to appropriate some of his charisma by frequently referring to "niggas" and "muthafuckas" in their routines. Others, such as Bill Cosby, were highly critical of this trend, and Pryor himself later vowed to never use the n-word in public. The controversy still festers, however. Within the larger show-biz community, whites and blacks generally agree that whites have no right to ever use the word. Furthermore, some black intellectuals and comedians argue that the word "belongs" to them—that it can be converted from an insult into a symbol of black pride or even a weapon against racism. Among most others, the prevailing attitude is less doctrinaire. Use of obscenities and the n-word depends on the situation, because, as most comedians have it, "anything goes as long as it's funny."

As Richard Pryor's career faded because of his health and emotional problems in the later 1970s, Eddie Murphy was already on his way to becoming "King Richard's" successor. While growing up in a middle class family in Long Island N.Y., he was a "natural" family fun maker and class clown. In his mid-teens he lied about his age and began performing routines copied from Richard Pryor in local clubs. At age twenty, he began a three-year run on TV, (1981–1984) as a featured performer on Saturday Night Live, where he became famous for acting out parodies of celebrities and for creating comic characters. His standup comedy concerts featured a more aggressive, confrontational style than had previously been typical of African Americans. He would come on stage with bold, often obscene, in-your-face routines ridiculing women, homosexuals, politicians, and any other convenient targets. Murphy's stance as a black performer was relatively unique and particularly attractive because he conveyed the impression of being immune and superior to any form of racism. It was as if he simply couldn't be bothered wasting his time over anything as silly or ignorant as race prejudice—except to occasionally make fun of it. In general, his unusually forthright standup persona as a brash, street-smart, pretty tough black man not only brought a special delight to black audiences but also defined a new era for African American comedy. There had always been a sensitive streak of vulnerability lurking in Richard Pryor's humor, but there was nothing of the sort to be seen in Eddie Murphy. After Murphy, standup performers were no longer concerned about coming on too strong in ways that might threaten whites. In this way, Eddie Murphy put the finishing touches on the assertive trend started by Richard Pryor while moving on to a movie career where he continued to portray strong and independent characters.[30] Between 1982 and 1989, he starred in seven major hit films, and his rise to Hollywood superstar status coincided with an explosive expansion of the standup universe.

THE ROARING EIGHTIES

Author and comedian Darryl Littleton did not exaggerate when he noted that "In the late '80s to mid-'90s everybody and his grandmother tried to be stand-up comedians, and the era came to be known as the 'black comedy boom.'[31] Comedy clubs and other venues for professional and amateur standup performers began opening up all over the country, and TV was not far behind with offerings such as *Def Comedy Jam, In Living Color,* and shows on Black Entertainment Television. Because of the sheer profusion of talented black standup artists emerging during this period, discussion must be limited to those who have stood the test of time and apparently had the greatest effect on the public and on other performers. They include Whoopi Goldberg, Chris Rock, Keenan Ivory and Damon Wayans, and Martin Lawrence. Along with a handful of others, such as Arsenio Hall, Robert Townsend, and Bernie Mac, these artists can be seen as having formed a critical mass of creative energy during the late eighties and early nineties that propelled standup comedy to the forefront of popular entertainment in America. And it is surely no accident that all of them are members of the sophisticated generation of black youths that came of age in the wake of the civil rights and integration struggles of the 1960s.[32]

It was 1957, for example, when eight-year-old Caryn Johnson, who would become Whoopi Goldberg, began her acting career in children's theater productions in New York. She grew up performing in a variety of small acting roles and working in improvisational drama and comedy groups. Her big break came when, almost by accident, she had to go on stage alone in a comedy club and act out the roles of different characters in a comedy sketch. It was surprisingly successful, and she proceeded to develop a portfolio of seemingly stereotyped characters—a drug addict, a valley girl, a West Indian maid, and so on—acting them out in comic monologues with unusual sympathetic twists in a one-woman show featured on HBO in 1985. The show, a sensational hit, came to define a new form of sustained, theatrical standup. There were criticisms from some comedians who saw it as more theater than standup. But it seems absurd to question the genuine standup status of someone who can get up alone on an empty stage and be funny for more than an hour. Whoopi also stands out as the single most prominent African American female comedian. Although Moms Mabley achieved national recognition toward the end of her career, her opportunities for wide exposure earlier on had been limited by segregation, and she never approached the superstar status of Whoopi Goldberg. There are certainly a number of talented young black women doing standup today, but as yet none of them has gained wide national recognition.[33]

Chris Rock exemplifies the by-now familiar sequence of success for standup artists: from small to larger club venues, then to theater concerts and TV, and finally to the movies. He was barely twenty-one years old and doing standup in New York clubs when Eddie Murphy saw his work and recommended him to perform in an HBO special. During the early nineties he became a comedy writer and performer on *Saturday Night Live*, and his major success leading to his career in Hollywood was an award-winning one-man HBO concert in 1996. His style of comedy has been described as a cross between Richard Pryor and George Carlin—that is, a mixture of hard-edged satire, spiced up with the usual n- and mf-words, and more intellectual, whimsical observations on the peculiar behaviors of human beings. A good deal of his act was often focused on the self-defeating activities of young African Americans. In this context, he became famous for the line "I love black people, but I hate niggas." He would go on to act in more TV specials and sitcoms and in supporting and starring roles in movies, also hosting the 2005 Academy Awards.[34]

NEW DEVELOPMENTS IN STANDUP

Starting in the late 1990s, African American standup began moving in a number of new directions. Some of these were simply matters of presentation, as when producer Walter Latham realized that instead of having a single superstar comedian performing on stage of an hour or more, it might work just as well to have four or five of them take turns doing fifteen minutes or so of their best material. Organized as a road show called the *Kings of Comedy*, comedians Steve Harvey, D. L. Hughey, Bernie Mac, and Cedric the Entertainer toured theaters around the country. In some respects, their show was reminiscent of the way performers toured on the old vaudeville circuits, and its success attracted Spike Lee to film the show, which was shown as an HBO concert in 2000. The pattern was repeated with women comedians—Laura Hayes, Mo'Nique, Sommore, and Adele Givens—who formed the group called *Queens of Comedy* in 2000 and 2001. The *Queens* were also successful on the road and in an HBO film but failed to gain the same celebrity as the *Kings*.[35]

The career of Keenan Ivory Wayans represents yet another new development in the field of African American standup. In this case, it involved both a new TV show venue and, perhaps more important, control over production of the show. Wayans's success seemed to come easily. After graduating from the Tuskegee Institute, he began doing standup in comedy clubs in New York in the mid-1980s and collaborated with Robert Townsend writing comedy scripts for films and TV. His standup career was soon put aside in favor of writing assignments for Eddie Murphy, and work on an original movie. The comic film *I'm Gonna Git You Sucka* was his first independent project, released in 1988. It was partly on the basis of this achievement that during the same year, producer, director, and starring actor Wayans was able to develop, produce, and star in his TV comedy show *In Living Color*, which consisted of a series of bizarrely funny, often outrageous skits involving stock characters played by himself, his brothers Damon and Shawn, and his sister Kim. Jamie Foxx, Jim Carrey, Chris Rock, and other rising comedians also gained exposure on the show, which remained a Fox channel hit for several years. Keenan and his brother Damon both went on to major Hollywood careers as actors, writers, and producers, but the larger significance of Keenan Ivory Wayans came about because of his status as the prototype for a new generation of black standup comedians who would become film and TV entrepreneurs.[36]

This career pattern, whereby successful comedians were able to transcend their performance careers and move into more central creative roles

In Living Color, 1990–1994. Shown: (back row) Jim Carrey, Tommy Davidson, Kelly Coffield, Damon Wayans, (front row) Anne-Marie Johnson, Keenen Ivory Wayans, T'Keyah Keymáh, Kim Wayans, David Alan Grier.

FOX/Photofest

as producers, directors, and writers, was already visible in some of the activities of Richard Pryor and Eddie Murphy. But, whereas they remained primarily performers, Keenan Ivory Wayans has become a near-full-time entertainment entrepreneur, and his success has decisively shattered the tradition of white producers, managers, and directors controlling the careers of black performers. A similar progression from standup success to the development and executive production of movies and TV shows can be seen among other black performers. On the strength of their bankable popularity, Martin Lawrence, Chris Rock, Bernie Mac, Jamie Foxx, and others have been able to gain an unprecedented degree of independent power in Hollywood. The same has been true of Dave Chappelle, who apparently chose, however, to move outside mainstream comedy while pushing the boundaries of standup in radical new directions.

Like Eddie Murphy, Chappelle began doing standup as a young teenager and, while later studying acting in Washington D.C. in the 1980s, performed in a number of local clubs. Subsequent to various film roles and TV appearances in the 1990s, and a successful HBO special in 2000, he developed his own TV series, *Chappelle's Show,* for the Comedy Central channel. The sketches played out on the show were bold, quirky satires that brought him both fame and notoriety. In one controversial sketch, *The*

Dave Chappelle: For What It's Worth, 2004.

Showtime/Photofest

Nigger Family, he tried to detoxify the n-word by showing its absurdity, but not everyone appreciated the ironic humor built into this satire on racist language. In another, Chappelle conceived a scenario in which the future could be foretold via the prophecies of a "Negrodamus." He also performed a scenario demonstrating the inhibitions imposed on middle-class blacks by their sensitivity to stereotypes, as exemplified in refusals to order fried chicken or watermelon in the presence of whites. This sort of material attracted a great deal of attention by simultaneously ridiculing the preconceptions of both blacks and whites. But in order to "get it," audiences had to be knowledgeable enough to recognize the often double-edged implications of the action. Then there was perhaps the boldest of Chappelle's satires, a piece analogous to "theater of the absurd," in which a blind black man becomes the leader of a white supremacist organization. It should not be surprising, therefore, that some whites and many African Americans who tended to focus on the superficial aspects of these skits—the mix of white and black racist attitudes and language they contained—began to criticize Chappelle for encouraging the prejudices his work was actually designed to ridicule.[37]

Nevertheless, the show was a great success until Chappelle abruptly quit in the spring of 2005 to spend several months on a personal retreat in South Africa. His subsequent comments suggest that he had experienced a type of midlife crisis brought on by overwork and anxiety about the meaning of his work. By 2006, he was back in the States, appearing on diverse talk shows, performing standup concerts, and planning new film and TV projects.[38]

Chappelle's recent career seems particularly significant because of his remarkable success and his current dominance over leading-edge black standup humor (Darryl Littleton has called him "the hottest comedian in the world"). Noteworthy too is his career's echoing that of his forebear Richard Pryor. Like Pryor, Chappelle has been a pioneer, extending the frontiers of standup to controversial new ground and gaining applause from many but sharp criticism from others for his n-word parodies of some black culture patterns. Also like Pryor, his edgy innovations have cost him a great deal of emotional stress leading to an existential crisis (Pryor took refuge in drugs; Chappelle found a better way by retreating to Africa). But he now seems to have found his way past this and has resisted big-money offers to work in the mainstream entertainment industry. Instead, he has returned to performing standup to live audiences, trying out new formats and styles of humor that can be complex and yet readily accessible. It remains to be seen whether he will keep on exploring new directions, but at the end of 2007, there seems no doubt that Chappelle defines the leading edge of African American standup.

CONTEMPORARY SIGNIFICANCE

Regardless of how standup comedy may develop in the future, it should be plain to any reader of this chapter that much of the contemporary significance of African American standup lies in its rags to riches history. This history has been nothing less than an outstanding against-the-odds national success story. No performance art in America has ever started lower or risen higher in the space of 150 years. And its movement into mainstream culture could not have happened unless African American standup humor had important value for *all* Americans. The most obvious value is simply the gift of laughter. This hardly needs any elaboration but to acknowledge that although some of the laughter may have been a disdainful manifestation of white racist attitudes, it is also only fair to suggest that among whites as well as blacks, a great deal of the laughter has been sympathetic in the past as it clearly is today. One merely has to observe the reactions of a mixed audience at, say, a Chris Rock concert to recognize that their reflexive bursts of laughter relate mainly to universal human frailties rather than racist attitudes.

A perennial question about the value of black standup comedy to African Americans centers on whether it helps or harms "the race." Influential middle- and upper-class blacks and whites, including Bill Cosby, have argued that by their use of the n-word and their exploitation of racist stereotypes, standup artists from Richard Pryor to Dave Chappelle have either supported race prejudices, profited from them, or made it seem "cool" to use insulting, hurtful language. The fact that these performers have been immensely popular among most African Americans has not convinced their critics to relent. Nor has the fact that it is more or less impossible to ridicule racist attitudes and stereotypes without mentioning and dramatizing them. But, setting aside the criticisms of the few, other values are associated with black standup that can hardly be questioned. It has, for example, clearly served an important social function by demonstrating how humor can provide any minority group, whether black, Hispanic, Asian, gay, Native American, or feminist, a way to vividly express their anxieties and frustrations. This can be most obviously seen in the rising number of diverse ethnic comedians who essentially use the standup paradigm developed by African Americans. Indeed, a good case can be made for the view that almost from their beginning, African American standup and other varieties of humor have often been the means whereby African Americans, and later other minorities as well, have been able to "speak truth to power" and to themselves.[39]

But truth can be a dangerous thing if people are not prepared to accept it. Black standup routines that invite audiences to laugh at themselves by presenting parodies of either black or white racist stereotypes can provoke anger rather than amusement if they aren't carefully calculated. Yet sociologists point out that such material can be particularly valuable to other African Americans. Thus, shared humor within a group, even when critical, tends to encourage group cohesion and morale. Self-critical laughter can be a healthy way to release social and emotional tensions, and parodies of stereotypes can be instructive by warning group members about the prejudices they are likely to encounter.[40]

No discussion of African American standup would be complete without paying tribute to the courage and creativity of its performers. All comedians, even those who perform conventional mainstream comedy, must accept the risks of public failure—the experience of what they call "flop sweat." But the risks have been far greater for black standup artists who have always had to perform under the shadow of implicit or explicit racism. When getting started, they have typically had to operate as road warriors, living by their wits as they moved from one club date to another. Nor could they be confident that a drunk would not suddenly pop up, shouting racial obscenities— or that whatever routine played well in Peoria would also play well in Philadelphia. And the risks have been still greater for the more creative performers who, from the days of minstrelsy to the present, have been pushing the boundaries of standup in new directions. To understand all this is also to understand why many performers fall by the wayside, undone by the stress they must endure or by the alcohol and other drugs that provide short-term relief from the stress. The challenge of performing standup is no small thing, and those who persist to finally achieve some lesser or greater degree of success fully deserve whatever rewards and respect may come their way.

NOTES

1. Preface to Ronald Lande Smith's *The Stars of Stand-up Comedy*, (New York: Garland Publishing Inc., 1986).

2. Gerald Nachman, *Seriously Funny: The Rebel Comedians of the 1950's and 1960's* (New York: Pantheon Books, 2003).

3. Jan Bremmer and Herman Roodenburg, eds., *A Cultural History of Humor: From Antiquity to the Present day* (Cambridge, UK: Polity Press, 1997), xi.

4. See the Bremmer chapter, "Jokes, Jokers, and Jokebooks in Ancient Greek Culture," 11–28, and the Fritz Graf chapter, "Cicero, Plautus and Roman Laughter," 29–39, both in Bremmer and Roodenburg, *A Cultural History of Humor*; this anthology also includes a valuable research bibliography on humor and history by Johan Verberckmoes, 242–252.

5. See Guy Halsall, "Funny Foreigners: Laughing with the Barbarians in Late Antiquity," 89–113, and Mark Humphries, "The Lexicon of Abuse: Drunkenness and Political Illegitimacy in the Late Roman World," 75–88, both in Guy Halsall, ed., *Humor, History, and Politics in Late Antiquity and the Early Middle Ages* (New York: Cambridge University Press, 2002); see also Robert Garland, "The Mockery of the Deformed and Disabled in Graeco-Roman Culture," in Siegfried Jakel and Asko Timonen, eds., *Laughter Down the Centuries*, Vol. 1. (Turku, Finland: Abo Academis Tryckeri, 1994), 71–84.

6. Mel Watkins, *On the Real Side: Laughing, Lying and Signifying—The Underground Tradition of African-American Humor That Transformed American Culture, From Slavery to Richard Pryor* (New York: Simon and Schuster, 1964), 63–65.

7. Halsall, *Humor, History and Politics*, 19.

8. Bronislaw Geremek, "The Marginal Man," in Jacques LeGoff, ed., *The Medieval World*, trans. L. G. Cochrane (London: Collins and Brown, 1990), 347–373; see also Marc Bloch, *Feudal Society*, trans. L. A. Manyon (Chicago: University of Chicago Press, 1968), 418.

9. Watkins, *On The Real Side*, 66; see also Langston Hughes and Milton Meltzer, *Black Magic: A Pictorial History of the Negro in American Entertainment* (Englewood Cliffs, NJ: Prentice Hall, 1967), 7–15.

10. Gilbert Osofsky, *Puttin' on Ole Massa: The Slave Narratives of Henry Bibb, William Wells Brown, and Solomon Nothrup* (New York: Harper and Row, 1969).

11. Hughes and Meltzer, *Black Magic*, 18. Their useful work describes the slave songs and dances, as well as how slaves made their own banjos and percussion instruments. Sketches, paintings, and photos of the better-known slave entertainers and later minstrel-show performers also feature largely in this book.

12. Watkins, *On the Real Side*, 86–95.

13. Joseph Boskin, *Sambo: the Rise and Demise of an American Jester* (New York: Oxford University Press, 1986), 85–92.

14. Hughes and Meltzer, *Black Magic*, 27.

15. Ibid., 67.

16. Watkins, *On the Real Side*, 156, 179.

17. Ibid., 164–180.

18. Ibid., 175, 179.

19. Darryl Littleton, *Black Comedians on Black Comedy: How African Americans Taught us to Laugh* (New York: Applause Theater and Cinema Books, 2006), 33–34. Littleton accurately sums up this period, noting: "The comedians of the day, though still in minstrel attire in many cases, were moving more toward authentic black humor while simultaneously keeping white audiences comfortable with the familiar image of the coon." (34)

20. Ibid., 52.

21. Watkins, *On the Real Side*, 292–293.

22. Gerald Nachman, *Seriously Funny: The Rebel Comedians of the 1950s and 1960s* (New York: Pantheon Books, 2003).

23. Watkins, *On the Real Side*, 485–486.

24. Gregory, *Nigger* (New York: E. P. Dutton, 1964).

25. Nachman, *Seriously Funny*, 563.

26. Ibid., 563–590; see also Watkins, *On the Real Side*, 503–508; Phil Berger, *The Last Laugh* (New York: Limelight Editions, 1985), 133; Darryl Littleton, *Black Comedians on Black Comedy*, 105.

27. For this and all the following material on Richard Pryor, I have drawn primarily on the works of Nachman, Littleton, and Watkins, noted above, and Phil Berger, *The Last Laugh: the World of the Stand-up Comics* (New York: Limelight Editions, 1989).

28. See my discussion of the similarities and parallels between the lives and careers of Bruce and Pryor in Leon Rappoport, *Punchlines: the Case for Racial, Ethnic and Gender Humor* (Westport CT: Praeger, 2005), 71–80.

29. Randall Kennedy, *Nigger: The Strange Career of a Troublesome Word* (New York: Pantheon Books, 2002.)

30. Watkins, *On The Real Side*, 563–565.

31. Littleton, *Black Comedians*, 187.

32. Watkins, *On the Real Side*, 565.

33. Mary Unterbrink, *Funny Women: American Comediennes, 1860–1985* (Jefferson North Carolina: McFarland & Co., 1987), 206–208; for more general perspectives

on women in comedy, see Linda Martin and Kerry Seagrave, *Women in Comedy: Funny Ladies From the Turn of the Century to the Present* (Secaucus NJ: Citadel Trade, 1986).

34. Littleton, *Black Comedians*, 256–258.

35. Ibid., 276–277.

36. Ibid., 227–228; see also biographical sketch on http://www.starpulse.com.

37. Ibid., 308–313; see also biographical sketch on http://www.starpulse.com.

38. Details available on the Chappelle Web page: http://www.davechappelle.com.

39. Mel Watkins, *On the Real Side*, 566–570.

40. Leon Rappoport, *Punchlines*, 35–36.

About the Editor and Contributors

Dr. Todd Boyd is the Katherine and Frank Price Endowed Chair for the Study of Race and Popular Culture, as well as Professor of Critical Studies in the USC School of Cinematic Arts. He is an accomplished author, media commentator, producer, and consultant. Dr. Boyd is highly regarded as one of the nation's leading experts on popular culture and is especially distinguished in this regard for his pioneering work on race, media, hip-hop culture, and sports. His many books include *The Notorious Ph.D's Guide to the Super Fly 70s* (2007), *Young, Black, Rich and Famous* (2003), *The New H.N.I.C.* (2002), and *Am I Black Enough For You?* (1997). Dr. Boyd was a producer and cowriter on the Paramount Pictures film *The Wood* (1999).

M. Keith Booker is the James E. and Ellen Wadley Roper Professor of English at the University of Arkansas. He has written or edited more than thirty books on literature, literary theory, and popular culture. His current research interests include film, television, science fiction, and comic books and graphic novels.

Don Cusic is Professor of Music Business at Belmont University in Nashville, Tennessee. He is the author of 18 books, including *The Trials of Henry Flipper: The First Black Graduate of West Point.*

Dr. Milmon F. Harrison is Associate Professor with the African American and African Studies Program at the University of California, Davis. He began his college education at Sacramento City College before transferring to UC Davis, where he completed his bachelor's degree in sociology, "with highest honors," in 1994. He received his Ph.D., also in sociology, in 1999 from UC Santa Barbara. Professor Harrison's research and teaching areas include African American culture, sociology of religion (with an emphasis on the black Church in America), racial and ethnic relations in the United States, and the sociology of culture (with an emphasis on representations of race in popular culture). His most recent publications include the book *Righteous Riches: The Word of Faith Movement in Contemporary African American Religion* (2005), which was chosen an "Outstanding Academic Title" for 2006 by *Choice Magazine.* He is currently working on two new books, one of which concerns the history of "prosperity gospels" in American culture; the other project looks at the production of contemporary black gospel music. Dr. Harrison has recently been selected as one of six recipients of the 2007–2008 Chancellor's Fellowship at UC Davis. In addition to substantial research funding, the award bestows upon him the title "Chancellor's Fellow" until 2012.

Cheryl L. Keyes is the author of *Rap Music and Street Consciousness*, which received a CHOICE award for outstanding academic books in 2004. She is a member of the faculty in the Department of Ethnomusicology at the University of California, Los Angeles. Her areas of specialty include African American music, gender, and popular music studies. Keyes has conducted extensive fieldwork on rap and hip-hop culture in Mali, West Africa; New York City; Detroit; Los Angeles; and London. Her research has been published in such major journals as *Ethnomusicology, Folklore Forum, Journal of American Folklore, Journal of Popular Music Studies,* and *The World of Music,* as well as in book chapters, numerous reference articles, and reviews.

Maureen Mahon, a cultural anthropologist, is Assistant Professor of Anthropology and Afro-American Studies at UCLA. She is the author of *Right to Rock: The Black Rock Coalition and the Cultural Politics of Race* (2004).

Carmen L. Manning-Miller is Associate Professor and Director, Graduate Program, in the Department of Journalism at the University of Mississippi. She is the coeditor, with Venise T. Berry, of *Mediated Messages in African American Culture* (1996), which received the Myers Center Award for the Study of Human Rights in North America. Her research interests include the structural biases of mass communication, particularly as relates to disability issues and people of color.

Dr. Ronald C. McCurdy is Chair of the Jazz Department and Professor of Music in the Thornton School of Music at the University of Southern California and serves as Past President of the International Association for Jazz Educations (IAJE). Prior to his appointment at USC, he served as Director of the Thelonious Monk Institute of Jazz at USC. He has served as Professor of Music and chair of the Afro–African American Studies Department and as Director of Jazz Studies at the University of Minnesota. In 1997, Dr. McCurdy served as Visiting Professor at Maria Sklodowska-Curie University in Lublin, Poland. In 2001 Dr. McCurdy received the Distinguished Alumni Award from the University of Kansas, where he served seven years as Director of Jazz Studies. Under the direction of Dr. McCurdy, the University of Kansas Jazz program gained national and international prominence. His instrumental and vocal ensembles performed at international and national music conferences and festivals throughout the world. Dr. McCurdy released his first CD, *Once Again for the First Time*, in 2001 and is coauthor of the vocal jazz improvisation series *Approaching the Standards* and author of the book *Meet the Great Jazz Legends*, both published by Warners Bros. He is currently touring The Langston Hughes Project, Ask Your Mama: 12 Moods for Jazz, a multimedia presentation featuring a jazz quartet, spoken-word pieces, and images from the Harlem Renaissance. Dr. McCurdy is in demand as a guest clinician, soloist, speaker, and director of honor jazz ensembles and choirs throughout the United States and Canada. He has directed All-State Jazz Ensembles in New York, Texas, Arizona, Vermont, Nebraska, Ohio, Nevada, Illinois, Oklahoma, and Florida, among others. Dr. McCurdy received his undergraduate degree from Florida A&M University and his master's and Ph.D. degrees from the University of Kansas. Dr. McCurdy is a consultant to the Grammy Foundation educational programs, serving as director of the National Grammy Vocal Jazz Ensemble and Combo. He has served as a consultant for the Walt Disney All-American Summer College Jazz Ensemble since 1990. While directing this program in Florida, he worked with many jazz artists, including Joe Williams, Rosemary Clooney, Leslie Uggams, Arturo Sandoval, Diane Schuur, Ramsey Lewis, Mercer Ellington, Dr. Billy Taylor, Maynard Ferguson, Lionel Hampton, and Dianne Reeves. He has also served as a member of the Jamey Aebersold Jazz Camp faculty. Dr. McCurdy is a performing artist for the Yamaha International Corporation.

Leon Rappoport received his Ph.D. in social psychology at the University of Colorado. After conducting research in Norway as an NSF Postdoctoral Fellow, he began teaching at Kansas State University, where he is now Emeritus Professor of Psychology. Author of many research aricles as well as books on personality, decision making, and eating behaviors, his recent (2005) work on humor is titled *Punchlines: The Case for Racial, Ethnic, and Gender Humor.*

Christopher Holmes Smith is a senior lecturer at the Annenberg School for Communication at the University of Southern California. His research, publication, and teaching interests concern modernity and the politics of identity, neoliberalism, the social formation of value, and entertainment's role in American public culture. He has written widely on pop culture and entertainment and has provided commentary and guidance on a variety of social and political issues for leading media outlets and governmental organizations worldwide. He is currently completing a book manuscript on financial capital and the ways that contemporary politics of money are influenced by American popular culture. He holds a Ph.D. in media and cultural studies from the University of Wisconsin–Madison and a B.A. in sociology from the University of Chicago.

Terrence Tucker is Assistant Professor of English at the University of Arkansas. His current work focuses on comedy and rage in African American literature in the twentieth and twenty-first centuries. He specializes in African American and contemporary American literature, and his research interests include pedagogy, drama, popular culture, and hip-hop.

Index